The Fate of the Revolution

the fate of the revolution

VIRGINIANS DEBATE THE CONSTITUTION

LORRI GLOVER

Saint Louis University

Johns Hopkins University Press | *Baltimore*

© 2016 Johns Hopkins University Press
All rights reserved. Published 2016
Printed in the United States of America on acid-free paper
9 8 7 6 5 4 3 2 1

Johns Hopkins University Press
2715 North Charles Street
Baltimore, Maryland 21218-4363
www.press.jhu.edu

Library of Congress Cataloging-in-Publication Data

Names: Glover, Lorri, 1967– author.
Title: The fate of the revolution : Virginians debate the constitution /
    Lorri Glover.
Description: Baltimore : Johns Hopkins University Press, 2016. | Series:
    Witness to history | Includes bibliographical references and index.
Identifiers: LCCN 2015034015| ISBN 9781421420011 (hardcover : alk. paper)
    | ISBN 9781421420028 (pbk. : alk. paper) | ISBN 9781421420035 (electronic)
    | ISBN 1421420015 (hardcover : alk. paper) | ISBN 1421420023 (pbk. : alk.
    paper) | ISBN 1421420031 (electronic)
Subjects: LCSH: Constitutional history—United States. | Virginia. Convention
    (1788) | Virginia—Politics and government—1775–1865.
Classification: LCC KF4512.V5 G57 2016 | DDC 342.7302/9—dc23 LC record
available at http://lccn.loc.gov/2015034015

A catalog record for this book is available from the British Library.

Special discounts are available for bulk purchases of this book.
For more information, please contact Special Sales at 410-516-6936 or
specialsales@press.jhu.edu.

Johns Hopkins University Press uses environmentally friendly book
materials, including recycled text paper that is composed of at least
30 percent post-consumer waste, whenever possible.

Contents

The Fate of the Revolution

prologue

ON 24 JUNE 1788 James Madison knew the debates were nearing the end. In fits and starts, after many digressions and quarrels, the 170 delegates elected to the Virginia Ratification Convention had finally made their way, clause by clause, through the proposed Constitution. The Richmond debates were the most important—and the most evenly matched—of all the state conventions called to decide whether to adopt or reject the US Constitution. Virginians had, in fact, been deliberating ever since word of the proposed new government reached the Old Dominion in late September 1787. The controversy over the Constitution consumed everyone in the state, as one man put it, "from the Governor to the door keeper." "Never," it seemed, "were eight months spent in such animated disputation."[1]

In all that time, neither the supporters of the Constitution nor the critics ever held a clear majority. In the March elections, Virginia voters split down the middle, matching the divisions among the state's revolutionary-era leaders. The representatives sent to Richmond were all determined to ensure the survival of the American Republic. But would the Constitution do that? Or would it spell the republic's doom? All month they appeared hopelessly deadlocked. As one edgy delegate calculated, "Were I to attempt to predict the fate of the constitution, it must be founded on conjecture." Spectators who overflowed the largest building in Richmond, a theater space known as the New Academy located on Shockoe Hill, shared the elected delegates' anxiety. "I see my Country on the point of embarking and launching into a troubled Ocean without Charts or Compass to direct them," said one observer, "one half the Crew hoisting sail for the land of *Energy*—and the other looking with a longing aspect on the Shore of Liberty."[2]

When Madison rose the morning of 24 June to offer his last formal contribution to the debates, he still wasn't sure if the supporters of the Constitution had the votes to ratify. He offered as heartfelt and emotional an appeal as he ever made in his life. Virginians held the future of the republic in their hands, Madison said: "It is a most awful thing that depends on our decision—no less than whether the thirteen States shall Unite freely, peaceably, and unanimously, for the security of their common happiness and liberty, or whether every thing is to be put in confusion and disorder!" The Constitution, he insisted, represented the only way forward for the American Republic, and voting against it would fracture the union of states with inevitable, perilous consequences. If, on the other hand, Virginians agreed to ratify, he continued, "I shall look upon it as one of the most fortunate events that ever happened, for human nature. I cannot, therefore, without the most excruciating apprehensions, see a possibility of losing its blessings—It gives me infinite pain to reflect, that all the earnest endeavours of the warmest friends of their Country, to introduce a system promotive of our happiness, may be blasted by a rejection."[3]

Madison was a shy, slight man but a relentlessly methodical thinker. He didn't lay down one idea to take up another until he considered all its implications and consequences. Many contemporaries considered him the most gifted intellectual of the revolutionary generation. Certainly no man in America had spent more time thinking about the Constitution. Madison's long study left him convinced that only through unity under the Constitution could the American Republic be saved. Rejecting it would force the states into separate, regionally based confederacies, which would fuel chronic conflict, economic and social turmoil, and likely foreign invasion, dooming republican government in America.[4]

As soon as Madison sat down, Patrick Henry stood up. Henry was the most politically powerful man in all of Virginia and a bold and dazzling orator. Even his critics marveled at Henry's unsurpassed ability to move an audience with his booming voice, agile mind, and intuitive grasp of what would inspire men to action. To many of his fellow Virginians, he epitomized the best of their sovereign state, and they admired his zealous commitment to Virginia's interests. Just a few short years before, he had, in a storied speech, inspired them to defend their liberty even at the cost of death. Now, with that same fierce passion, he again called on Virginians to safeguard their rights: to refuse to submit Virginia to the powers of the proposed federal government.[5]

In the summer of 1788, James Madison and Patrick Henry found in one another an almost perfectly matched, polar opposite. The two men had clashed before, most notably just a few years earlier over whether to disestablish the Anglican Church in Virginia. From dearly bought experience they knew well one another's strengths, weaknesses, and political convictions. Both wanted a republican government that protected the rights of citizens. But they disagreed vehemently over what form the government should take and where sovereignty should reside. Madison saw Henry as a prime example of the parochial interests afflicting the country, throwing up ill-informed obstacles to the creation of an energetic, effective government—a "more perfect union." Henry, meanwhile, was appalled that a fellow Virginian would work so hard to undermine the state's sovereignty with so little apparent regard for how his plan jeopardized citizens' long-held and treasured rights.

Throughout the convention, Henry made no bones about his opinion on the Constitution: "I despise and abhor it." As Madison tried to convince the delegates that the Constitution was the fulfillment of the Revolution's noblest ideals, Henry worked tirelessly to show that it was "incompatible with the genius of republicanism." "He tells you of important blessings which he imagines will result to us and mankind in general, from the adoption of this system," Henry said of Madison, but "I see the awful immensity of the dangers with which it is pregnant—I see it—I feel it."[6]

As Henry spoke on 24 June, storm clouds gathered over Richmond. "Our own happiness alone is not affected by the event," he reminded the rapt audience. "All nations are interested in the determination," he proclaimed, his voice ringing out as thunder rumbled. Suddenly, with a crash of lightning, the skies opened up, and a deluge rained down on the New Academy. To stunned delegates and spectators, the rising storm seemed to score Henry's ominous warnings about the future of mankind. As the wind roared, a clap of thunder shook the whole building, and delegates scrambled for cover. At that moment, the ever-unbendable Patrick Henry called out: "The consequent happiness or misery of mankind . . . will depend on what we now decide!"[7]

Were Madison and Henry exaggerating the importance of the Virginia convention outcome? Technically, of course, any nine states could ratify the Constitution and legally replace the Articles of Confederation. In reality, the matter was considerably more complicated. The states were not created equal, and the process was anything but smooth. In the winter of 1787–88 four of the smallest states (Delaware, New Jersey, Georgia, and Connecticut) quickly voted in favor of ratification. Pennsylvania, influential because of its population and location, did too. But that early enthusiasm soon stalled. Massachusetts, the crucible of political radicalism in the 1760s and 1770s, held its convention in February, but the resulting vote—187 for and 168 against—hardly seemed a resounding endorsement of the proposition that the Constitution would save the Revolution. Maryland and South Carolina ratified in the spring of 1788, but Rhode Island, which had refused to send a delegation to Philadelphia, declined to call a convention. New Hampshire's convention, called in mid-February, abruptly adjourned when advocates of ratification saw they did not have the votes to win. In New York, an essential state because of its economy and location, opponents to ratification held a comfortable majority. The same was true in North Carolina. Ratification, then, remained in doubt in the summer of 1788. And the biggest question of all centered on Virginia.[8]

Many well-informed Americans believed that Virginia's rejection, regardless of which other states ratified, would sink the proposed Constitution. Virginia was the most populous of all the states in the confederation, home to one in six Americans. It was also the largest, controlling no less than one-fifth of the land in the United States, right in the middle of the Atlantic seaboard. If Virginia refused to accept the Constitution, what would happen next? Virtually no one in 1787–88 thought retaining the existing Articles of Confederation was a viable long-term solution to America's problems. Some changes were essential, and soon. Could representatives gather again and somehow agree to a different revision of the Articles? Or would the states devolve into separate confederacies and wind up as divided and fractious as Europe?

Then there was the weight of history. The patriot cause emerged in the streets of Boston in the 1760s. But designing a civic culture to replace the colonial order American patriots overthrew—that mammoth task fell to a

small cohort of Virginians. The values that moved the revolutionary generation from rebellion to republicanism, the ideas that laid the foundation for
an independent country, the practical designs of government—these came
principally from men occupying the great houses of Virginia. George Mason conceived the first bill of rights and first state constitution among the
breakaway colonies. His work served as a template for many other states and
for the Second Continental Congress's Declaration of Independence. A fellow Virginian, Thomas Jefferson, was the architect of that document, drawing on his friend Mason's ideas and even his language. Jefferson and Mason's
friend, George Washington, led the Continental army through the ordeal of
the Revolutionary War. By 1777 he was widely acclaimed as the "father of his
country." If the home of Jefferson and Mason and especially Washington was
not in the United States, was there a United States at all?

When Americans first read or heard about the Constitution, many automatically assumed that, if it passed, George Washington would become the
president. In our present cynical and divisive political climate, it is hard to
imagine the nearly universal respect Washington enjoyed. In the late 1780s,
Americans saw him as the savior of their country and the embodiment of
their highest ideals. He was beloved and, more importantly, trusted.[9] The
idea of a President Washington turned many skeptics of the Constitution into
cautious supporters of ratification: perhaps, they reasoned, everything would
work out under his steady hand. And his enthusiasm for the Constitution
was widely known. But if Virginia did not ratify, Washington would not be
a citizen of the United States and so could not become president. Such an
outcome would have dealt a crippling, perhaps fatal blow to the proposed new
government. For all those reasons, Virginia was a game changer.

When most Americans think about the creation of the Constitution, they
envision the convention in Philadelphia, that who's who of revolutionary era
heroes working though the sweltering summer of 1787 to forge a new government.[10] We celebrate Constitution Day every September 17, the day nearly all
the delegates signed the finished document. It's a public memory centered
on learned men reasoning together to reach consensus around a plan of government that survives, now in the third century after it was created, and has
become a model for representative democracies around the globe. The Philadelphia meeting marked a signal moment in American history. It deserves
study and celebration.

But we should not forget that the Philadelphia Convention was only the start of a long conflict with an uncertain outcome. Ratification was not automatic—far from it. The preamble to the Constitution indicated that the government derived its power from "we, the people." So, in what soon became a remarkable and unprecedented outpouring of public debate, *the people* had to decide whether the secretly created plan out of Philadelphia would become law. As important as the men in Philadelphia were, even James Madison understood that their work "could never be regarded as the oracular guide" to the Constitution. "As the instrument came from them," he reasoned, "it was nothing more than the draught of a plan, nothing but a dead letter, until life and validity were breathed into it, by the voice of the people, speaking through the several state conventions." To find the real meaning of the Constitution, Madison explained, "we must look for it not in the general convention, which proposed, but in the state conventions, which accepted and ratified the constitution."[11]

Actually, the story runs even deeper than the formal debates within the state ratification conventions. Americans fiercely contested the language, implications, and powers of the new government from the moment it was first revealed. Those popular debates—"out of doors" to borrow language of the eighteenth century—drove both perceptions of the Constitution and the election of delegates to state conventions. Newspapermen and printers shaped public opinion, too, as they circulated nuanced commentaries on the Constitution alongside vicious rumors about advocates on all sides of the debates. Whereas the focus in Philadelphia had been on consensus building among a few dozen well-connected men, in the states tens of thousands of citizens played hard-ball politics.[12]

These popular deliberations preceding the state convention debates were at once political, theoretical, and personal—and a vital civic duty. Citizens held themselves responsible for reasoning through every part of the Constitution. As one Virginia essayist pleaded: "Let no citizen of the United States of America, who is capable of discussing the important subject, retire from the field."[13] To understand the ratification of the Constitution in Virginia—and for the United States—it is essential not only to appreciate the discussions that took place in Richmond in June 1788 between property-owning white men, mostly slaveholders. We must also understand the perceptions of the farmers, artisans, shopkeepers, and planters consumed with debating the Constitution between late September 1787, when copies of the Constitution reached Virginia, and the opening days of the formal convention the following June.

The speeches convention delegates gave were not spontaneous. Rather many grew out of long conversations with allies and political enemies, aggressive newspaper wars, and networks of correspondence that ran from Georgia to New England. Some new issues emerged in June, but others had been well rehearsed in taverns and around dinner tables.

In our mind's eye, "the founders" often appear etched in amber, a small cadre of familiar men dressed in powdered wigs and velvet knee-britches. The truth of the creation of the United States is far more complicated, interesting, and relatable. Men like George Washington, James Madison, Patrick Henry, and George Mason took the lead in designing and debating the Constitution, but they certainly did not act alone. They were shaped by their constituents who by 1787 felt every bit as invested in the fate of the American Republic as the self-styled gentlemen patriots. Citizens respected the leading founders' experience, but they were not reflexively deferential. And even if the "lesser sort" wanted to defer to elites, which ones should they follow? James Madison said that Virginians supporting ratification faced a far greater challenge than their friends in Massachusetts, where all the "men of abilities, of property, of character" favored ratification. By contrast, he knew, "the same description of characters are divided and opposed to one another in Virginia."[14]

Virginia's political leaders often disagreed during the revolutionary era, both about policy decisions and because of personality conflicts. The debates of 1787–88 bore the marks of those earlier philosophical and temperamental disagreements. But never before had the divisions been so deep or the stakes so high.

Happily, the surviving evidence from those momentous Virginia debates— both in the formal convention and "out of doors"—is remarkably bountiful. From the day the Philadelphia Convention adjourned until the opening of the Virginia Ratification Convention, Virginians interrogated the merits of the Constitution, strategized over the best tactics, and gossiped about who stood where and why. One of the great editorial projects of early American history derives from those discussions. Thanks to *The Documentary History of the Ratification of the Constitution*, published by the State Historical Society of Wisconsin, we can read the letters, pamphlets, treatises, and newspaper articles that Americans wrote during the ratification contest. The Virginia volumes run almost 1,800 pages.[15] That extraordinary resource exists because of preservation efforts started in the eighteenth century by the most famous founders. Many obsessed over their historical significance and copiously documented their political careers. Madison and Washington in particular spent the latter years of their lives systematically compiling their correspondences, which ran into the tens of thousands of letters and included a wealth of writings from 1787–88.[16] There was no secrecy pledge in Richmond as there had been in Philadelphia, so during the weeks the delegates met, letters passed from Richmond to Mount Vernon and back, across the state of Virginia, and to correspondents watching from as far away as Europe.

In Richmond, an attorney from Petersburg named David Robertson jockeyed for a seat nearly every day of the June convention. Most states did not allow their deliberations to be recorded, but the Virginians—keenly aware of their place in history—agreed to let Robertson take notes. Sometimes he got pushed toward the back of the cavernous theater, and the throngs of spectators occasionally drowned out the speakers, particularly James Madison. Later, men disappointed with how they appeared in the published record of the proceedings complained about Robertson's editorial license. George Mason, for example, accused him of giving some pro-Constitution speakers the chance to edit the transcriptions. Robertson insisted he "was governed by the most sacred regard to justice and impartiality," even as he admitted that he sat in the gallery far from the speakers and was often distracted by the comings and goings of members of the audience. Robertson also occasionally passed over rambling parts of speeches and from time to time even stopped taking notes and editorialized that the speaker droned on. He had to miss some speeches, and a far less conscientious man took his place. So the transcripts are hardly perfect. Still, they are a wonder: the most complete on-the-spot records of the entire ratification process.[17]

Thanks to all of these impressive preservation efforts, we can trace, in real time and with confidence, the wide-ranging, evenly divided, and sometimes shockingly raw contest in Virginia that decided the future of the American Republic. We can return to Virginia in 1787–88 and witness simultaneously venomous arguments, brilliant political moves, craven manipulations of fears, reasoned debates about philosophy, history, and law, and an astounding clash of wills. Historians have tried to explain the final, razor-thin vote on the Constitution in Virginia in many ways (easterners vs. westerners, nationalists vs. localists, established gentlemen vs. up-and-comers, commerce vs. agriculture, youth vs. experience, aristocracy vs. democracy).[18] Present-day readers entering the fascinating, nearly yearlong controversy that culminated in that vote almost invariably disagree. Some things are clear, though. Virginians were the most important and divided players in one of the greatest human dramas in American history. In no gathering during the entire revolutionary era was there so vigorous a contest between so many talented, famous, and committed leaders. The "father of the Constitution," James Madison, aided behind the scenes by George Washington, took on the most eminent and experienced opponents to ratification in the United States: Patrick Henry and George Mason. The outcome was unpredictable, but the consequences were crystal clear: Virginians faced "one of the most serious and important subjects, that ever was agitated by a free people." Before them lay "not the fate of an individual, but that of millions . . . not the welfare of a state, but, that of mankind."[19]

1 Fall 1787, First Reactions

The plan of a Government proposed to us by the Convention affords matter for conversation to every rank of beings from the Governor to the door keeper—& the opinions appear to be as various as the persons possessing them.

George Lee Turberville, 28 October 1787

THEIR DUTY FULFILLED ON 17 SEPTEMBER 1787, George Washington and George Mason were in a hurry to get home from Philadelphia. Like their colleagues throughout the states, they felt worn out by the summer's long labors. But fatigue was hardly their main motivation. Although it would be many months before representatives from the state of Virginia formally considered whether to ratify the new Constitution drafted in the Philadelphia Convention, both men understood that the contest would commence as soon as news of the radical restructuring of the union of states reached the Old Dominion. More work lay ahead, then, and every hour lost was precious.

Mason and Washington had been neighbors, business partners, and friends for decades. They lived close to one another, on sprawling, picturesque estates overlooking the Potomac River in Virginia's Northern Neck—Mason at Gunston Hall and Washington at Mount Vernon. They led quintessential Virginia gentry lifestyles, bought and paid for by the scores of African Americans they held in bondage. The two friends visited often, and when their children were young they played together. Though neither man was particularly religious, they served together on the local vestry and bought neighboring pews at Pohick Church. In the 1770s, the American Revolution pulled them from their happy, parochial lives onto the stage of history. Washington, ambitious and dashing with a naturally imposing presence, became the heroic commander of the Continental army. The intellectual, sometimes irascible, and slightly hypochondriacal Mason took the lead in drafting Virginia's first constitution. The two corresponded often during the dark days of the Revolutionary War and in 1781 celebrated the proud achievement of American independence. Mason made no attempt to hide his frequent frustration with the drawn-out war, and he eagerly anticipated Washington's return to northern Virginia, so that he could "sit down at his Ease under the Shade of his own Vine, & his own fig-tree, & enjoy the Sweets of domestic Life!" Washington, his military days behind him and his long-sought fame secure, fully expected that he would "move gently down the stream of life, until I sleep with my Fathers."[1]

Both men prospered after the war; their diversified holdings made them the two most successful planters in Fairfax County. Mason focused his attention on his family and neighbors, while Washington remained connected to a national network of friends and protégés through letters and by hosting visitors at Mount Vernon. Both men enjoyed being celebrated by their countrymen as visionary patriots, Washington in particular. Neither strayed far from home. But events of 1787 forced Mason and Washington to abandon their retirement from politics. They reluctantly left Virginia for the crucial business of a continent-wide convention to revise the faltering Articles of Confederation. Sixty-one-year-old Mason had never traveled outside the Chesapeake before he agreed to serve as a member of Virginia's delegation in Philadelphia. He did so understanding that "the Revolt from Great Britain" seemed "nothing compared with the great Business now before us."[2] What neither Mason nor Washington knew as they headed north was that Philadelphia would end their long friendship.

George Washington presided over the deliberations that summer, which created a far stronger central government than Americans expected. (The gathering was only subsequently called the Constitutional Convention; creating a new constitution was not its charge.) Though Washington rarely spoke during the debates, he was a strong supporter of the resulting plan. The outcome seemed to him "little short of a miracle."[3] That was *not* what the majority of Virginia delegates thought, however, and it was certainly not the opinion of George Mason. Like many Virginians, Mason was a staunch believer in decentralized government power as the surest protection of citizens' liberty. A man forthright to the point of abrasiveness, Mason refused to sign the document because of the authority granted the new government. He was one of three holdouts—and announced on the floor of the convention that "he would sooner chop off his right hand than put it to the Constitution." According to James Madison, Mason left Philadelphia "in an exceedingly ill humour indeed." Not surprisingly, Washington, who had urged a stronger national government since the early 1780s, did not travel home with him.[4]

The Philadelphia Convention drew revolutionary icons from all the states— Benjamin Franklin (who lived within walking distance from the meeting hall), the Pinckney cousins from South Carolina, Roger Sherman from Connecticut. But even in that illustrious gathering, the Virginians stood out for their abilities and their fame. George Washington, the most honored man in America, was joined by James Madison, the intellectual force behind the gathering and the principal architect of the resulting Constitution. George Mason, an experienced constitution writer and the author of Virginia's widely influential Declaration of Rights, also attended. Rounding out Virginia's delegation was the state's popular young governor Edmund Randolph; John Blair, a leading Williamsburg attorney who had been involved in virtually every part of Virginia politics since 1770; and George Wythe, one of the greatest legal minds in America. At the College of William and Mary, Wythe trained a generation of notable Virginians, including John Marshall, James Monroe, and Thomas Jefferson. (Jefferson missed the Philadelphia gathering because of his diplomatic assignment in France.)

The Virginia delegation arrived first and met daily as other states' delegates trickled into the city. Once a quorum was reached, the Virginians took the lead. Convention delegates almost immediately scrapped their charge to revise the Articles. The plan was too deeply flawed, they concluded, and the technical process for amending the Articles impossible to achieve. So, delegates set to creating an entirely new government. They worked off the "Virginia Plan"—conceived by James Madison and formally introduced by Edmund Randolph.

James Madison. Pendleton's Lithography, from the portrait by Gilbert Stuart. Prints and Photographs Division, Library of Congress

Madison's design created a strong national government with sovereignty vested in that central government. This was a critical shift in power since under the Articles the states were clearly sovereign. Among other proposals strengthening the central government, the Virginia Plan called for the national legislature to hold veto power over state laws or, as Madison usually called it, a "negative." Throughout the nearly four-month-long debates, a series of compromises whittled away at this clarity within the Virginia Plan, resulting in a constitutional design in which sovereignty was shared and more ambiguous.

Most men (unlike James Madison) arrived in Philadelphia not knowing exactly what specific changes they wanted in their government. But one thing was clear in their minds. Delegates resolved to seek consensus—to rigorously reason together to create the best possible plan that met with everyone's approval. Though frustrated with some of the compromises made to his original design, Madison was temperamentally well suited to this approach. His state's delegation was another matter. As the deliberations proceeded, Virginians became increasingly and openly divided, even as they remained at the center of the convention. Madison, Mason, and Randolph numbered among the most vocal and powerful of all delegates. Madison spoke the most—161 times, followed closely by Mason, with 136 contributions.[5]

The divisions among the Virginians that deepened as the weeks passed in Philadelphia were disappointing though hardly surprising. After all, it had been a struggle in Virginia even to field a delegation. The state legislature had tried to appoint Patrick Henry, the most influential man in Virginia and greatest orator of his age, but he declined. He claimed family obligations, as he did from time to time when he wanted to avoid an office. Henry fathered sixteen children by two wives, and Philadelphia was too far to travel from his family, he said, and too distracting from his law practice. A nineteenth-century biographer claimed that Henry refused the appointment because he "smelt a rat." The story is often repeated with the words put in Henry's mouth, but there is no evidence he ever said it. The state of Virginia had no stronger defender than Patrick Henry. Had he really suspected what some delegates intended, Henry would have been more, not less, likely to attend. Henry's son-in-law attributed his absence to finances. While serving as governor of Virginia in 1784–86, Henry's expenses greatly exceeded his income; he was not a wealthy man and supported his large family through his legal work.[6] But when Patrick Henry was really keen on something, he found a way to make it happen. The simple fact was that nothing drew him to the Philadelphia meeting. He was not a gifted political theorist and not particularly concerned with confederation politics. His interests lay with his family and in Virginia. In the summer of 1787, Patrick Henry had every reason to believe that, whatever happened in Philadelphia, Virginia would continue to be a sovereign state. Why should he leave home?

Virginia's legislature had turned next to Thomas Nelson Jr., a Revolutionary War veteran and former governor, but he refused, too. So did Richard Henry Lee. Lee, an heir to one of Virginia's most renowned families and a long-standing political leader, served as president of the Confederation Congress in 1785, and he was still a representative in 1787. Eventually, Virginia legislators settled on James McClurg, a prominent physician, to fill the last seat in their delegation.

Even George Washington had been reluctant to attend. He wanted to stay home with Martha and the two young grandchildren they were raising. Washy and Nelly Custis's father, Jack, died at the close of the Revolutionary War, and their overwhelmed mother kept their two younger siblings with her and sent Washy and Nelly to live with their grandmother and step-grandfather. Washington was also editing his writings for posthumous publication. During the Revolutionary War he came to realize that he was so connected to the American cause that future generations would want to know about his life from his own pen. So he set about shaping a narrative for them. At the end of the war he shipped several wagonloads of his papers to Mount Vernon—the easier water passage seemed too dangerous for such precious cargo. And he brought wartime protégés home with him to work as secretaries on the project. Apart from these pressing obligations, Washington feared that attending the Philadelphia gathering would compromise his standing as a paragon of republican service. Signing on to a failed or, worse, scandalous effort to fix the Articles of Confederation would damage that hard-earned reputation. He was eventually coaxed into going by friends, including James Madison. Madison cautioned Washington that his refusal to attend might undermine the two friends' shared vision of what the United States should become: a stronger, more unified country, capable of protecting its citizens' rights, ensuring domestic stability, and warranting the respect of foreign nations.[7]

During the Revolutionary War, General Washington felt the perils of decentralized power, and he emerged from his military service convinced that the Articles of Confederation jeopardized the republic. Like many military leaders and diplomats, Washington came to believe in the necessity of "a firm and permanent Government for this Union." The biggest obstacle, he said, lay with provincial men, deeply loyal to their states, who refused to "yield to a more enlarged scale of politicks."[8] His friends' appeals convinced Washington that, if he refused to serve in the Philadelphia Convention, the essential work of strengthening the government would be lost before it even began—an accurate reading of his tremendous influence in the young American Republic. During the debates in Philadelphia, Washington grew confident that the new government created under the Constitution would save the republic for which he had sacrificed so much for so long. By the close of the convention, he saw his reputation and place in history linked to the prospects of the plan. The Constitution had found its most formidable friend.

James Madison was perfectly aligned with George Washington in 1787, except that he could hardly wait to get to Philadelphia. He had been urging a redesign of the United States government long before the Confederation Congress sanctioned the gathering to revise the Articles. In fact, he had spent the better part of a year studying history and political theory to understand the problems facing the Confederation Congress and to design a remedy. The result of that long and considered investigation was "Vices of the Political System of the United States," in which Madison concluded that too few checks on local concerns were destroying the greater interests of the union of states. A stronger, central government was essential for the republic to survive. This conviction set James Madison at odds with many of his fellow Virginians who were committed to Virginia's sovereignty and their own local prerogatives. Madison, however, took a more capacious view, and he saw worsening social disorder and looming international threats. If Americans stayed the course under the Articles, the republic would be done in, perhaps by social unrest or economic collapse, or perhaps by foreign intrigues or regional alliances. Men in other parts of the United States reached similar conclusions. Even diplomats in Britain, France, and Spain speculated in the mid-1780s that the union of states would not survive much longer.

When Congress agreed to a gathering in Philadelphia, Madison was more than ready. He was thirty-six, almost twenty years younger than Washington and twenty-five years younger than Mason and Wythe—a child of the Revolution, he sometimes said, whereas they had been on the front lines. But he took the lead in Philadelphia. Madison arrived early and with his specific plan not to revise the Articles but to create an entirely new government. Although parts of his design were changed in significant ways, some of which, especially the veto issue, he strongly opposed, Madison deserves to be known as "father of the Constitution." He guided the delegates through months of intense deliberations. Though sometimes aggravated and on the losing end of votes, he nearly always remained his usual even-tempered, intellectually curious self.[9]

Through the long hot summer, led by Madison, the Philadelphia delegates adeptly negotiated compromises between central and state powers, forged a working if morally repugnant deal over slavery's future in the United States, and settled seemingly intractable controversies over representation. They examined every part of the design, from terms of office for judicial appointments to the mechanism for impeaching the president to funding a navy. They had little to say about religion. Subsequent generations of Americans have sometimes read Christian theology and providential design into the results of their deliberations. But, in fact, the Constitution they produced only mentioned religion once, in Article 6: "No religious Test shall ever be required as a Qualification to any Office or public Trust under the United States."[10]

The work was hard, particularly the struggle to balance, as Madison put it, "a proper stability & energy in the Government with the essential characters of the republican form." Even to the brilliant minds gathered at the convention, this proved "as difficult as it was desirable." It was an uphill battle, and many times the men simply tabled an issue in hopes that tempers might cool and a compromise be reached.[11]

Everyone saw that the two main leaders of the convention, Madison and Washington, faced the most trouble within their own delegation. George Wythe generally agreed with them, but he left a month into the convention to care for his sick wife and never returned. Dr. McClurg also believed in the necessity of a stronger government, but he left Philadelphia not long after Wythe, frustrated with the deep divisions among the Virginians. He wrote Madison that he had concluded "my vote could only operate to produce a division, & so destroy the vote of the State." During the Philadelphia meeting—and all continent-wide gatherings up to 1787—representatives voted by state caucus. Each man spoke his own mind, but when it came to formal votes, each state got one vote, representing the majority opinion of state delegates. McClurg decided that his further participation in the Virginia caucus "would certainly be useless, perhaps injurious," so he did not go back to Philadelphia.[12]

Madison and Washington must have hoped that George Mason would quit, too, but they had no such luck. Mason spoke often during the debates, and the further delegates moved through the plan, the more critical he became. A republic, Mason became convinced, could never operate on so large a scale as the Constitution attempted to establish and with so little real representation of citizens' interests. Near the end, he raised the need for a bill of rights. Without such guarantees, Mason said, he could never support the Constitution. The majority of delegates thought adding a bill of rights to the Constitution was unnecessary because, they believed, the new government's limited powers could never extend to infringing on state bills of rights. Mason didn't press the matter, but he remained unconvinced. Appeals to compromise, political maneuvering, even the personal intervention of George Washington could not change his mind. Though his opposition cost him dearly, Mason never looked back. "In this important trust," he told his son, "I am truly conscious of having acted from the purest motives of honesty, and love to my country." He felt confident that "my conduct . . . will administer comfort to me in those moments when I shall most want it, and smooth the bed of death." Mason left Philadelphia determined to keep Virginia out of what he saw as a dangerously powerful government that he feared would quickly degenerate into "a Monarchy, or a corrupt oppressive Aristocracy."[13]

Edmund Randolph, the governor of Virginia, joined Mason in declining to add his signature, but he took a very different tone. "In refusing to sign the Constitution, I make a step which might be the most awful of my life," he conceded. But he felt compelled by his conscience.[14] Thirty-five years old, rather "portly" and handsome, Randolph was a canny judge of popular opinion. Some contemporaries found him a bit too attuned to the opinions of others. A French diplomat dismissed him as motivated by "egotism, of the consuming desire to lead." He always wanted "to become the hero of a new scene." Randolph's own cousin likened him to "a chameleon on an aspen: always quaking, always changing."[15]

Randolph was a political moderate, and the changes in the Constitution were, he understood, radical: no term limits, a standing army, a powerful chief executive, minimal electoral representation. The method of evaluation—a straight up or down vote by state—would surely spark controversy. Randolph suggested a second convention, to meet after the states had the opportunity of reviewing the Constitution and recommending changes. Without a second convention, Randolph said, it would "be impossible for him to put his name to the instrument." Whether he would oppose ratification back home, he would not say. According to Madison's notes from the Philadelphia Convention, Randolph announced that "he would not deprive himself of the freedom to do so in his own State, if that course should be prescribed by his final judgment."[16]

A consummate politician, Randolph knew a political firestorm lay ahead. Indeed, many men left Philadelphia worried about how their neighbors would view their conduct and proposal. Randolph understood why some citizens would welcome the stronger structure and the economic stability the Constitution promised. But many others, he knew, would feel betrayed by this profound (and secret) change to the government. He wanted to figure out which way the wind was blowing in Virginia before committing himself. Eager to leave himself room to maneuver back home, he told the delegates in Philadelphia that "he did not mean by this refusal to decide that he should oppose the Constitution without doors."[17] In other words, he was no George Mason.

It was a commentary on Virginia politics that a man of Randolph's political savvy could not predict public reaction. When the Constitution was finally signed—but not by George Mason, Edmund Randolph, or Elbridge Gerry of Massachusetts—two of the three men who formally withheld their support came from Virginia. John Blair, who did not contribute to the debates but often sided with Mason and Randolph, did decide to sign. Otherwise, Virginia—home to the convention's president and the Constitution's originator—would not have supported the Constitution at its creation.

From the late colonial era until the Philadelphia meeting, Virginia's leading revolutionaries—Patrick Henry, George Washington, George Mason, Edmund Randolph, John Blair, Thomas Jefferson, James Madison, Edmund Pendleton, Richard Henry Lee—had been friends, business partners, political allies, and brothers in the patriot cause. Sometimes rivalries and clashing personalities made their bonds tenuous, and they even quarreled with and conspired against one another. But their political connections did not come apart until they confronted the Constitution.

And Philadelphia was only the start.

It took only a few days for the proposed Constitution to arrive on the desks of members of the Confederation Congress, meeting that year in New York City. Representatives immediately saw that the men sent to Philadelphia had egregiously violated the express charge given them by Congress. The plan they offered created an entirely new kind of government, which, if approved, would end the sovereignty of the very states members of Congress represented. Faced with this stunning turn of events, congressmen had to make a hard choice. Should they legitimize that work, knowing that doing so might well destroy the body in which they were serving? And if they did, what would the citizens of their respective states—voters who entrusted them with their political positions—think?

Virginia's representatives were influential leaders in the Confederation Congress, and they split as sharply as the state's delegates had in Philadelphia. William Grayson and Richard Henry Lee opposed the Constitution. Edward Carrington and Henry "Light-Horse Harry" Lee III, a relative of Richard Henry Lee's, supported it. They were joined by James Madison, who resumed his seat in Congress the week after the final vote in Philadelphia. Other states' delegates divided on the question, too, and they also included men who had helped design the controversial plan.

Ten delegates to the Philadelphia Convention were sitting members of the Confederation Congress, and all of them supported the Constitution. Their return in late September put them in the odd position—some critics said it was unethical—of judging their own actions. Their conduct was particularly galling to Richard Henry Lee. He had declined an appointment to the Philadelphia Convention because he thought it inappropriate to serve at once in both bodies. "This opinion," Lee informed his friend Samuel Adams, "was fully verified, when the members of Convention came to Congress."[18]

Lee, tall and patrician, was educated in England and part of a long family line of military officers. A stalwart patriot and never one to shy away from a confrontation, he offered the formal resolution for American independence in the Continental Congress in 1776 and continued in prominent political positions for the next decade. He'd disfigured one of his hands in a hunting accident and always kept it covered in black silk. Some men thought this added to Lee's dramatic flair. Opponents found him relentless and sometimes imperious, while friends praised his sharp mind and candor, all of which he displayed in the Confederation Congress that September as he led the first campaign against the Constitution.

Just as Richard Henry Lee anticipated, the proposal out of the Philadelphia Convention "could not have a dispassionate and impartial review in Congress; nor, indeed, had it." Despite the efforts of Lee, Grayson, and prominent New Yorkers Robert Yates and John Lansing, the returning Philadelphia delegates enjoyed a decided advantage in advocating for their proposal: they composed nearly a third of all congressmen (ten of the thirty-three considering the Constitution on 26–27 September). They had spent all summer reasoning through the plan and so arrived back in New York with well-rehearsed answers to critics' questions.[19]

Although he was frustrated with the compromises that changed his initial constitutional design, Madison led the cause in Congress, as he had in Philadelphia. He was an introverted intellectual, just over five feet tall and prone to speaking barely above a whisper about complex, even esoteric top-

Richard Henry Lee. Special Collections, John D. Rockefeller Jr. Library, The Colonial Williamsburg Foundation

ics. It is easy, looking back and in light of larger-than-life characters such as Benjamin Franklin, George Washington, and Patrick Henry, to underestimate Madison. But he was steel-spined and tenacious. He was also perfectly prepared and thinking two steps ahead of the skeptics in Congress. And he had an important practical advantage: the Confederation Congress had, after all, sanctioned the Philadelphia meeting because virtually everyone agreed that retaining the Articles unchanged was untenable. Richard Henry Lee commiserated with George Mason about getting strong-armed. "It was with us, as with you, this or nothing," he complained.[20]

The pressing practical issue before the Confederation Congress was whether to send the Constitution to the states and, if so, with what directions. Richard Henry Lee and William Grayson argued that the document should only be forwarded to the states along with a clear statement that it violated the thirteenth article of the Articles of Confederation, which required unanimous consent of all state legislatures to amend the Articles. They also wanted to underscore the unauthorized conduct of the Philadelphia delegates by including the original charge of the meeting: "for the sole and express purpose of revising the Articles." James Madison and Edward Carrington, meanwhile, lobbied Congress to formally approve the Constitution and notify the states of their endorsement.[21]

Within days and despite strong opposition, congressmen voted to submit the Constitution to the states for their consideration. The decision was forced, Richard Henry Lee wrote George Mason, by "a coalition of Monarchy men, Military men, Aristocrats, and Drones whose noise, impudence & zeal exceeds all belief."[22]

The two sides did manage to compromise on the language of the notification to the states, agreeing to make no mention of whether Congress approved or disapproved of the Constitution. Or so Lee and his allies thought. As was customary after divisive debates, congressmen took a vote to signal their consensus on the narrow matter of sending the document to the states for their deliberation. At that point, supporters of the Constitution in the Confederation Congress made an extraordinarily savvy move—or a duplicitous one, depending on one's perspective. They inserted the word "unanimously" into the notice to the states. The wording left the impression of unanimous approval of the Constitution itself, not just the process of having states debate the proposal. Richard Henry Lee saw, too late, the strategy: zealous advocates of the Constitution wanted "to have it mistaken for an Unanimous approbation of the thing." George Washington congratulated James Madison on the clever move. "This apparent unanimity will have its effect," he predicted. "Not every one has opportunities to peep behind the curtain," Washington understood, so "the appearance of unanimity in that body . . . will be of great importance."[23]

To brand their cause, supporters of the Constitution also seized on a potent word: *Federalist*. In fact, it was the critics of the Constitution, the men who championed a design of government that recognized the sovereignty of individual states, joined in a confederation to advance limited, specific powers, who were federalist in the then-common meaning of the word. Whatever men read into the more ambiguous parts of the Constitution, it was abundantly clear that the design did not retain the sovereignty of individual states. A more accurate divide might have been drawn between *Federalists* and *Nationalists*—the former those who favored revisions to the Articles of Confederation and the latter those advocating the Constitution. But by the time they arrived in New York, supporters of the Constitution had claimed the far more favorable, familiar name for themselves and their governmental plan. They then branded skeptics of the Constitution *Anti-Federalists*. The negative-sounding and distortive name was never embraced by opponents to ratification, but it stuck—emblematic of the ability of Constitution advocates to seize the momentum and define the parameters of debate. Historians still use the terms today, for, though fraught, they remain the most familiar and succinct way of explaining divisions over ratification.

Opponents of the proposed Constitution—those who came to be called Anti-Federalists—intuited yet another manipulative tactic: Federalists intended to use time to advance their agenda. "The plan," Richard Henry Lee saw, "is, to push the business on with great dispatch, & with as little opposition as possible; that it may be adopted before it has stood the test of Reflection & due examination." This might work in small states, acting out of weakness, or among men awed by the heroes who signed the Constitution. But New York, Pennsylvania, and especially Virginia could stand against this strategy, Lee believed. He therefore urged Virginians doubtful about the proposed government to try their best to slow things down in the Old Dominion.[24]

Lee lost the first fight against the Constitution in New York City. He and like-minded representatives were caught off guard, outargued, and outpoliticked by their better-prepared opponents. In many ways, that brief struggle in the Confederation Congress was a rehearsal for the larger drama that lay ahead. Men disagreed over the best structure for government and the precise meaning of constitutional language: their quarrels were philosophical, legal, and theoretical. They were especially divided over the balance of power between the state and federal governments and how shared sovereignty might work. But the contest was also political, presaging the manipulation of language, public opinion, and timing that would drive ratification debates in all the states.[25]

As Richard Henry Lee struggled against James Madison in New York, George Mason and George Washington headed to Virginia. Though traveling separately, Mason and Washington, by strange coincidence, both survived potentially fatal accidents on the journey home. Mason's driver overturned their coach outside Baltimore. Though not crippling, the injury Mason sustained to his neck was serious; several weeks passed before he saw the effects wear off. Washington's carriage crashed into a river when a bridge suddenly collapsed. Luckily, he had decided to walk across, which saved him from a likely deadly fall.[26] Perhaps the accidents seemed an ominous prediction of what lay ahead. But the brushes with death didn't temper either man's zeal to get to Virginia and persuade others to adopt his point of view.

Washington and Mason arrived back in Virginia to a terrible drought. In Fredericksburg farmers endured "the dryest Summer remembered by the oldest Men in this Country," and though tobacco fared well, the corn crops were "shorter than ever known." James Madison worried that, come harvest, "there will be scarcely subsistence for the inhabitants" of Orange County.[27]

The news Mason and Washington brought from Philadelphia ran like wildfire across Virginia and swept aside most men's concerns about their crops. Kept in the dark all summer long, Virginians, like all Americans, could not wait to learn about the new plan of government. And men with firsthand knowledge of events in Philadelphia were eager to seek out their friends and spread the news. The first copies of the Constitution arrived in late September, and newspapers began immediately publishing the document so that Virginians could enter into informed debate about the future of America's government. In mid-October and to that same end, the state legislature bought five thousand copies of the Constitution to distribute across the Old Dominion.

George Mason actually started his fight against ratification before he left Philadelphia. Near the end of the convention, Benjamin Franklin urged all the men still harboring doubts to refrain from going home and sowing dissent. If every delegate shared his particular grievances with his neighbors and constituents, Franklin said, it could undermine the good work of the convention. Furthermore, Franklin hoped that every man with strong reservations would "on this occasion doubt a little of his own infallibility" and sign the Constitution. To make the matter easier, signatures did not signify personal support for the plan. Men signed only as representatives of states and "in witness" of the "unanimous consent of the States present." How many wavering delegates Franklin persuaded is unknown. In the end, only three men resisted his appeal.[28]

George Mason, though he respected Benjamin Franklin, was not about to sign the Constitution—not as a supporter, a witness, or under any other circumstance. He was already at work cataloging the flaws he saw in the Constitution, and the day after Franklin's plea he announced his dissent. Before he headed home, Mason mailed Richard Henry Lee a detailed account of his objections to the Constitution.

James Madison suspected that once George Mason returned to Virginia he would feel "under the necessity of justifying his refusal to sign" and so could be counted on to "muster every possible" reason.[29] He was right. Thinking about the Constitution doubtless consumed Mason's trip home. Despite his injury, once he got to Gunston Hall in late September, he immediately set about refining the criticisms he'd shared with Lee. In early October 1787, when he was satisfied with the revisions, Mason privately circulated his treatise among friends and neighbors.

Mason had slowly come to his skepticism in Philadelphia, but with "Objections to the Constitution of Government Formed by the Convention," he leveled a thoroughgoing, unqualified condemnation of the proposed new government. In the first place, and now suddenly displaying grave alarm, he announced, "there is no Declaration of Rights." That was only the start of his myriad concerns. In the House of Representatives sixty-five men would presume to reflect the interests of all the diverse states. Clearly, Mason reasoned, "there is not the Substance, but the Shadow of Representation." The Senate held too much unchecked power. The judiciary promised to allow "the Rich to oppress & ruin the Poor." The president had no council but unrestrained power to pardon. The executive and legislative branches were dangerously combined. Because a simple majority within the national legislature could decide commercial policies, southern states would, Mason predicted, "be ruined." The Congress faced no term limits, knew no boundaries to authority, and could "extend their Power as far as they shall think proper." And, returning to where he started, Mason repeated: "There is no Declaration of any kind preserving the Liberty of the Press, the Trial by jury in civil Causes, nor against the Danger of standing Armys in time of Peace." This was, he understood, a recipe for tyranny.[30]

George Mason joined Richard Henry Lee, Elbridge Gerry, Robert Yates, and John Lansing at the forefront of a diverse group of Anti-Federalists whose influence spanned the continent. Although citizens opposed ratification for varied, often inconsistent reasons, these men's writings were widely reprinted, and their ideas shaped debates throughout the states.[31]

While Mason spread his grave misgivings, George Washington campaigned to win converts to his point of view. Like Mason, Washington worked across the states, but he was connected to a far more unified network that ran from New England to the lower South. Unlike Mason, Washington's first order of business in Virginia was courting the state's most powerful men. On 24 September, Washington wrote three former governors, Patrick Henry, Benjamin Harrison, and Thomas Nelson Jr., sending along a copy of the Constitution to each. "I accompany it," Washington misleadingly said, "with no observation." He assured each man, in identical letters, that "your own Judgment will at once discover the good, and the exceptional parts of it." But the letters did not end there. Washington offered a great deal of "observation" and not a little advocacy. "I sincerely believe it is the best that could be obtained at this time," he wrote, adding that adopting the Constitution "is in my opinion desirable." Another "observation" followed, this one dire and, he hoped, motivating: "It appears to me that the political concerns of this Country are, in a manner, suspended by a thread."[32]

Washington wanted to appear above the fray, so publicly he disavowed any firm opinion on the outcome of the ratification contest. But that was a posture to protect his reputation, not a reality. Once at Mount Vernon, he immediately shared with trusted friends and correspondents his enthusiasm for the federal plan and contempt for its critics. While especially concerned with his home state, Washington kept up a vigorous campaign elsewhere, eager to use his influence in crucial and divided states such as New York and Massachusetts. One visitor to Mount Vernon in early October remarked, "I never saw him so keen for any thing in my Life, as he is for the adoption of the new Form of Government."[33]

A small cohort of lawyers and wealthy landowners framed the Constitution, but it could become law only after citizens weighed in. Because citizens would elect representatives to the state ratification conventions, every voter needed to inform himself about the historic decision confronting the country. Americans took that duty very seriously, and upon learning about the federal plan, they set about scrutinizing every part of it.

Although the signatures of so many leading lights of the Revolution—including the "father of his country"—gave advocates for ratification an initial boost in public opinion, deliberations transcended the self-styled "better sort" who usually controlled politics, particularly in southern states. All across the

United States, ratification debates prompted an unprecedented level of participation by citizens. And Americans' reactions to the proposed government did not simply filter down from the elites who attended the Philadelphia Convention. Citizens took it upon themselves to weigh the merits of the Constitution, judging and not simply parroting the opinions of political insiders. The result was a staggering, continent-wide outpouring of curiosity and conversation.[34]

In Virginia, between the unveiling of the Constitution in late September 1787 and the start of the ratification convention on 2 June 1788, discussions about the federal plan resounded on "the court green, the race-course, and the muster-field." Virginians understood they were living in an era that would "be the most interesting you ever saw, or ever will see." Not surprisingly, "the state of our affairs at present, is of such moment, as even to rouse the dead." A Pennsylvania visitor to southwest Virginia marveled that "even in these remote wilds the people are deeply engaged in that science. The new Constitution is the subject of universal discussion."[35]

The conversations might have been universal, but participating in deciding was not. Constitution making was under the exclusive purview of property-owning white men because suffrage was strictly limited in eighteenth-century Virginia. The Declaration of Rights proclaimed "that all men, having sufficient evidence of permanent common interest with, and attachment to, the community, have the right of suffrage." Under long-standing colonial law, which Virginians retained in their 1776 constitution, "permanent common interest" specifically meant owning one hundred acres of undeveloped land or twenty-five acres with a house and farm. Not every white male citizen of Virginia, then, had the right to vote—only the landowners.[36]

Some white women relished witnessing and contributing to the discussions about the Constitution, but they had no direct role in formal politics. Whatever white women thought about the proposal out of Philadelphia, their votes were certainly not solicited and their voices are mostly lost in the past. Martha Washington, as experienced with and committed to the revolutionary cause as any woman in America, made a telling observation about both men's zeal for and women's place in debating the Constitution: "We have not a single article of news but pollitick which I do not concern myself about."[37]

African American men and women were at once a part of the design of the American Republic and apart from it. They were excluded from participating in civic culture in eighteenth-century America, even though their forced labor drove the country's economy. Their systematic legal debasement also underlay assumptions of white male equality during the revolutionary era; a perpetual racial divide ensured that all white men could be free and equal. At the same time, more and more white citizens recognized in the wake of American independence that slavery could not be reconciled with their republican principles. As a result of these two fundamental and contradictory impulses, the institution of racial slavery became a controversial, divisive issue in the 1780s. In Philadelphia, despite tense disagreements, those committed to maintaining America's racial order ultimately carried the day. African Americans' fates were written into the document, but Virginia's 290,000 slaves played no direct role in deciding whether the Constitution became law—nor did black men (and certainly not black women) in any state in the union.[38]

Across America, however, property-owning white men saw debating the Constitution as a political and patriotic act—an inviolable civic duty. In advance of their respective state conventions, they studied the document and meticulously refined their varied perspectives. Private correspondences, newspaper stories, and pamphlets flew across the states, filled with fierce arguments, sometimes scholarly and sometimes venomous, over the proposed change in government. By the time of the Richmond meeting—in a pattern duplicated across America—these ideas, rehearsed by citizens for months, were polished to a high sheen.

In early commentaries on the Constitution one sees many of the controversial issues that would drive men to oppose ratification at the formal conventions. The previously sovereign states ceded too much authority to the central government. The president held too much power, most distressingly over a standing army. The legislative and executive branches were too connected, particularly with the vice president, "whose sole business" complained the critics, "seems to be to intrigue." There was barely the illusion of representation in Congress. The framers failed to codify citizens' rights. Taxation powers seemed unlimited. As vast a territory as the United States could never be governed as a single republic. And, of particular concern to southern planters, their states "will be little more than appendages to those to the northward."[39]

Likewise, one hears from the earliest public debates claims that Federalists would make in the ratification conventions. The most learned and distinguished patriots across America cooperated to create the Constitution—as brilliant a work as was ever produced by human hands. The new plan solved all the problems plaguing the unworkable Articles of Confederation. It cre-

ated a stable and just government that would earn the respect of foreign nations and ensure the financial stability of the United States. Citizens' rights,
threatened by social upheaval in recent years, could now be protected. Small-
minded critics of the proposal offered no alternative, only endless complaints.
Their rejection of the Constitution would invite foreign invasion or force the
states into separate, regionally based and inevitably fractious confederacies.
In sum, without the Constitution, Americans' experiment in republican government would collapse. George Washington warned that "this, or a dissolution of the Union awaits our choice, & are the only alternatives before us."[40]

Virginians were not alone in confronting this trial; but the question of
ratification was thrown into high relief in the Old Dominion because it was
the single most important as well as the most evenly divided state in the
union. Virginians also took an especially long time, both in the lead-up to the
formal debates and at the state convention itself, to work through their ideas.
And because so many influential and prolific advocates lived in Virginia, they
amassed quite a record of their opinions about the federal plan.

As Virginians worked through every element of the Constitution, sometimes their conversations took a formal turn. Some residents called town
meetings to discuss the Constitution, for example, and others issued formal
directions to their representatives in the House of Delegates. The "Political
Club" of the town of Danville, the unofficial capital of the Kentucky district
in the western regions of Virginia, met almost every week for nearly three
months to debate and revise the Constitution.[41] Virginians also engaged in
countless casual discussions in their homes and with their neighbors. The
records of most informal exchanges, alas, cannot be recovered. But a wealth
of personal correspondences and published writings has survived from the
eighteenth century—the largest cache of materials on the ratification controversy anywhere in the country. These sources show how profoundly troubled
Virginians were about their future and that, in searching for a solution, they
often turned on one another.

The longer they talked about the Constitution, the more often Virginians
decided that men who disagreed with them did not simply hold different,
misguided opinions; instead, they posed a mortal threat to the American Republic. This represented a major change in political traditions. Quarrels and
rivalries had marked the American cause from the outset of the Revolutionary
War, but patriots tried to treat differences within their own ranks according to

rules of civility: good and honorable men could disagree. Not so in 1787–88. The demand from Philadelphia that states vote yes or no—with no alterations and no middle ground—had a polarizing effect on civic culture. Virginians also became convinced that they were gambling with the future of republican government, for themselves, for the union of states, and for the entire world. Though they actually held a range of reactions to the Constitution, the political culture soon pushed Virginians toward an "us vs. them" mentality. They then carried out a vicious war of words—of character assassination, exaggerations, rumor mongering, and jingoism—in personal letters and the pages of Virginia's newspapers.

Zealots on both sides used fiery rhetoric because they agreed on what was at stake: everything they had spent twelve years trying to build. "The moment is at hand," read one typical letter published in October in the *Virginia Independent Chronicle*, "when America will rise respected and affluent, or sink into contempt, anarchy, and perhaps a total dissolution of our short existence as a nation." Similar language was elsewhere, to be certain, but because of the tremendous influence of Virginia, it really did seem that, more than any other state, its voters would determine "not the fate of an individual, but that of millions . . . not the welfare of a state, but, that of mankind."[42]

But what decision should patriotic Virginians make?

Federalists pronounced the country in "a distressed and ruinous state," with the economy collapsing, civic virtue in a freefall, and society barreling toward anarchy or foreign invasion because of the failings of the Articles of Confederation. The only hope of survival lay in quickly ratifying the Constitution. Anti-Federalists countered that the only imminent mortal danger facing Americans was the Constitution. Certainly, most conceded, the Articles required revision. But the solution was surely not a distant, consolidated government that destroyed the sovereignty of the states and the liberty of citizens. If Americans ratified the Constitution, Anti-Federalists predicted, they would soon find themselves "broiling in a Hell of Slavery."[43]

Lost on the writer was the awful irony of a generation of slaveholders fretting over the "Hell of Slavery" they would endure if they made the wrong decision about the Constitution. He would have known that every major player in Virginia politics—Federalist and Anti-Federalist alike—held slaves, and that they did so while fully acknowledging that slavery violated their republican ideals. On the eve of the Revolution, Patrick Henry condemned slavery as "a principle as repugnant to humanity, as it is inconsistent with the bible and destructive to liberty." At the Philadelphia Convention no less, James Madison criticized making "the mere distinction of colour" the basis for "the most oppressive dominion ever exercised by man over man." Still, in Virginia, it was February 1788 before any newspaper article pointed out that "it would better become us all as men and Christians" to end the cruel exploitation of slaves already in Virginia "than to permit any more to be subjected to the like sufferings," which the Constitution allowed by sanctioning the international slave trade. That appeal was strategically made to court Quaker voters.[44]

Though reluctant about or indifferent to discussing slavery's place in the Constitution, newspaper editors provided immediate and ceaseless coverage of the Constitution, spreading and deepening the rancor between Federalists and Anti-Federalists. Printers held strong convictions about the proposal, felt a civic obligation to inform the public, and wanted to make money by meeting Virginians' demands to know more about the Constitution. By publishing news and commentaries, Virginia papers heightened public awareness of all the issues surrounding the Constitution.

Newspapers also lowered the political discourse by publicizing inflammatory screeds. Within weeks of the revelation of the Constitution, writers filled Virginia's newspapers with "fulsome panegyric" and "low lifed invective." Occasionally printers ran forged articles misrepresenting the attitudes of leading men or edited essays to change the context and even the meaning of an author's ideas in order to skew public opinion. But usually they did not need to resort to such tactics. Editors received more than enough blistering submissions to overflow the pages of their papers.[45]

Newspapermen gave supporters of the Constitution a key advantage in their efforts to influence public opinion. Nationally nearly 90 percent of American newspapers sympathized with the Federalists. Most newspapers— and certainly the most widely read—were published in eastern cities: Boston, New York, and especially Philadelphia. City dwellers, who composed less than 15 percent of the American population, overwhelmingly supported the Constitution because most made their living off commerce and saw the financial advantages of a stronger federal government. These commercially minded advertisers and readers pushed editors toward the Federalist camp. Though Virginia was less one-sided than most states, Anti-Federalists in the Old Dominion were still at a distinct numerical disadvantage in the newspaper wars.

Federalists routinely used sympathetic papers to publicly malign the character of men who did not share their views on the Constitution, dismissing their questions as absurd and condemning them as "either consummately impudent, or consummately ignorant." Writers insisted again and again that Anti-Federalist objections were fabricated. Their real motivations, editorialists claimed, were selfish. Some dreaded the loss of their personal political power. Such men, one proponent of ratification complained, "would indignantly trample on the freedom and happiness of mankind, rather than relinquish the dangerous power of ruling an extensive state with unbounded authority." Others were just greedy: they "fear that good order and regulations once established, will lead to the payment of public and private debts."[46]

At the same time, Federalists published fawning tributes to the Philadelphia Convention, hailing it an achievement unrivaled in the annals of history. One enthusiast likened it to "the dazzling splendor of the sun." "My admiration," he gushed, "knows no bounds." Another supporter calculated that "had the united wisdom of the universe been collected into one center," the results could not have surpassed the Philadelphia Convention. "I may venture to foretell," wrote yet another, "that the *Bible* and the *Federal Constitution* will be read and reverenced, when the arguments, insidiously employed against them, are forgotten."[47]

Men who could not see the merits of the Constitution, or would not because of self-interest, were blasted in the press as treacherous conspirators. Federalist writers warned readers that a "dangerous Junto" was trying to mislead them. Wise voters should ensure that opponents to ratification "meet with that execration and contempt they so justly merit." Some flatly condemned Anti-Federalists as "enemies to their country."[48]

More subtle Federalists used their influence with printers to invidiously compare the Constitution to the Articles of Confederation. The majority of Americans had lost confidence in the Articles, and many thought retaining the confederation government posed an imminent existential threat to the young country. As with the "yes or no" demand out of Philadelphia, Federalists succeeded again in framing public debates around a dichotomy of their making: either you were for the Constitution or for the Articles. They also played up in friendly newspapers the natural advantage of having a clear plan, which the Anti-Federalists lacked.

Even with all these disadvantages, however, Anti-Federalists kept forcing Federalists on the defensive. Federalists constantly complained that their opponents hurled one unsubstantiated accusation after another. Malicious

assaults against the Constitution should not, writers urged, dissuade voters from considering its many benefits or from seeing the dire alternatives.
"When I reflect upon the fatal consequences which will inevitably follow the
rejection of this government," announced one typical essayist, "I am tortured
with doubt and anxiety." If voters were seduced into sending to the Virginia
Ratification Convention men opposed to the Constitution, he predicted, "dissolution of the present feeble confederacy would be the first and smallest
evil; anarchy would quickly follow." Remember, he cautioned, "a fool may ask
more questions in half an hour, than a wise man can answer in seven years."[49]

Anti-Federalists trying to shape public opinion found in that sort of criticism a key advantage of their own: they didn't necessarily need to offer a
better plan but only to create enough doubts in voters' minds to prevent ratification. In the fall of 1787, opponents to ratification were fairly successful in
doing just that while evading questions about what they ultimately wanted
to happen. Even for voters paying close attention, it was difficult to see what
Anti-Federalists sought beyond a rejection of the Constitution. The questions
were asked, to be certain: If Anti-Federalists succeeded and ratification failed,
what did they want to do next? Would Congress call a second convention?
Could such an undertaking ever succeed? Would the states break apart into
separate confederacies? When answers did come, though, they were varied,
sometimes contradictory, and often opaque.

Anti-Federalists were far clearer and more unified in condemning the
stunning innovations in the Constitution. Presenting themselves as the faithful defenders of the Revolution, they depicted the plan out of Philadelphia as
an abject and intentional betrayal of the recent, noble past. In the words of
one contributor to a Winchester paper, the Constitution was "incompatible
with, and subversive of, those virtuous plans established by our brave and
worthy patriots of the late revolution."[50]

Even with fewer newspapermen on their side, Anti-Federalists had little
problem questioning in print every part of the proposed government. The
creation of a permanent army under the authority of the new chief executive, for example, shocked them. Eighteenth-century Americans had long
seen standing armies as the ultimate threat to personal liberty. Capturing
the widespread perceptions of that age, one essayist reminded his readers
that "standing armies in times of peace are dangerous to a free country." Pro-
fessional soldiers were "generally composed of the dregs of the people," and
"unfit for any other employment" because "the unconditional submission to

their commands of their superiors" made them "instruments of tyranny and oppression."[51] The plan for a standing army, wrote another critic, would "rivet the chains of perpetual slavery upon us." Free government and a standing army were "absolutely incompatible." If the Constitution passed, he warned, "every soul in America will be an absolute slave."[52]

Other criticisms—of the presidency, Senate, federal taxation, number of representatives, treaty powers, and absence of a bill of rights—all followed this same design. No wonder advocates for ratification feared it would take seven years to answer the Anti-Federalists' barrage of complaints!

With writers raising question after question about the Constitution, public opinion started to slip through the Federalists' hands. When Virginians first heard about the Constitution and all the powerful men, including George Washington, who supported it, many inclined to see the best in the plan. But, as James McClurg and others told James Madison in late October, time "caused this disposition to subside." In place of first-blush confidence, "every man's mind is turn'd to a subtle investigation of the plan." Madison then shared with Washington the concerning reports that cast "the enthusiasm in favor of the new Constitution as subsiding, and giving place to a spirit of criticism."[53]

The "father of his country" was flummoxed by this turn of events. Although he continued to affect an air of disinterest, by November George Washington was clearly upset by this growing "spirit of criticism"—which he took quite personally. From his point of view, Federalists were not only right about the structure of government, they were also more virtuous and honorable in their efforts to inform citizens. They took the high road, thoughtfully, dispassionately presenting their (correct) ideas about the Constitution. Conversely, Washington repeatedly charged in private letters, Anti-Federalists used every low tactic they could imagine to "alarm the apprehensions of the ignorant or unthinking." Criticisms of the Constitution were, he complained, not just mistaken but "addressed to the passions of the people; and obviously calculated to rouse their fears."[54]

Although many Virginians voiced their skepticism about the redesign of the government, Washington, a gentleman and accustomed to deference, assumed the problem originated with other gentlemen, namely his former friend George Mason. A tussle between Washington and Mason in the pages of Virginia newspapers in November reveals a great deal about the contest for public opinion and how deep the ambition to arouse "the passions of the people" ran.

The long friendship between Mason and Washington came to a fast close when Mason circulated within the local gentry his "Objections" to the Constitution. Out of respect for Washington, Mason sent him a copy. "My Objections are not numerous," Mason wrote, "tho' in my Mind, some of them are capital ones."[55] Sending the letter was a mistake. With the help of his personal secretary, Tobias Lear, Washington immediately started networking to undermine Mason, both in Virginia and throughout the states. He sent a copy of Mason's "Objections" to James Madison, who was still in New York City, to gather a rebuttal. And he made sure a powerful speech given by James Wilson in Philadelphia got reprinted in the Virginia papers. Wilson's defense of the Constitution, Washington believed, "will place the most of Colo. Mason's objections in their true point of light."[56]

Washington and Lear knew that Mason was a formidable player in Virginia politics, and they tried to diminish his influence by damaging his reputation, a long tradition among Virginia gentry. They spread the false rumor that Mason's conduct in Philadelphia had cost him the respect of his neighbors. He was, Washington told James Madison, "obnoxious" in Philadelphia and "reprobated in this County." They also dismissed the substance of Mason's criticisms. The few ideas that had any legitimacy had been responsibly settled in Philadelphia, they claimed. As for the majority of Mason's objections, Washington and Lear insisted, in language they often used against their rivals, that they "seem to be calculated only to alarm the fears of the people."[57]

Washington and Lear's campaign did not slow Mason, however. He continued privately sharing his "Objections" as growing numbers of Virginians reached similar conclusions about the Constitution. Many men found Washington's criticism of Mason's ideas unpersuasive. In fact, Mason's "Objections" became one of the most widely circulated of any of the Anti-Federalist writings—though that was *not* Mason's plan.

In eighteenth-century political culture, men rarely disclosed their names when publishing advocacy pieces. Pseudonyms were traditional and respectful: a man of George Mason's influence putting his name to a published lobbying campaign would have appeared heavy-handed—an unseemly attempt to exploit the ideal of deference and exert undue influence over other men. Since he was so respected, the logic went, he should not push other citizens to adopt his view by using his name. Writing under a pseudonym allowed readers to decide based on the merits of the ideas, not the reputation of the author. Nearly all newspaper writers followed that tradition. Mason went even further. He decided not to publish his essay at all, choosing only to circulate it in manuscript form and with friends. Of course those friends shared Mason's ideas with their friends who shared with their friends and so on.

In late October 1787, with his influence widening, George Mason arrived in Richmond to take his seat in the House of Delegates. He was the only Virginian who attended the Philadelphia Convention serving in the state legislature. This afforded Mason great power to shape others' views, both the legislators who would need to discuss the Constitution and the public closely observing their actions. The second delegate from Fairfax County was David Stuart, a George Washington ally. Washington, assuming Mason would use the occasion to publicly reveal his "Objections," provided Stuart with a copy of James Wilson's brilliant defense of the Constitution to directly rebut Mason. But Stuart never got the chance.

Though manuscript copies of Mason's "Objections" had long since reached Richmond, Mason declined to formally publicize his opinions within the legislature. "At a proper season," he announced, the fullness of his concerns "should be communicated to his countrymen."[58] He also decided not to seek a printer. The informal means of communicating his "Objections" seemed to be working just fine.

Tobias Lear, frustrated and clearly acting with the approval of George Washington, had had enough. He delivered Mason's "Objections"—with Mason's name—to the editor of the *Virginia Journal*, followed by a point-by-point rebuttal, penned by Lear. Though he disclosed Mason's name, Lear chose for himself the telling pseudonym "Brutus."[59]

When he saw the newspaper, Mason was understandably livid, and his supporters retaliated. Two weeks after the *Virginia Journal* published George Mason's "Objections"—without Mason's permission or foreknowledge—"Philanthropos" rose to his defense in the same paper. Far from seeking to push an agenda, Mason had, Philanthropos insisted, declined to publish his essay out of an abundance of respect for his countrymen and the political process: "He wishes every man to judge, and form an opinion for himself." Philanthropos was appalled that Brutus charged Mason with attempting to "alarm the fears of the people." He refuted all of Brutus's criticism and matched him step for step in terms of character assassination. "Beware my countrymen!" Philanthropos warned his readers, of "our enemies" and their "ambitious schemes." Philanthropos predicted the worst of all outcomes from too hasty a move toward too powerful a government: a civil war, when "fathers and sons, sheath their swords in one another's bowels in the field, and their wives and daughters, are exposed to the . . . lust of ruffians."[60]

Barely two months after the Constitution arrived in Virginia, the newspaper wars had reached the highest echelons of society—and the divide between two of the state's most distinguished patriots was laid bare for everyone to see. Brutus and Philanthropos moved the disagreement between Washington and Mason from the parlor to the papers, a reflection of the broadening—and intensity—of the contest for Virginia voters.

As the ruckus over the Constitution got louder and louder, the most politically influential man in the state remained conspicuously silent. For a month after the Constitution arrived in Virginia, Patrick Henry said nothing. It was a surprising move from a man universally admired for his oratorical talents, and one at odds with the ceaseless, fiery debates roiling Virginia. Patrick Henry had always been an unwavering advocate for Virginia, but he was not an ideologically driven man. His contemporaries could not predict whether he would think Virginians' interests and liberty would be better served by the Constitution or not.

When Patrick Henry told no one his opinion, speculation filled the void. Partisans on both sides searched for any sign that he agreed with them: they gossiped about his finances, his friends' views, and his past conduct to glean some insight into his reaction to the Constitution. As press coverage and strategizing escalated, rumors about Henry multiplied. Still he kept his own counsel. "The Sentiments of Mr. Henry," George Washington told James Madison in early October, "are not known in these parts."[61]

No one at the time knew what to make of this uncharacteristic discretion, which was exactly what Patrick Henry wanted. In retrospect, while his fellow Virginians were playing checkers, he was playing chess.

On 19 October, Henry finally broke his silence in a long-delayed reply to George Washington's letter sharing the Constitution. It was unusually, strategically taciturn. "I cannot bring my Mind to accord with the proposed Constitution," Henry told Washington. Perhaps, he allowed, "mature Reflection may furnish me Reasons to change my present Sentiments." For now, he closed, "The Concern I feel on this account, is really greater than I am able to express."[62] It was a stunning loss for words from the Revolution's leading orator and a crushing blow to the friends of the Constitution, for there was no denying the power Patrick Henry exerted over Virginia politics. Henry soon found his tongue; within days of writing Washington, he began assailing the Constitution and its supporters. Anti-Federalists rejoiced as momentum swung their way.

Patrick Henry's opposition to the proposed Constitution raised a fresh question: *Would* Virginia plan a convention? Even as citizens quarreled and newspaper accounts reached a fevered pitch, Virginians assumed their government would take the next formal step. In many of the largest counties citizens had already directed their representatives in the legislature to call for a convention. And in some counties, men were gathering to debate which way their convention delegates should vote. But in October, that all suddenly seemed premature. Federalists gossiped that Patrick Henry might stonewall the Constitution by convincing members of the state legislature to simply refuse to call a convention. That was an accurate reading of his political power, but a gross underestimation of his political skill. Soon enough, Virginia Federalists would realize that Patrick Henry was even cleverer than they feared.

2 Winter 1787–1788, Jockeying for Power

Every corner of the city resounds with politicks.

James Breckinridge, 31 October 1787

FROM THE VERY START OF HIS LEGAL CAREER, Patrick Henry knew how to enthrall a jury and leave them, as he did in a storied trial in the 1760s, "so delighted with their captivity, that they followed implicitly, whithersoever he led them, that, at his bidding, their tears flowed from pity, and their cheeks flushed with indignation."[1] Henry brought that same magnetism to state government, where he served off and on nearly his whole adult life. His political principles, except for his unwavering commitment to Virginia, were fluid or, according to some critics, inconsistent. But his political genius was unrivaled in the state. Henry commanded more respect in Virginia than any man other than George Washington—and he surpassed Washington in some quarters. Though not a particularly gifted legislative thinker, he inspired men to follow him and was a brilliant strategist.

Among Patrick Henry's many political talents was an intuitive mastery of the art of timing. He calculated his entry into the public debates about the

Constitution to exert the greatest influence at the most significant moment. In the initial frenzy to share and shape public opinion on the Constitution, he shrewdly bided his time. Revealing his views too early would have squandered a rich opportunity. Why hand others the chance to challenge his opinions? So he waited.

As citizens continued their interrogation of the proposed Constitution, it fell to the Virginia General Assembly to make the next substantive move. As was traditional, representatives convened in mid-October, after the crops were in and as the weather was turning. Fall 1787 was the first session operating under a new law that fined absent members—a frequent problem that sometimes meant there was not a quorum and no business could be conducted. But absenteeism was not a problem during this session. The better than normal turnout was likely owing as much to the business before the Assembly as to the new election law.

The men who designed Virginia's state constitution did so in the midst of the Revolution, when fears of distant, unchecked governmental powers were pervasive. Like most other states, power in Virginia was decentralized, and the structures of the government reflected Virginians' commitment to preserving their dearly bought rights. The governor exercised little independent authority. In the state's bicameral legislature, the House of Delegates held far more power than the Senate. All laws originated in the House of Delegates; the Senate could approve their actions or not, but could amend bills only with the consent of the House. So, when Virginia's state government needed to formally respond to the letter from the Continental Congress requesting it call a convention to debate the Constitution, all eyes turned to the delegates. Among those men, Patrick Henry held tremendous sway. The delegates were scheduled to discuss the Constitution on 25 October. A few days earlier, on 19 October, Henry broke his silence: it was just enough time to ensure the news spread far and wide but not so much as to allow a robust Federalist rebuttal.

There was time for wild speculation, though, and word spread that Henry would try to block the Constitution by manipulating other legislators into refusing to sanction a convention. Since more legislators were skeptical of than enthusiastic about the Constitution, such an audacious move seemed possible—especially if Henry led it. An adept vote counter could see a path for Henry if he decided to stop the process before it even started. Rhode Island had already made that choice, so it was not unprecedented.

Refusing to call a convention fit the political narrative that Federalists wanted to create: critics of the Constitution were self-interested, scheming, and untrustworthy; they would resort to any political stunt to have their way, even if it meant undoing the republican experiment. But Henry did not play into their hand. He disarmed his critics by proclaiming that "it transcended our powers to decide on the Constitution; that it must go before a Convention."[2] Without saying as much, Henry was creating his own narrative: that he, unlike the men in Philadelphia, followed the rules of Congress, sought an open airing of ideas, and trusted the people. His actions implied that secrecy and intrigue were the tactics of the Federalists, not the Anti-Federalists.

Henry's call for an official debate won universal support among the legislators, Federalists and Anti-Federalists alike. Although citizens were generally "divided and extremely agitated" over the Constitution, holding a convention was one thing on which Virginians mostly agreed. Members of the House of Delegates nervous about the high stakes and tensions surrounding the Constitution felt good about making a decision so in line with public opinion.[3]

But the questions kept coming. Who could serve? How would representatives be chosen? When should they meet? These practical choices held profound political implications—they might, in fact, decide the ratification vote.

As legislators turned from *whether* to *how* to plan a convention, their consensus evaporated. When Francis Corbin, a strong supporter of the Constitution, made the motion that "a Convention should be called, according to the recommendation of Congress," Patrick Henry and George Mason immediately objected. That language, they charged, allowed Virginians only to vote up or down on the Constitution.[4]

Mason and Henry wanted convention delegates to be empowered to make changes to the federal plan before ratifying it. Henry proposed and Mason seconded an addition to Corbin's resolution specifically allowing the convention to draft conditional—what critics of the Constitution usually called "previous"—amendments. Other Virginians favored requested (or "subsequent") amendments: changes proposed by the state conventions but not required as a condition of ratifying. And still others thought any discussion of changes, before or after ratification, should be avoided. As legislators deliberated, Mason could not resist launching a brief, preemptive assault on the Constitution, making excellent use of vivid, even inflammatory language. He had not, he announced, supported the federal plan in Philadelphia, because "I thought it repugnant to our highest interests." Had he signed, he continued, "I might

Patrick Henry. Portrait by George B. Matthews. Prints and Photographs Division, Library of Congress

have been justly regarded as a traitor to my country." By "my country," Mason meant Virginia, not the union of states. Many men in the audience felt the same way. Recurring to the graphic imagery he had employed in Philadelphia, Mason closed by insisting, "I would have lost this hand, before it should have marked my name to the new government."[5]

George Nicholas balked at the Mason-Henry motion because, he protested, it implied that the legislature thought amendments necessary. Nothing in the phrasing of the original motion, he said, prohibited discussion of amendments, whereas the change in language would be leading—and in a direction he feared. Nicholas descended from one of Virginia's most powerful families. He and his brothers, all wealthy and politically connected, were legislators and judges on the rise, the kind of men usually inclined to support the Constitution. Nicholas, who represented Albemarle County in the House

George Mason. Portrait by Louis Mathieu Didier Guillaume. Virginia Historical Society

of Delegates, was also good friends with James Madison, so he had an added personal motivation to fight Henry's move.

The tussle over how to word the instructions to the ratification convention showed that Virginians had learned a lesson from what transpired in the Confederation Congress the month before. In New York, opponents to ratification saw too late the advantage Federalists gained by misleadingly inserting the word "unanimous" into Congress's directions to the states. They did not intend to make the same mistake twice. Federalists, meanwhile, reaped the benefits of that clever move and hoped for a repeat in Richmond.

In addition to an object lesson in political posturing, the debate on 25 October perfectly captured how this generation of Americans thought about language: words and ideas had transcendent power and should not be casually thrown about.

When John Marshall offered a thoughtful compromise between these polarizing positions, his fellow legislators listened. A wartime protégé of George Washington, Marshall read law with George Wythe and rose quickly through the ranks of Virginia society. His peers found him good-humored, intelligent, and forthright. Marshall urged the House of Delegates to employ language that neither encouraged nor precluded amendments—that gave the future convention "the fullest latitude in their deliberations." His suggestion for the charge was that the proposed Constitution "be submitted to a Convention of the people for their full and free investigation, discussion, and decision."[6]

The vote on that language was unanimous, but the Anti-Federalists must have felt they won a strategic victory. The agreed-upon language raised a specter that James Madison and his allies had dreaded since Philadelphia. "Virginia has set the example," Madison fretted, "of opening a door for amendments."[7]

Federalists understood that ceding ground on the up-or-down voting directions to the states weakened their chances of success. Defining the debates as an all-or-nothing proposition was an important tactic for them. It also reflected the conviction of men like Madison that the Constitution represented the best ideas of the best minds in America working in the best manner. The representatives in Philadelphia had created the Constitution in a spirit of compromise, conceding local biases and ambitions to achieve the common good. If states insisted on inserting their narrow interests into the plan, it would foment tension and breed rivalries. If every state adopted that kind of provincial inflexibility, no union of the states would ever be possible. This problem lay at the heart of the failures of the Articles of Confederation—the crux of what Madison saw as the "vices of the political system." Federalists had philosophical as well as political reasons, then, for flatly rejecting the idea of conditional amendments. In fact, they had hoped to avoid even requested amendments. Now, they saw, Anti-Federalists had opened that dangerous door and did so in the most influential state in the union.

As the hours passed, legislators negotiated all the terms of the convention elections, the details fraught with political implications. They eventually decided that, just as in the House of Delegates, each county would elect two representatives to the ratification convention, and the two cities represented in the legislature—Williamsburg and Norfolk—would each choose one delegate. This made the Virginia convention more than three times the size of the Philadelphia gathering: 170 men. They would all come from Virginia's landed elite: the same property qualifications for service in the General Assembly applied to convention representatives.

Members of the House of Delegates abandoned other political traditions as it suited them. Convention representatives could hold another elected office concurrently, a practice generally forbidden in Virginia. That way, sitting legislators made sure they remained eligible for election to the convention. Another key change ensured that particular men got a seat in the convention: representatives could reside outside the county that elected them. This too was disallowed in the General Assembly. In fact, "virtual representation"—allowing men from one district or province to represent men from another—had been the source of much colonial complaining in the 1760s and 1770s. Accepting it in 1787 was important, however, especially for George Mason. His views differed starkly from most of his Federalist-leaning neighbors in Fairfax County, and he could not hope to get elected there. Anti-Federalists needed him at the convention, so they insisted on allowing virtual representation. Federalists went along because they too had otherwise unelectable men they wanted at the convention. Besides, they reasoned, why keep such worthy Virginians from participating in this momentous decision?

It was clear from the late October deliberations in the General Assembly that many legislators wanted to quiet the public storm over the Constitution. Without confidence in their leaders, who knew what residents might resort to? The dread of their political quarrels inadvertently inviting social unrest of the sort perpetuated by Daniel Shays and his backcountry neighbors in Massachusetts was a powerful motivation to Virginia's leading men. In 1786, indebted western Massachusetts farmers, squeezed by land foreclosures and taxes, had taken up arms against the Boston bankers and elites they thought were oppressing them. Virginia's planter class wanted to avoid at all costs a repeat of that occurrence in the Old Dominion. Consensus building was also the ideal of republican government. In a well-functioning republic, citizens' representatives worked together to agree on the best interest of the whole commonwealth. This, Federalists repeatedly reminded their critics, was exactly what produced the proposed Constitution.[8]

Even as they sought consensus, though, legislators debating how to proceed to a convention could not avoid political maneuvering. They understood that the choices they made would influence and might even decide whether Virginia rejected or ratified the Constitution. That decision, in turn, could either ruin or save the American Republic. As much as they wanted accord, they would not sacrifice their future for it.

No choice loomed larger than the timing of the Virginia Ratification Convention. Anti-Federalists believed from the start that Federalists planned to rush a decision. Richard Henry Lee warned from the Confederation Congress in early October that advocates of ratification did not want to allow time for "Reflection & due examination." Gouverneur Morris, a strident supporter of the Constitution, conceded as much. The more "the people have time to hear the variety of objections," Morris allowed, the more doubtful ratification became.[9]

Virginia Anti-Federalists believed that, given enough time, citizens would look past the seduction of a quick fix to the country's problems and their admiration of men like George Washington to see the fatal flaws in the Constitution. They favored a long period of consideration, time for voters to educate themselves and to reflect on what the Constitution actually said—not just what its proponents claimed. Surely, they thought, after deep and dispassionate study, Virginians would refuse to give over so much of their state's power to the proposed federal government. Extending the date also allowed opponents of ratification to better organize within the Old Dominion—they lagged behind the Federalists on that score.

But as would often be the case, the strongest advocates for ratification were thinking beyond Virginia, to the larger continental picture. From that perspective, Federalists concluded that time might be their best friend.

Some Federalists thought that a summer 1788 meeting for the Virginia Ratification Convention could work to their advantage. By putting off the decision until June, they calculated, most of the other states would have concluded their conventions. The weight of the outcome in those states might force Virginians to ratify despite their reservations. Or, as George Washington put it, of all the arguments Federalists might make in the Richmond convention, "none will be so forcible . . . as that nine States have acceded to it." John Breckinridge saw the same thing. Virginians, he predicted, "will have little to deliberate on by the Time they meet. Nearly all the States will have met . . . & this State will agree with the Majority."[10]

James Madison, still in New York as a member of the Confederation Congress and lobbying for ratification there, heartily supported a summer meeting for Virginia. Although he remained apprehensive about public opinion back home, he saw "a very strong probability that nine States at least" would ratify in the winter of 1787–88. "What," he pondered, "will become of the tardy remainder? They must be either left as outcasts from the Society to shift for themselves, or be compelled to come in." If confronted with only these unhappy alternatives, he expected reluctant states like Virginia to adopt "a prompt and manly determination to support the Union." Of course, this all rested on the optimistic presumption that other states would act quickly and decide in favor of the Constitution.[11]

Anti-Federalists who considered the larger continental picture expected no such unanimity. They believed that scrutiny of the federal plan would produce a divided electorate, which would result in rejection in some states and close votes in others. Virginians could then turn that division into the impetus for reform. By the summer, they hoped, Virginia would be well positioned to force meaningful changes in the Constitution through conditional amendments and a second continent-wide convention.

In the end, members of the House of Delegates reached unanimity on when to hold the ratification convention not because of some idealistic compromise but only because of coinciding interests. Both the Anti-Federalist majority and the Federalist minority thought a delay until the following summer worked to their side's advantage. They then agreed to schedule elections in March, on the first court date in each county. Because court days varied from county to county, election returns would come in for nearly the entire month of March. Citizens in counties holding late elections would know the results of early elections before they voted. The drawn-out elections to a far-off convention ensured fervent public debates would continue apace and for many, many months.

Delegates initially set the meeting for Richmond, on the fourth Monday in May. This was the only important part of the House proposals that the Senate wanted to revise. It recommended a move to the first Monday in June, and the House agreed to this seven-day extension. By 31 October, the General Assembly's work was done. It sent its "Resolutions Calling the State Convention" to the newspapers, which quickly circulated the news throughout the Old Dominion and the other states: Virginians would convene for their "full and free investigation" on 2 June 1788.[12]

After the General Assembly concluded its official responsibilities of planning the ratification convention, legislators returned to the routine business of governing the still-sovereign state of Virginia. But it was hardly business as usual in Richmond that fall and winter. As the early frosts gave way to the first snow, the town buzzed with excitement. Residents studied newspapers from across the continent, and around the fires in the taverns and parlors talk inevitably turned to the Constitution. The question, Washington wrote a friend, "seems to have absorbed all lesser matters." Inside the statehouse, powerful representatives, especially Patrick Henry, saw ripe openings to drive public opinion of the Constitution. Henry used his position in the Assembly to make a number of adroit political moves, calculated to control the debates going forward and, ultimately, to keep the Constitution from becoming law. "This gentleman," one aggravated Federalist groused, "fires his shot at the new constitution every opportunity."[13]

A great opportunity arose in November, when the House of Delegates needed to appropriate money to pay the expenses of representatives to the ratification convention. Samuel Hopkins Jr. moved that the legislature arrange to fund both the June convention *and* a second continental meeting to design amendments "in case such a convention should be judged necessary." Patrick Henry and George Mason immediately seconded the motion. Hopkins may have introduced the proposal, but it had Patrick Henry written all over it. Henry "conducted this business," one Federalist informed James Madison, adding something Madison already knew: when it came to politics, Henry's "art is Equal to his talents for declamation."[14]

Federalist-leaning legislators cried foul. They insisted that Anti-Federalists were misusing the legislative process to promote their desire to demand changes to the Constitution. In response to those complaints, Henry's supporters doubled down: they suggested setting aside money to help neighboring states fund the costs of sending representatives to a second convention.[15]

In the fall of 1787, a decisive majority of the members of the House of Delegates opposed the Constitution. According to George Washington, "the powerful adversaries to the Constitution are all assembled at that place, acting conjunctly."[16] So they had the votes to carry the measure. But they wanted to influence, not overawe. Hopkins's motion did not need to pass formally to work politically anyway. The conversation alone was sufficient to present amendments as a viable option to unconditional ratification. The point won, Anti-Federalists sought out some middle ground with Federalists, agreeing, in the interest of preserving "the most friendly sentiments towards each other," to strike any specific reference to a second convention from the appropriations bill. They retained in the language of the appropriations measure, however, a commitment to funding whatever future expenses derived from the ratification convention. Most important, they reminded Virginia voters that their choice in June was not simply "yes" or "no."[17]

Outnumbered in the legislature, Federalists informed James Madison of their distressing situation. "I fear," wrote Archibald Stuart, "since they have discovered their Strength they will adopt other Measures tending to its [the Constitution's] prejudice."[18]

Madison was concerned, but he tried to calm his friends in Virginia. He seldom impugned the motives of his opponents in the ratification debates; he just insisted they were wrong. His reply to Stuart sounds at once generous and condescending: "I am persuaded that the scheme of amendments is pursued by some of its patrons at least, with the most patriotic & virtuous intentions. But I am equally persuaded that it is pregnant with consequences, which they fail to bring into view."[19]

What Madison saw (and assumed Anti-Federalists did not) was that "conditional amendments or a second general Convention will be fatal."[20] Previous amendments, he reasoned, would not only reveal but deepen—probably irreparably—the divides between states. What one state demanded, another would refuse. Incorporating changes into the federal plan before ratification would be a logistical nightmare, requiring a second national convention, which could never hope to duplicate the secrecy and success of the first. Without unconditional ratification, Madison feared the union of states devolving into separate confederacies or inviting out of weakness some foreign invasion.

Anti-Federalists, however, saw a closer threat, created by the Constitution as it stood: Virginia's well-being could be sacrificed to other states, especially the commercial interests of northeastern merchants.

These regional and economic fears lay behind Patrick Henry's next move in the Virginia legislature. He used a recent episode in the West to remind Virginians about the perils of trusting the Northeast. After the 1783 Treaty of Paris, which settled the terms of the Revolutionary War, Spain tried to close the Mississippi River to American shipping. This slowed the migration of Americans to southwestern settlements in present-day Kentucky and Tennessee and left the people already living there in a much more precarious position, in terms of both economic opportunities and safety. (Kentucky and Tennessee became states in 1792 and 1796, respectively. During the confederation era, Kentucky remained part of Virginia, but settlers were actively seeking independent statehood with the support of tidewater Virginians.) Closing the Mississippi also threatened the interests of seaboard planters, who wanted river access to ship their products to market. To force American acceptance of the demand, Spain denied US merchants access to its ports. The Confederation Congress assigned John Jay, secretary of foreign affairs, to negotiate a solution. In August 1786, Jay notified the Congress that he had succeeded in getting Spain to agree to open its ports to American trade. But the cost was steep: Americans had to cede use of the Mississippi River for twenty-five years.

The Confederation Congress immediately split along a bitter, sectional divide. Northeastern merchants desperately wanted to resume trade with Spain, and representatives from those states pushed hard to accept the admittedly damaging mandate to give up the Mississippi River. Southern politicians were furious that northerners would even consider sacrificing their peoples' interests: they needed to use the Mississippi to carry their agricultural goods and foster greater migration into the Southwest. When Virginia legislators learned of Jay's conduct, they felt betrayed and in November 1786 acted to defend the economic interest of the state, especially their western citizens in the Kentucky district. The House of Delegates sent to the Confederation Congress a unanimously approved resolution, condemning Jay's proposal and asserting the rights of Virginians to the "free and common use" of the Mississippi River. To Virginians, the affair laid bare the perils of centralized commercial power and the stark differences between northern and southern states.[21]

While legislators fumed over the Mississippi controversy in late 1786, James Madison remained at work on his plans for revising the confederation government, and he immediately saw the two were connected. He warned George Washington in December 1786 that the support they hoped to garner in Virginia for changes in the union of the states would now depend on keeping the West open: "I am entirely convinced from what I observe here, that unless the project of Congress can be reversed, the hopes of carrying this State into a proper federal System will be demolished." "Many of our most federal leading men," he added, "are extremely soured with what has already passed." Just the *idea* of sacrificing southern agricultural interests to northern commerce was enough to turn many Virginians against plans for greater centralized power.[22]

In the end, neither the northern nor the southern delegations in the Confederation Congress had the votes required to prevail in the Mississippi dispute, so the matter was dropped. (Many Americans pointed to this gridlock as yet another example of the "imbecility" of the Articles of Confederation.) Resentments lingered. Feeling blindsided by the betrayal of their supposed friends in the northern states, Virginians decided that the five southern states had to maintain the veto power over all international treaties they held—and in this case exercised—under the Articles of Confederation.

A year later, many Virginians remained "extremely soured" over the controversy. In case anyone had forgotten the lessons of the aborted Jay negotiations over the Mississippi River, Patrick Henry offered up a reminder in November 1787. He introduced in the House of Delegates a proposal to petition Congress to seek access to the Mississippi River. The 1787 proposal duplicated the resolution of November 1786 and had no practical meaning. But everyone in Richmond saw the strategic significance. John Pierce, a friend of George Washington's, explained, "Mr. Henry introduced it to shew in a forcible manner how the commercial interests of the Southern States are sacrificed by the Northern whenever its suits their convenience."[23] Now, however, the matter was far more pressing, since the proposed Constitution gave the president power to negotiate treaties, and he needed to secure only a two-thirds majority of a quorum of senators to approve his actions—a far more dangerous situation than existed in 1786. Commercial laws would require only a simple majority to pass the new Congress. What Virginians had feared and stopped in 1786 would, Anti-Federalists anticipated, become an immutable fact under the Constitution of 1787.

Within days, critics of the federal plan picked up on Henry's cue. In the *Virginia Independent Chronicle*, one writer claimed that Virginia risked "being made the subject of a ruinous monopoly in the commercial or carrying states" because under the Constitution "their interests would be always paramount to ours."[24] Again and again, in private letters and newspaper essays—and later in the formal debates—Anti-Federalists pointed to the navigation of the Mississippi River as a prime example of the dangers facing Virginians under the Constitution.

From his vaunted position in state government, Patrick Henry seized every opportunity to capitalize on Virginians' state pride and their skittishness about losing out to northeasterners. He also wisely calculated that if Anti-Federalist legislators could mobilize enough voters in the right counties, they could spoil the Federalists' well-laid plans. In raising the incendiary issue of the Mississippi River, Henry hit a rich target: voters in the Kentucky counties. They always demanded their representatives protect the West, and enough citizens lived there to swing the convention outcome. By Thanksgiving, Henry and the Anti-Federalists had cause to celebrate their successes in shaping the terms of the political debates about ratification. And there were still three months to go before the first vote was cast in the spring elections.

"Did it ever enter the mind of any one of you," asked one incredulous Virginia writer, "that you could live to see the day, that any other government, but the General Assembly of Virginia, should have power of *direct taxation* in this state?" He was hardly alone. As the weight of the proposed constitutional changes settled in, Virginians saw how profoundly it recast long-standing republican principles—not only about taxation and representation but also about sovereignty, balancing liberty and power, and the nature of the union of the states. Virginians expressed dismay at the many sacrifices their sovereign state would have to make to the federal government, starting with the collection of taxes. From dearly bought recent experience, Virginians knew what tolerating unchecked taxation power in a distant government could cost. "Are we not to expect," the essayist scoffed, "that New England will now send us revenue officers, instead of their onions and their apples?"[25]

Widespread apprehension about what might happen to their beloved state benefited Virginians trying to fight ratification. Most voters thought first about local concerns, and localism was a constant theme in the political maneuverings of Anti-Federalists. "Consider," one essayist movingly asked, "whether you are willing to see the state of Virginia dwindle into the insignificance of a town corporate."[26]

Anti-Federalists' ability to explain the implications of ratification in local terms was of a great advantage over Federalists, whom they often depicted as betrayers of Virginia's sovereignty. The Mississippi River would be just the start, they predicted. "If Congress can take upon herself this Power," one Kentucky Anti-Federalist reasoned, "she may stretch her arbitrary hand to Private Property, & . . . reduce us to a State of Vassalage—We have no Security to Barr her Tyrinnical hand, or prevent lawless thirst of Dominion." The Constitution threatened everything that Virginians prized, starting with their most basic freedoms. "We cannot but perceive," they warned, "that we are forging fetters for Virginia."[27]

Federalists countered that patriotic citizens needed to think about the financial and international perils facing all the states, Virginia included. A pro-Constitution writer in the *Virginia Herald* complained that under the Articles of Confederation "our credit in Europe began so rapidly to decline, that our ministers were viewed with the utmost contempt by the foreign courts." The Philadelphia Convention had, they proclaimed, designed an elegant solution to such international perils.[28] Anti-Federalists' tendency to prioritize local interests at the expense of the larger needs of the country would, Federalists warned, be America's undoing. European powers were more likely to invade a weak, insolvent country and would ignore or take advantage of them in trade relations. While always reminding voters that the Constitution would ensure republican government for generations to come, most advocates for ratification also emphasized national economic and foreign policy benefits. The proposed government was, one typical supporter proclaimed, "eminently calculated to promote the happiness, the grandeur and importance of America, until time shall be no more."[29]

Opponents seized on this emphasis on the greatness of the United States. Anti-Federalists felt deeply suspicious of promises of "grandeur and importance" not because they doubted the power that Americans might achieve through the Constitution but because they feared it. A republic, they believed, should promote liberty, not power.

In response to Anti-Federalist criticisms that the Constitution bought national security with individuals' liberty, Federalists claimed that Anti-Federalists were the ones clamoring for power. Their real ambition was to force separate confederacies in the various regions of North America. That way they could maintain their influence in Virginia. Edward Carrington gossiped, for example, that Patrick Henry did not want to improve the Constitution through amendments or even work out the failings of the Articles of Confederation. Instead, he sought "a dismemberment of the Union."[30]

Carrington was typical: many Federalists saw their opponents' state pride and local allegiances as arrogance and parochialism. They disparaged Anti-Federalists as eager to cast aside their fellow Americans, the people with whom they had defeated Britain to build the American Republic. Richard Henry Lee and George Mason, for example, were publicly condemned for unpatriotically inflaming Virginians' prejudices against their northern "brethren."[31]

Virginia's future mattered as deeply to Federalists as Anti-Federalists, but advocates for ratification believed the state could not thrive apart from the union. "Virginians," George Washington concluded, "entertain *too* high an opinion of the importance" of their state. Virginia was the largest and most populous state, but, he perceived, "in point of *strength*, it is, comparatively, weak."[32] Federalists continually reminded voters that the state could not stand alone. Now, as in the Revolutionary War, they argued, Virginia's future was tied to the union of states.

How, Federalists wondered, could Anti-Federalists claiming that northeasterners wanted to take advantage of southerners have such a short memory? Had they forgotten the bond with Massachusetts that allowed the patriots to prevail over Great Britain? Now they seemed bent on jeopardizing the unity that had made the Revolution possible.

As they fought for the political upper hand, both Federalists and Anti-Federalists insisted they acted only out of republican principles whereas men holding opposing views indulged in political machinations. Firebrands on both sides went further than predicting dire consequences of a wrong decision: they claimed those outcomes were actually the secret goals of their opponents. In fact, the allegation that Anti-Federalists planned to abandon the union and preside over a separate southern confederacy was as false as the claim that Federalists were conspiring to reduce Virginia to a "state of vassalage." Mischaracterizing the opposition was for some men a result of confusion and fear and for others a political strategy. To be certain, sometimes men from the two sides reasoned together, as their political ideals taught. But more often they used their political speech to jockey for power, convinced that the other side was wrong, dangerous, and, worst of all, intentionally undermining the noble experiment in republican government. In the closing months of 1787, men on both sides of the ratification contest seemed less and less willing to give one another the benefit of the doubt and more and more eager to win votes.

Although there had been some flurries earlier in the month, the first real snow of the season fell at Mount Vernon on 22 December. By then, the last of the potatoes were in, and the African Americans enslaved on George Washington's plantations were set to wintertime work, such as repairing fences and slaughtering hogs. Wintery weather sometimes slowed mail deliveries to Virginia, but it did not chill debates over the Constitution. All winter supporters and critics of the Constitution kept a close watch on other states, wanting to learn about their political processes, to understand which strategies worked, and to see if they had been right in setting the Virginia Ratification Convention so late.[33]

In December 1787, tensions in Pennsylvania, the first major state to hold a convention, spilled over into Virginia. Pennsylvania Federalists succeeded brilliantly at using time to their advantage. They set the convention to start on 20 November, and delegate elections were so rushed that voter turnout suffered. Federalists also used their printer allies to suppress criticism of the Constitution in the newspapers in the weeks before the Pennsylvania Ratification Convention. Once gathered in their convention, Federalists outmaneuvered the Anti-Federalist minority at every turn and sped toward a vote, despite overwhelming evidence that skepticism of the Constitution was growing fast within the state's population. By a two-to-one margin, Pennsylvania delegates voted in favor of ratification two weeks before Christmas. (Federalists there had tried desperately to be the first state to ratify, but Delaware beat them.) The defeated Pennsylvania opposition remained angry about the high-handed tactics of Federalists and refused to let the matter drop.[34]

Just three days after Pennsylvania ratified, dissenters published an essay explaining their many grievances, starting with the secrecy of the debates that produced the Constitution and concluding with the intimidating tactics of the Federalists at the state convention. Pennsylvania Anti-Federalists sent copies to their friends in Virginia; by mid-January, a pamphlet of "Dissent of the Minority of the Pennsylvania Convention" was selling in Richmond. A few weeks later the editor of the *Winchester Virginia Gazette* began running it in installments. Anti-Federalists may have lost the fight in Pennsylvania, but they and their Virginia allies had hopes for a resurgence in the Old Dominion.[35]

Federalists in Virginia, seeing that the Pennsylvania essay was helping Anti-Federalists gain steam, took to the newspapers, too. Alexander White, a Winchester planter serving in the Virginia House of Delegates, published a venomous rebuke of the Pennsylvania dissenters. He warned his neighbors that their essay "appears to be the mere ebullition of embittered minds, intended to mislead your judgments, inflame your passions, and stifle in your bosoms the noblest of all human faculties, reason." The Pennsylvanians, White charged, had no limits to "how far they are willing to degrade themselves, in order to inflame the minds of the people." They invented "a direful train of evils" in order to "induce the ignorant" into believing that the federal government would deny them their basic rights: of freedom of religion, speech, and the press. This was, White concluded, completely "out of the jurisdiction of Congress."[36]

White's assertions about the limits of federal powers held no water with Anti-Federalists, who complained bitterly about the absence of a bill of rights. And they pointed to the conduct of Pennsylvania's majority as a sign of things to come if Virginians submitted to the Constitution.

On 9 January 1787, delegates from across Massachusetts made their way into Boston through freezing rain and snow to begin deliberations. Theirs was the first convention in a state with a large, perhaps majority opposition to the Constitution, and Virginians were anxious to learn the outcome. Word had already reached the Old Dominion that most of Massachusetts's leading men advocated for the Constitution, but artisans, shopkeepers, and farmers, especially those living outside Boston, were not so convinced. Like Virginians, Massachusetts residents thought of themselves as paragons of the American Revolution, holding a special obligation to make sure the proposed government would preserve and did not destroy the political movement sparked on Boston Commons and at the city's wharves. Citizens from other states respected the many sacrifices Massachusetts patriots had made on behalf of the American cause and eagerly anticipated their judgment on the Constitution. If the opponents to ratification prevailed in Massachusetts, it would surely embolden critics attending later conventions in divided states. On the other hand, an endorsement out of Massachusetts would be a signal accomplishment for Federalists.[37]

The very popular and widely respected Governor John Hancock presided over the largest political gathering in the history of Massachusetts: 364 delegates. The election returns had reflected a sharply divided citizenry, and most observers were at a loss to predict which side held the numerical advantage. As they settled into the Long Lane Congregational Church, where the galleries could hold at least six hundred spectators, supporters of Shays's Rebellion sat (uncomfortably) alongside Boston merchants.[38]

Virginians apprehensively waited for reports out of Massachusetts, "for on her," Edward Carrington said, "every thing seems to depend." Rufus King, a strong Federalist and Massachusetts convention delegate, kept James Madison informed about events in Boston, and Madison passed the news on to George Washington. In fact, Madison wrote Washington seven times between

20 January, when he received his first report from Massachusetts, and mid-February, when news of the outcome reached him. Until the end, Massachusetts delegates remained evenly divided, so that each report he got, Madison said, "rather increases than removes the anxiety produced by the last."[39]

Federalists dreaded a domino effect if Massachusetts rejected the Constitution. Joseph Jones watched Massachusetts with Madison, and he warned that, should the state "give it a negative," its rejection would all but guarantee failure in New York and "strengthen the opposition in the States that are yet to consider the measure"—including Virginia.[40]

Near the end of the Massachusetts deliberations, with the convention still deadlocked, John Hancock proposed a compromise: Massachusetts should unconditionally ratify the Constitution *and* direct its representatives in the first Congress to "exert all their influence" to pass nine specific amendments, mostly aimed at reining in federal powers. The move divided opponents to ratification. Some thought Hancock's proposal a damning admission of the Constitution's flaws, giving even more cause to reject the federal plan. Others found it a welcome concession that made the Constitution safer. When they voted on 6 February, Hancock's compromise moved enough men toward ratification to prevail, though hardly by a resounding majority. Only 19 votes among 355 delegates separated the two sides: 187 in favor and 168 opposed (9 delegates were absent).[41]

Virginia Federalists breathed a huge sigh of relief. Madison still worried about the precedent of discussing amendments, but George Washington saw cause for optimism. The outcome in Massachusetts might, he hoped, deliver "a severe stroke to the opponents of the proposed Constitution" in Virginia. Federalist-leaning newspapers in Virginia quickly hailed the vote as an act of patriotism. "The true friends of union," the *Virginia Independent Chronicle* announced, "that is, to liberty, happiness and national glory, are those who wish to go hand in hand with Massachusetts." Raising again the danger of separate confederacies, the editorial warned that "if we pull one way and Massachusetts another—both of us may lose what each may have in view."[42]

If Massachusetts offered Federalists hope, New York provoked worry. New York was the commercial center of the United States; rejection there would economically imperil as well as physically divide the other states. James Madison was in New York City in the winter of 1787–88 as a representative in Congress, but he felt so concerned about the prospects of the Constitution in

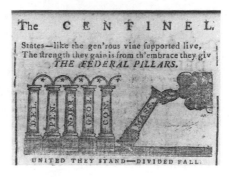

The Federal Pillars. The "pillars" of the republic became a popular motif for Federalists. Here a divine force is lifting the sixth pillar, Massachusetts. *Massachusetts Centinel*, 30 January 1788. Serial and Government Publications Division, Library of Congress

New York that he remained longer than his legislative obligations required— to the dismay of many Virginia Federalists who needed him back home. New Yorkers called their convention for June 1788, too, so they had plenty of time to debate the merits of the federal plan. Madison put his considerable political talents to lobbying for ratification in New York, keeping updated on Virginia through letters with friends. He understood that if the Constitution was to gain legitimacy, not just the requisite number of state votes, New York, alongside Virginia and Massachusetts, had to ratify.

Federalists faced an uphill battle in New York. Governor George Clinton shared much in common with Patrick Henry. Both men had tremendous influence within their states and a steely resolve to use all their power to fight ratification. The Anti-Federalists also held the popular majority in New York, and they were as well organized as the Federalists.

In hopes of countering all this enthusiasm for the Anti-Federalist cause in New York, James Madison, Alexander Hamilton, and John Jay produced a series of essays, eventually eighty-five in number. They all wrote their extended commentaries under the same pseudonym, Publius, and published them serially in New York City newspapers beginning in late October 1787. Their initial intention was to answer the many questions raised by New York citizens. Eventually, the result of their efforts, *The Federalist*, became celebrated as the most sophisticated and important work of political theory ever produced in the United States.[43]

Madison, Hamilton, and Jay's production of essays increased exponentially in the winter of 1787–88, and Madison sent copies of his writings to Virginia, to friends like George Washington, and with the clear intent that they be shared with sympathetic newspaper editors. Some of the essays began to appear in Virginia in January 1788, but distribution was slow. New York City papers operated in the most populous city in North America and published as many as four issues a week. Virginia was rural and its towns far-flung, so the state's papers were all weeklies. Because Virginia's newspapers could not keep pace with New York, printers made plans to publish the entire series as a book. The first thirty-six essays were offered for sale in book form in April 1788—after the Virginia convention elections. The direct impact of the essays on Virginians' perceptions of the Constitution was negligible, because despite its prominence after 1788, most Virginians did not see *The Federalist* in the winter of 1787–88.[44]

In fact, *The Federalist* did not have much political influence in any state outside of New York. Then, as opposed to now, readers knew the essays were not an impartial intellectual inquiry into the federal design. They were planned as advocacy pieces, political statements crafted to negate criticisms of the Constitution. But that plan did not work very well, because most of the essays did not get published outside New York in time to shape other state debates. They didn't even have the desired effect of persuading New Yorkers to abandon Anti-Federalism. When the New York convention gathered in mid-June 1788, delegates met in the Anti-Federalist stronghold of Poughkeepsie, and representatives who were avowed opponents to ratification constituted a majority.

Virginians kept abreast of political goings-on in these other states by drawing on long-standing networks of kinship, friendship, and political alliance, all safeguarded by letter writing and the US mail. From the colonial period, elites traveled throughout British America, often building business ties and sometimes intermarrying. In the 1760s and 1770s leaders of the various colonies became increasingly immersed in a continental-wide network of political and personal partnerships. Americans forged close bonds and a sense of solidarity as they pursued the patriot cause and then fought the Revolutionary War. When they couldn't be together, they sent letters that correspondents shared with other relatives and friends and, in time, passed down to their heirs. (The papers of men like Thomas Jefferson and James Madison numbered in the tens of thousands.) Such correspondences preserved and extended family, business, and political networks, bridging the distances between friends and allies. So as soon as the Constitution was unveiled, men began mailing their far-flung contacts to air out ideas and garner support. The mails carried, too, newspapers and political treatises. Information traveled no faster than horse or wagon in eighteenth-century America, and commerce, like politics and news, depended on reliable mail. The mail service was so important to the American Republic that the Continental Congress appointed no less than Benjamin Franklin to serve as the first postmaster general.[45]

The best connected Virginian opposed to the Constitution was Richard Henry Lee. Lee's close contacts spanned America: in his efforts to stop ratification in the various states, he corresponded with his brother-in-law, Philadelphia doctor William Shippen, and good friends like Sam Adams of Massachusetts. Among like-minded relatives and friends, Richard Henry Lee circulated in mid-October a long list of grievances, which was eventually published in newspapers. Lee's paramount concern was, he said, that "this new constitution is, in its first principles, highly and dangerously oligarchic." In his objections, Lee laid out a litany of complaints about the powers of the federal government and offered up several structural changes he thought essential for the system to work. The cornerstone of his proposed revisions was a bill of rights, guaranteeing freedom of the press, trial by jury, and freedom of religion. Richard Henry Lee then turned toward proposing a political strategy for Anti-Federalist success. The best tactic, he believed, was for opponents of ratification to demand amendments rectifying the egregious violations of republican government and ensuring citizens' rights. They also needed to insist that ratification be contingent on calling a second convention to consider those amendments.[46]

James Madison, the best situated Virginian to coordinate a national Federalist network, disagreed on every point. From his perch in New York City, Madison corresponded with men throughout America, including Rufus King of Massachusetts and Tench Coxe of Pennsylvania, and with Thomas Jefferson in Paris. Madison saw Alexander Hamilton regularly, as well as politicians from New York and others in the city for the Confederation Congress. And, of course, he kept up a steady correspondence with close allies in Virginia, starting with George Washington. Washington and Madison were convinced that no quarter could be given to the idea of amendments or a second convention: the Constitution represented the *only* path forward.[47]

These rival networks became public because of printers and newspapers.

Virginia had ten weekly newspapers in 1787–88: three in Richmond with the rest spread across the state in Alexandria, Petersburg, Fredericksburg, Norfolk, Winchester, and the Kentucky district town of Lexington. Federalists held an advantage in circulating their ideas, because most of the newspaper and commercial printers appeared to favor ratification. Though many papers published essays supporting both sides, they ran considerably fewer Anti-Federalists pieces. Federalist-leaning editors also seemed to be better connected to a network of like-minded newspapermen throughout America. A telling example came in March 1788, when the *Virginia Independent Chronicle* ran an incendiary article extolling the "great and good patriots in America" who supported the Constitution and condemning men who "suffer themselves to be branded with the *odious* and *disgraceful* appellation of *antifederalist*." The essay went on to blast anyone who even raised the question of amendments before ratification for "low cunning" and "wickedness." The essay was reprinted in fifteen newspapers across the United States, and parts of it appeared in no less than two dozen. There was nothing comparable among Anti-Federalist essays.[48]

As the sharing of this *Virginia Independent Chronicle* essay revealed, Americans were captivated by Virginia's contentious politics. Politicians and voters across America, whether in New York City, Philadelphia, Hartford, Baltimore, or Boston, gossiped about and waited anxiously for news from Virginia. Even foreign diplomats watched to see what would happen next in Virginia. "Holding the first rank among the 13 States of the Union," explained one French emissary, "its influence against the Constitution is particularly feared." Spanish diplomat Don Diego de Gardoqui speculated in December that Virginia would not ratify. "In the meantime," he explained, "there is an infinite amount of writing pro and con."[49]

Among the most widely discussed topics, in both personal letters and newspapers, was the position of leading Virginia politicians. In fact, gossiping about politicians' actions became a political strategy. Pennsylvanians, for example, circulated the false but sticky rumor that George Mason and Patrick Henry were conspiring in Virginia to promote a southern confederacy. A Pennsylvania newspaper also reported in mid-October that George Mason "has been treated with every possible mark of contempt" for his refusal to sign the Constitution. That story was refuted in a New York paper twelve days later. That author charged that the attacks on Mason were typical of the scheming supporters of the federal plan, who used "*force, fraud and falsehood*" to advance their political agenda.[50]

As far away as Connecticut, writers condemned Virginian politicians who stood against the Constitution. Advocates of ratification insisted that in that most critical of states "the opposition wholly originated in two principles; the madness of Mason, and the enmity of the Lee faction to General Washington." One Connecticut essay reprinted in the *Virginia Independent Chronicle* vilified Richard Henry Lee as the author "of most of the scurrility poured out in New York papers against the new constitution." The writer attributed Lee's opposition to "his implacable hatred to General Washington—his well known intrigues against him in the late war" and his generally "factious spirit." As for George Mason, the same writer asserted, he was "pompous" and obsessed with advancing the agricultural interests of the southern states at all costs. "A man governed by such narrow views and local prejudices," the essayist charged, "can never be trusted."[51]

Anti-Federalists spread rumors across the states, too, including that men favoring ratification were cravenly seeking power for themselves at the expense of their countrymen's liberty. They also gossiped that George Washington was the only prominent Virginian who supported ratification. "It must mortify the General exceedingly," speculated one Philadelphian, "to see all his sensible countrymen differ in opinion with him."[52]

The biggest rumor about Washington centered not on his waning popularity, however, but on his future plans. Within days of the Constitution being revealed, Americans gossiped that "General Washington has given assurances, that he will serve as President." Since no one heard this directly from Washington, curiosity about his ambitions grew with each passing week. When a friend visiting Mount Vernon sounded him out on the question in early October, Washington pleaded reluctance because of his age and love of retirement. But the man left Mount Vernon, as he put it, "fully of opinion he may be induced to appear once more on the Publick Stage." Speculation spread as far as France. In the spring of 1788, Lafayette wrote Washington to ask about his intentions should the Constitution pass muster. Washington was smart enough to avoid refusing an office that might never exist. Always affectionate with Lafayette, whom he considered an adoptive son, Washington joked about appearing like the fox in a popular fable, who "is represented as inveighing against the sourness of the grapes, because he could not reach them."[53] Despite Washington's posturing to protect his reputation, Americans believed he would make an excellent president and assumed he would take the position if asked. After all, he had never declined to serve his country before. Why would he change at this most fateful hour? At the same time, Americans understood that if Virginians rejected the Constitution—which seemed as likely as not in the winter of 1787–88—George Washington would not be a citizen of the United States and so could not become president. What would happen then? Such apprehensions and rumors were in abundant supply all winter.

As the days grew longer and the daffodils began to appear, it remained unclear which way the Old Dominion might turn. Perhaps, those watching and wondering speculated, the coming spring elections would predict Virginia's choice and America's future.

3 Spring 1788, Electing the Delegates

The plot thickens fast. A few short weeks will determine the political fate of America for the present generation and probably produce no small influence on the happiness of society through a long succession of ages to come.

George Washington, 28 May 1788

ON 17 MARCH 1788, as was his custom, George Washington rose early. The temperature was only 37 degrees that morning, but the skies were clear and the wind light—a good day to ride to the county elections. David Humphreys, a wartime protégé and now personal secretary to Washington, accompanied him on the trip to Alexandria, around ten miles north of Mount Vernon. Washington had made the trek many times before: the courthouse was the seat of civic life in the county that he had called home for well over thirty years. Washington was a man of exceptional talent and means, and his neighbors routinely called him to positions of leadership in Fairfax County. But that spring day the most famous man in America was fulfilling only a simple if solemn duty: he was voting.[1]

In his diary, Washington made little mention of the day spent in Alexandria, but he was surely pleased at the election outcome. Two strong Federalists, Charles Simms and David Stuart, won unanimously. Simms had been an officer in the Revolutionary War under Washington's command. After the war, he ran a thriving law practice in Alexandria and remained personal friends with Washington. Stuart was even closer; after Washington's stepson Jack Custis died, Stuart married his widow, and the two men worked together on all sorts of family matters.

After voting, Washington and Humphreys enjoyed a celebratory meal but returned home before nightfall. James Madison was arriving at Mount Vernon the next day, on his way home from New York for his own county elections, scheduled for 24 March. Madison spent the night with the Washingtons and the next one, too. Unlike Washington, Madison had decided to stand for election to the Virginia Ratification Convention, and unlike Fairfax County, Orange County posed a serious problem for Federalists. Much to Madison's dismay, citizens in his home county seemed, he complained, "filled with the most absurd and groundless prejudices" against the Constitution. Hopefully, Madison thought, he might turn the tide once he got to the Orange County courthouse and shared with his neighbors his deep understanding of the Constitution.[2]

Thousands upon thousands of Virginia men made similar journeys as Washington and Madison did that March. Voting at court days—and socializing with friends and neighbors, making business deals, and settling legal cases—was commonplace in citizens' lives. Today, Americans prize the secret ballot and enter polling places under precise laws that protect the privacy of individual voters. Campaign workers, for example, must remain at a physical distance from voters. Often we feel offended if directly asked how we voted. But this was not so in the eighteenth century, where viva voce was the rule. Usually the county sheriff presided over elections. He called the name of every man who met the property qualification, and each voter came forward to openly declare his preference. Sometimes, voters joined in a chorus, offering public acclamation. Either way, neighbors knew where one another stood and which candidate got whose support. These rituals were familiar to everyone who went to county court days. But court day in March of 1788 was anything but normal: voters gathered to elect delegates to a state ratification convention that had just one purpose. Most Virginians, like George

Washington, believed that convention would "determine the political fate of America."[3]

By the time voters went to their county elections, Virginians had spent nearly six months debating the structure of the Constitution, the nature of republican government, and whether ratification lay in Virginia's best interest. But the elections raised a new controversy: On what basis should men vote?

York County offered one kind of solution. On the day of the county elections, Federalists and Anti-Federalists both put up two candidates, and citizens gathered to choose between the sides. But when the sheriff called for the men to cast their votes, "an old man by the name of Charles Lewis step'd forward." He addressed the Federalist candidates, General Thomas Nelson and Joseph Prentis. Lewis said he had voted for Prentis and Nelson in the past, never with the slightest cause for regret. He came to the courthouse planning to vote for them again. But along the way, his thinking changed. He did not want to vote on the basis of his confidence in individual men but rather on his personal opinion about the Constitution. Alas, he admitted, "all his examination had not satisfied him what opinion he ought to express upon this question." The ratification convention had only "a single and a known proposition to be settled." And that proposition was "the most important of any that had come before the people, since the question of Independence." Lewis thus decided not to vote for any man who already had a firm opinion, but rather to support only representatives "who should be well qualified to determine wisely, what they were prepared to examine impartially." With that in mind, he proposed as alternative candidates "two fellow Citizens": George Wythe and John Blair. Both men had represented Virginia at the Philadelphia Convention. But because Wythe came home early and Blair never spoke (though he did sign the Constitution), their precise views on the federal plan were not publicly known.

Thomas Nelson, seeing how Lewis moved the crowd, immediately sprang from his seat, thanked Lewis "in the warmest terms for what he had said and done," and directed the sheriff to cast his vote in favor of Wythe and Blair. Prentis, though apparently caught off guard, "followed General Nelson in this course." Soon Wythe and Blair were unanimously elected by the voters of York County.

Nelson, seizing the political opportunity he saw in his failed candidacy, took the lead in forming a procession of voters to go to Williamsburg to tell

Wythe and Blair what had happened. Littleton Tazewell, who years later became governor of Virginia and a US senator and wrote about this event in a family memoir, was then a thirteen-year-old boy, reciting a Greek lesson in George Wythe's study, as the York County men knocked on the door. When Wythe went outside, "An hundred voices exclaimed at the same time, 'Will you serve?'" Wythe stood on his steps and wept, and Tazewell started to cry, too. Finally, Wythe gathered himself enough to consent, and the happy crowd continued on to John Blair's home.[4]

From time to time in the months leading up to the elections, Virginians raised the very solution that Charles Lewis offered his neighbors struggling to sort out *how* to vote (rather than simply *whom* to vote for). In late January, for example, an essayist called on voters to choose only "men of enlightened understandings, and impartial principles; and who do not violently, on all occasions, declare their opinions." The best interest of the republic, some authors believed, lay in electing undecided men who "will deliberate with coolness."[5]

But the York County story of consensus and disinterestedness was not repeated in most elections. Voters were both conflicted about their own views and in disagreement with their neighbors. Should voters send to the Richmond convention leaders they'd often elected before, in effect deferring to respected, experienced men? Or should they instead cast their ballots for men they knew shared their opinion on the Constitution, turning the election into a referendum?

The March 1788 elections thus laid bare a larger question about the nature of representation. Should voters elect proxies who shared their specific views or leaders who deserved their respect? Were representatives supposed to reflect the majority opinion of voters? Or did they act independently, to advance the best interest of the whole community? Confronting these choices forced Virginians to decide whether deference still had a place in state politics.[6]

In the colonial era, politics followed social custom: men deferred to their superiors. Codes of conduct defined how the "lesser sort"—shopkeepers, farmers, artisans—acted around the "better sort," which in Virginia meant rich, well-connected planter-patriarchs. Rank even determined how colonists dressed: sartorial laws forbade nonelites from wearing purple and velvet. As a teenager, George Washington used conduct books to create for himself a personal guide that he called "Rules of Civility and Decent Behaviour in Company and Conversation." His 110 exacting rules covered everything from eating to hygiene to clothing. He needed to avoid such low behavior as excessive laughing, crossing his legs, and raising one eyebrow higher than the other. Washington's rules emphasized proper interactions with gentlemen, whose station in life deserved his deference. According to his guidebook, the "better bred and quality of the person" the more deference owed (no. 26). Men sat according to rank (nos. 28 and 106) and walked to the left side of a social better, "but if three walk together, the mid place is the most honourable" (no. 30). If asked a question by "those of higher quality . . . stand upright, put off your hat, & answer in few words" (no. 85). Number 37 stipulated: "In speaking to men of quality, do not lean nor look them full in the face, nor approach too near them, at least keep a full pace from them."[7]

This ritualized conduct shaped politics in colonial Virginia, too. Small landowners cast their votes for their county's leading planter-patriarchs, reflexively trusting them to make decisions. When the Revolution challenged the colonial order, it also ushered in new attitudes about political power, prizing self-determination and equality. Some Virginians, mostly Federalists, still wanted to continue the long-standing tradition of political deference in the 1788 elections. "An Old Planter," writing to middling-rank voters in the late winter, believed that men who had only "a scanty education," were incapable of "judging soundly of abstract principles of government." Meanwhile, he said, "the wisest and most virtuous men on the continent" had endorsed the Constitution "with an unanimity almost unknown in the history of mankind." In this traditional mindset, supported by more Federalists than Anti-Federalists, farmers and artisans had no basis on which to question let alone contradict the opinions of such high-ranking men.[8]

Anti-Federalists certainly respected the reputations and past service of the men who had gathered in Philadelphia in the summer of 1787. However, to their minds admiration for such men did not require automatic agreement with them. As one editorialist explained it, the Philadelphia Convention drew together many of America's "choicest sons" who deserved the "reverence" of their fellow citizens. But voters still needed to independently evaluate the Constitution. A responsible citizen should never substitute another man's judgment for his own—regardless of rank, experience, or fame. Addressing the "freeman of Virginia," the author challenged citizens to turn away from "over-weaning reverence for men" and fulfill their duty to defend the liberty of posterity. Otherwise, he warned them, "you are no longer worthy to bear the name of *freemen.*" His hope was that "every freeman in Virginia will . . .

nobly dare to think for himself, and will not be lulled, perhaps into a fatal stupor, by the whistling of any names whatsoever."[9]

The author's dismissal of the "whistling" of famous names reflects an extraordinary move against many of America's most powerful men, including the "father of his country." Everyone in Virginia knew that George Washington presided over the Philadelphia Convention and signed the Constitution. That in the face of Washington's support Virginia voters might reject the Constitution shows how deep the Revolution cut into the long-standing tradition of political deference. By the turn of the new year, Edmund Pendleton was cautioning James Madison that "a considerable Revolution has happened in the minds of the middle & lower Class's of the people." At first they "warmly" supported the Constitution, Pendleton said, "from a confidence in the wisdom & Integrity of their representatives." But growing numbers were being led astray by what they read and heard from Anti-Federalists, who he characterized as "designing men" who were "decrying powers as dangerous to liberty."[10]

This widening reluctance to defer to delegates at the Philadelphia Convention in general and George Washington in particular stunned and galled Federalists. During the Revolution, they reminded voters, Washington had been "the Saviour of America." It seemed preposterous that Anti-Federalists would now reject his leadership or, to use Federalists' outsized language, that they would either directly or by implication "charge him with being a Conspirator against the liberties of that very Country which he so lately saved from the all grasping hand of a haughty Tyrant." Alexander White, writing in a Winchester paper, urged voters to recall that among the Philadelphia delegates "was a Washington, whose hair has become grey and eyes dim in watching over your safety" and "a Franklin, whose philosophical and political abilities have procured him the admiration of the world." "Is it possible," he wondered, "that a Washington and a Franklin could conspire to enslave their country?" Again and again, Virginia Federalists held up Washington and Franklin as paragons of republican sacrifice and virtue—proven leaders far above the petty skepticism of ordinary men. A typical essay in the *Norfolk and Portsmouth Journal* dismissed as "monstrous absurdity" the mere suggestion that "such characters as *Washington* and *Franklin*, who by a long life of virtue and patriotism, have acquired reputations not to be extinguished but with the world" would allow "the sanction of their names to establish a system of tyranny!"[11]

Looking back, it's hard to know how much of this outrage was genuine and how much was strategic. Federalists saw an electoral advantage in linking support for the Constitution with a defense of George Washington's integrity and Benjamin Franklin's intelligence. They were clearly selective in their indignation about criticism leveled at the revolutionary leaders. Federalists freely lambasted George Mason in the newspapers for his "absolutely puerile" depiction of constitutional powers. Another tract, dripping with false sympathy, mocked Mason as a "poor old man" who had "worn his judgment entirely thread-bare and ragged in the service of his country." They excoriated Patrick Henry, too, claiming that he manufactured opposition to the Constitution to force "a dismemberment of the Union" and aggrandize himself. Such assaults on the integrity of renowned patriots like Mason and Henry didn't seem to worry Federalists at all.[12]

In any event, George Washington's reputation forced Anti-Federalists to seek out creative ways to publicly disagree with his support for the Constitution without disrespecting his service—which they well understood would hurt them at the polls. Responding to Federalists' repeated invocation of Washington's name to attract voters, Anti-Federalists insisted that judging the Constitution on its merits was not only their right but their responsibility. They bristled at the idea that reflexive deference was owed to any man—even George Washington—and denounced such conduct as beneath a virtuous citizen.

Fortunately for Anti-Federalists, no other man in Virginia merited this sort of delicacy; everyone else was fair game. And though they handled Washington gingerly in the newspapers, in both publications and private letters Anti-Federalists openly derided Federalists' expectation of political deference. Reasoned dissent, proclaimed one Alexandria Anti-Federalist, "is a Right I claim as a Citizen & which I never did or will Surrender."[13]

The speed with which ordinary farmers and artisans challenged the views of prominent men rattled even the usually unflappable James Madison. The turnabout struck him as "wonderful"—by which he meant shocking, not delightful. Before the ratification debates, he knew, "the mass of the people have been so much accustomed to be guided by their rulers on all new and intricate questions." Now, Madison marveled, ordinary men decided to "not only go before, but contrary to, their most popular leaders." More incredible still, Madison added, the question at hand "certainly surpasses the judgment of the greater part of them."[14]

Perhaps advocates for ratification should have anticipated citizens balking at what they saw as high-handed tactics and cunning manipulations aimed at instituting a tyrannical government. This was, after all, precisely what the patriots charged Parliament and George III with doing the decade before.

That powerful men like Patrick Henry, Richard Henry Lee, and George Mason stood against the Constitution doubtless emboldened critics from the middling ranks of Virginia society. Some voters, in fact, concluded that divisions among long-standing leaders of the state warranted rejection: until they agreed, no governmental change should be made. But the matter ran deeper than simply reaching a consensus among elites or even deciding which gentlemen to defer to. Seizing on the ideas of the Declaration of Independence, critics of the Constitution trumpeted the equality of all citizens, regardless of rank or experience.

The lead-up to the 1788 elections in Virginia revealed the efforts of independent citizens to educate themselves and make the right choice for their country, even if that meant questioning the motives of accomplished leaders. While Federalists tended to prefer a more traditional, deferential approach to voting, they found themselves pushed toward echoing Anti-Federalists on the matter of voter autonomy. "When we take a view of the respectable names who met upon this occasion, and composed this plan of government," explained one Federalist writer, "we ought to approach it with deference and respect." But, he quickly added, "not in such a manner as to deprive us" of individual opinions.[15]

When Federalists agreed with Anti-Federalists that no man should substitute another's judgment for his own, they also asked: What about the collective judgment of the most learned and respected men in America? Federalists repeatedly urged voters—as they weighed for themselves the merits of the Constitution—to balance their personal perceptions against the great majority of members of the Philadelphia Convention. Wasn't it more likely, one essayist asked, "that a single reader, even of great capacity, should be mistaken, than that so respectable a body as the Convention" would be wrong? "A Freeholder," writing in a Richmond newspaper, repeated the point. It should seem more probable to a reasonable man, he suggested, that critics were mistaken in their bleak reading of the Constitution than that "the members of the late grand convention should have ignorantly contrived a foolish plan, or have basely framed a mischievous one, with design to enslave their country."[16]

Lobbying for reasoned deference to the Philadelphia Convention delegates fit with the Federalists' general depiction of the ratification question. In the opinion of many strong Federalists, critics of the Constitution were confused at best. At worst, they willfully deceived the ignorant, manipulated the masses, and exploited the lower ranks. Edward Carrington warned James Madison in mid-February about the insidious influence he expected Patrick Henry's seductive oratory to exert over "weak Men" elected to the convention.[17] Conversely, Federalists depicted themselves as experienced leaders serving the common good: men of larger, more capacious minds who knew better than their parochial neighbors. This rhetoric revealed how class played into Virginians' disagreements over the Constitution. It also subtly encouraged middling-rank voters who wanted to see themselves as gentlemen-in-the-making to identify with elites and not with the so-called rabble. Voting for Anti-Federalist delegates, Federalists cautioned, would only fuel social chaos, which jeopardized all citizens' rights.[18]

Federalists trying to persuade skittish voters to adopt their view insisted that the Constitution was the only chance to foster the stability the United States desperately needed and preserve the liberty Virginians treasured. The path to peace lay in standing firm together. If voters filled the Richmond convention with representatives opposed to ratification, insisted one typical writer, "anarchy would quickly follow." If, on the other hand, voters elected men committed to the Constitution, they would be governed not by a corrupt oligarchy, as the Anti-Federalists wrongly feared, but by an "aristocracy of talent"—the most virtuous, learned, experienced, and trustworthy men in the country. "If power cannot be trusted in the hands of men so appointed," reasoned one writer, "it can be trusted no where." Another asked his readers: "Do you really believe that you cannot choose men who will faithfully promote your happiness in the discharge of the duties of their respective offices?"[19]

Anti-Federalists likewise used the debates about the basis for voting to press their central criticism of the Constitution: the federal plan sacrificed individual liberty for governmental power—which could never be trusted in any man's hands as it was inherently corrupting. Anti-Federalists tended to favor a referendum approach to the elections. They advised voters that if they sent to Richmond men who supported the Constitution just because powerful men said they should, they could expect continued marginalization of citizens' voices and a federal government controlled by elites. What use was order under such tyranny? The Constitution, critics believed, created a distant, consolidated government that held unchecked powers over citizens and privileged the wealthy and well-connected. Under this plan, "the common people, who are the best and greatest supporters of government, will be slaves." "Now," they alerted voters, "is the time to secure, or to bid eternal farewell to liberty."[20]

As election fever spread, "common people" bent on securing liberty increasingly challenged the power of Virginia's leading gentlemen. This included the first man in America. George Washington understood the reputational perils of appearing overeager for the government he expected to lead, so he played the part of an eighteenth-century gentleman. He refused to serve in the Virginia Ratification Convention, campaign for Federalist candidates, or even publicly comment on the elections. This facade did not, however, keep Washington from deeply involving himself in the elections. He monitored debates in other states and stayed in close contact with James Madison about the prospects of the Constitution nationally. His proxies, especially Tobias Lear and David Stuart, used Virginia newspapers to assail Anti-Federalists' views. And visitors to Mount Vernon got his message loud and clear.

This behind-the-scenes approach could not last in Virginia's fast-changing political climate. On 14 December, Washington wrote a private letter to Charles Carter praising the Constitution. "My *decided* Opinion of the Matter," he told Carter, "is, that there is *no Alternative* between the *Adoption* of it and *Anarchy*." As for the opposition, Washington dismissed their questions and criticisms as "addressed more to the Passions than to the Reason."[21]

Two days after Christmas, Washington was shocked to see parts of that private letter published in the *Virginia Herald*. His name was withheld, but his identity was clear. Carter, it turned out, had shared the letter with several friends—always with express directions to keep it from the newspapers. But apparently some member of Carter's circle showed it to a printer. Or, perhaps, it fell into the hands of a skeptic of the Constitution. In any event, excerpts of that personal letter, Washington complained to Carter, were "running through all the news papers." A Baltimore editor added Washington's name, removing all doubts and deniability. By March, Washington's letter, usually carrying his name, appeared in *forty-nine* papers and in every state except North Carolina. While he was not ashamed of his views, Washington told Carter, he certainly did not appreciate seeing "the hasty, and indigested production of a private letter, handed to the public."[22]

George Washington never received much of a formal education, which was unusual among Virginia gentlemen, and he remained prickly about the shortcoming throughout his life. It bothered him that the Carter letter lacked what he called "a proper dress"—more polished prose. Furthermore, if his views were going to be published, he wanted to mount a more rigorous defense of the Constitution than appeared in the quickly composed letter. He would have, Washington told Carter, "assigned some reasons in support of my opinions, and the charges against others."[23]

Carter promised he played no part in the publication and profusely apologized, and Washington accepted. What else could he do? Washington confided to James Madison that he felt "hurt by the publication" and disappointed that Carter's "zeal in the cause" overran his discretion.[24]

Madison saw an upside to Washington's embarrassment: newspapers printing Washington's dire predictions of anarchy if ratification failed "may have been of service."[25] Federalists routinely pointed out that Americans stood on the precipice of political and social collapse. Anti-Federalists, while acknowledging problems with the Articles of Confederation and agreeing about the need for change, recoiled from what they saw as Federalist hysteria. Advocates for the Constitution, they charged, exaggerated threats to stoke fear and win votes. Madison understood that Washington's prediction gave Federalist warnings renewed credibility among voters.

At the same time, Madison commiserated with Washington over "the scandalous misinterpretations . . . which have been attempted." Included in the published parts of the letter was Washington's concession that "I am not a blind Admirer (for I saw the imperfections) of the Constitution." He described the federal plan as "the *best that can be obtained at this Time*." Anti-Federalists pounced on those statements both to question the merits of the Constitution and to undercut the endorsement of George Washington.[26]

Even as the Carter letter spread across the continent, Washington maintained his (now incredible) public posture of detachment and objectivity. In the weeks leading up to the March elections, he told a former Continental army soldier that he was "perhaps less qualified to give an opinion upon" the outcome in Virginia "than almost any one, as I very seldom ride off my farms." He made the same spurious claim to John Jay: "I am incompetent to judge, never having been six miles beyond the limits of my own Farms since my return from Philadelphia."[27] Left unsaid was his extended correspondences with a host of men and the fact that his many visitors included leading figures from across America like Charles Cotesworth Pinckney of South Carolina, Robert

Morris of New York, and Gouverneur Morris (who had relocated from New York to Pennsylvania), and well-connected fellow Virginians such as Henry Lee and Arthur Lee, Edward Carrington, and James Madison. Washington had no cause to travel beyond Mount Vernon since everyone came to him.

Anti-Federalists knew better than to publicly challenge George Washington's pretense of disinterestedness. Instead, they tried to twist his words to their advantage. And, when other men held Washington up to defend the Constitution, ratification opponents proclaimed their right to decide for themselves. Anti-Federalists would have lost more than they gained by going any further. But other leading men, on both sides of the debate, were not so fortunate: they found their reputations assailed, including by writers who proudly proclaimed themselves "plain" and "unlettered" plowmen.

In late January, one such "plain, unlettered man" took on Richard Henry Lee for his published critique of the Constitution. In a scorching rebuttal addressed directly to Lee, "Valerius" openly derided Lee's idea of a second convention to debate amendments.[28]

Feigning the deference that he charged Lee with arrogantly expecting from fellow citizens, Valerius sarcastically contrasted Lee's "superior knowledge" with his own "humble opinion." He then declared Lee "the *dupe* of your own sophistry" and guilty of trying to manipulate citizens with "low arts." The language could scarce get more accusatory: "For shame! Sir, for shame!" On the specific issue of representation, which Lee complained was inadequate under the Constitution, Valerius insisted, "the description is as false, as the language is vulgar."[29]

"Cassius" followed suit in a series of blistering letters soon published in the *Virginia Independent Chronicle*. The author dared Richard Henry Lee to defend his opinion of the Constitution and made no bones about his contempt for Lee, who, he insisted, was either "*totally* ignorant of the subject" on which he wrote, or willfully trying "to deceive the people." The hammering continued: "Many of your objections, sir, are so extremely puerile and absurd, that I can, scarcely, reconcile it to myself you are serious." The next week's edition brought another installment of vitriol. "Alternately impelled by the weakness and fury of your passions," Cassius charged Lee, "you go on, in a rapid progression, from error to error, without giving your reason a moment's interval, to exert itself." Lee was also accused in the pages of the *Petersburg Virginia Gazette* of "egregious errors and gross misrepresentations" in his "arrogant and inflammatory" criticisms of the Constitution.[30]

Lee's reaction hinted at the condescension his critics loathed. Although taken aback by the attacks, he dismissed the "Scribblers in the Newspapers" as beneath his consideration. "My attention to them," he told Edmund Pendleton, "will never exist whilst there is a Cat or a Spaniel in the House!"[31]

Governor Edmund Randolph likewise found himself on the receiving end of an onslaught of criticism—not for his position but because he refused to explain it. In late 1787, Randolph seemed to exemplify his critics' harsh judgment: he acted cagey, self-protective, and politically driven. As French diplomat Martin Oster saw it, Randolph "is of a character that bends according to how his interest varies, and in addition that always follows the strongest party."[32]

Unlike Patrick Henry, who used circumspection to great political effect, Randolph seemed to annoy other men. To begin with, Randolph, unlike Henry, directly participated in the Philadelphia Convention. He made the controversial decision not to sign the Constitution and then, once home, refused to explain his actions. His public silence also dragged on, long after Henry announced his fierce objections to the federal plan. And, finally, Randolph seemed to tell advocates on both sides of the debates what they wanted to hear. In late September, for example, he wrote Richard Henry Lee that, unless amended, the Constitution would devolve into a monarchy or an aristocracy. By January, he was begging James Madison to come home, lest ratification flounder.[33]

Randolph's critics thought he played politics even before he left Philadelphia. When he decided to withhold his signature from the Constitution, Randolph wrote Lieutenant Governor Beverley Randolph that his reasons would be better explained in person than in a letter. Shortly thereafter the Richmond papers reported that Governor Randolph would not be able to return to the city as soon as he hoped "owing to the Indisposition of his Lady." On 10 October, Randolph apparently composed a letter to the Speaker of the House of Delegates explaining why he refused to sign the Constitution. But he did not send the letter. Two and a half months passed before it saw the light of day, and only then under tremendous political pressure.[34]

Meanwhile, the state legislature reconvened on 18 October, for its first session after the Philadelphia Convention. Members of the legislature were bewildered when the governor offered no explanation for his conduct and no comment on the Constitution. At the end of that month, he wrote to James Madison about the variety of opinions on the Constitution and his continued

Edmund Randolph. Portrait by John Angel James Wilcox. Prints and Photographs Division, Library of Congress

determination "to postpone my explanation of myself, except in private" until after the state legislature finalized plans for the ratification convention. But even then, he kept silent.[35]

Detractors saw this conduct as entirely self-serving. Randolph's term as governor was nearly up: the next vote in the legislature for the governorship was scheduled for 23 October. (Virginians did not directly elect their governor until the 1850s.) If Randolph intended to use his silence to his political advantage, it worked. He was reelected governor by the state legislature even though no one knew for sure what he thought about the most important issue facing Virginia. And the margin was stunning: 137-3. Political deference was not dead in Virginia after all.[36]

Randolph did not divulge his opinion even after retaining his position as governor, although his personal correspondence with James Madison in the fall revealed his leanings. He congratulated Madison on being reelected to the Confederation Congress in late October, and admitted that he and Patrick Henry "have had several animated discourses" during the legislative session. Publicly, though, Randolph stayed on the fence.[37]

Finally, in early December, a group of legislators gave Randolph an ultimatum. Several powerful state leaders wrote him that "the time is passed, when you might with propriety" have informed the legislature of "what objections could induce you to refuse your signature" to the Constitution. Randolph had already told them his thoughts "in private." After so long a delay, they explained, "we hope, you can have no objection to enable us to make them public through the medium of the Press." In other words, Governor Randolph could act or they would.[38]

His hand forced by these legislators, Randolph finally agreed to disclose his thoughts, and in late December a sixteen-page essay, printed as a pamphlet and in newspapers, hit Virginia. By January it appeared in sixteen newspapers, in Maryland, Pennsylvania, New York, Connecticut, Rhode Island, and Massachusetts.[39]

To Virginians aggravated by the governor's gamesmanship, the essay perfectly captured Randolph the political trimmer: he waffled, dodged, and dissembled from the first paragraphs. In blatant contradiction to his actions over the past two months, he proclaimed his "disdain to conceal the reasons" for his refusal to sign the Constitution and added, incredibly: "I have always been, still am, and ever shall be, ready to proclaim them to the world."[40]

Randolph began a long and by his own reckoning "tedious" lead-in to his explanation with the misleading claim that, before the Philadelphia Convention, he believed "the confederation was not so eminently defective, as it had been supposed." In fact, Randolph had fairly begged George Washington to attend the 1787 convention by reminding him that "every day brings forth some new crisis." Then, when he introduced the Virginia Plan at the Philadelphia Convention, he dismissed the Articles as "totally inadequate" and promoted a new design of government as an "absolute necessity."[41]

Throughout his account, Randolph repeatedly invoked the Revolutionary War, in an apparent attempt to play to readers' patriotism. He also predicted dire consequences if Americans did not stand together, though exactly what standing together meant he did not say. Two-thirds of the way into the essay, when readers still could not discern his opinion on the Constitution, Randolph announced, "I am fatigued with summoning up to my imagination the miseries, which will harass the United States, if torn from each other." Some readers doubtless felt fatigued, too.

Finally, in the last quarter of the essay, Randolph explained that his real objection was to the ratification process itself. He wanted states to be able to debate and make amendments, and he believed that if he signed in Philadelphia he would be "bound to be silent as to amendments" in Virginia. "I was afraid," he continued, "that if the Constitution was to be submitted to the people, to be wholly adopted or wholly rejected by them, they would not only reject it, but bid a lasting farewell to the union."

In the end, Randolph said that "if after our best efforts for amendments they cannot be obtained," then he would accept the Constitution. And he closed with another hollow claim: "I affect neither mystery nor subtlety, in politics."[42] After arguing for this middle ground, Randolph appeared to ally himself squarely with James Madison. George Mason was appalled at Randolph's turnaround, which he counted as a craven betrayal.

Mason was far from alone in his contempt for Edmund Randolph's conduct. On 13 February, the Virginia Independent Chronicle published an essay by "A Plain Dealer," which rebuked Randolph's political waffling. Advocates of the Constitution almost immediately assumed that the author was Spencer Roane, the son-in-law of Patrick Henry. Roane was a long-serving state politician, a lawyer and planter, and, it turned out, quite a vivid writer. To Randolph's specious claim that he needed to refrain from sharing his views earlier because of his possible reelection as governor, "Plain Dealer" offered this reproof: "I did not know that the being, or not being, Governor of Virginia . . . was sufficient to deter, a real patriot, from speaking . . . in behalf of the liberties of his country."[43]

"Plain Dealer" pointed out that in the fall of 1787 Randolph had concluded that, left unchanged, "either a monarchy or an aristocracy will be generated from the proposed Constitution." Just a few months later, he publicly announced his determination to support the Constitution, even if amendments could not be secured. "Good God!" exclaimed the author, "how can the first Magistrate . . . declare that he will accept a Constitution which is to begat a monarchy or an aristocracy." At least the "respectable characters" who signed the Constitution in Philadelphia did so, "Plain Dealer" allowed, from a position of integrity, misguided though it was. None of them would have accepted the Constitution if they actually believed it would destroy the republic. The same could not be said, however, for Governor Randolph.[44]

Virginia's fractious political climate made it easy for partisans to disparage Randolph's wobbliness. But a more dispassionate reflection on his behavior sheds different light on Randolph and, by extension, Virginians' attitudes toward the looming elections. What if Randolph wasn't Machiavellian at all but rather a pragmatic moderate?[45]

The requirement that voters in each county elect two men who, in turn, would vote for or against ratification pushed Virginians toward stark positions in the lead-up to the elections. This polarization obscured the complexity of voters' opinions. In fact, views on the Constitution ran across a wide spectrum. "The opinions," remarked one Virginian, "appear to be as various as the persons possessing them."[46]

Within that diversity of opinions, Virginians held a consensus on several crucial points. No one in Virginia in 1787–88 disputed the need for some fundamental governmental reform. The Articles, they saw, required significant alteration. Likewise, everyone agreed that any changes had to protect Virginians' liberty and their economic interests. Virginians feared standing armies and public debts; they recoiled from the idea of a consolidated government that forfeited their financial interests to northeastern states; they were determined to protect westward expansion.[47]

That governmental changes were necessary the Virginians understood: what changes to make and when and how to make them was where they disagreed. What kind of structure should bind the union of states? How should sovereignty be shared between the states and the central government? What was the proper balance between individual liberty and governmental power? Some men fawned over the Constitution, hailing it as a panacea for all of America's problems and the pinnacle of governmental thought: "the rising SUN of the western world." Others blasted it as irredeemably flawed: "replete with shackles for the free born sons of America." But most Virginians found themselves somewhere between those two extremes. Although their voices often got drowned out by the thundering rhetoric of hardline Federalists and Anti-Federalists, men often said there were no easy answers to the challenging questions facing the Old Dominion.[48]

At the end of 1787, James Madison saw three general camps emerging out of this complex picture. One group of Virginians supported ratifying without amendments. Another did not object to the basic structure of the Constitution but wanted to see amendments expressly securing the rights of individuals and clarifying the roles of the states. A third, including Patrick Henry, demanded changes "such as strike at the essence of the System." There was no doubt in Madison's mind that Henry "is the great adversary who will render the event precarious." If Virginia voters shared Henry's attitude, Madison speculated, the resulting convention would not ratify. That decision would consequently drive the states toward separate confederacies—ending the union of states and sending Americans down the road of ruin.[49] Unlike some of his contemporaries, Madison did not claim this was the intent of men like Patrick Henry. He did not doubt their patriotism, only their judgment. Rather than their plan, a shattered union would be the inevitable, if unintentional, result of Anti-Federalists' campaign to defeat ratification.

The many Virginians who wanted some revisions to the Constitution divided over the process of effecting change. Some men lobbied for "previous" amendments: Virginia should demand changes *before* ratifying the Constitution. Others wanted to follow the example of Massachusetts, which ratified and forwarded a list of "subsequent" amendments that the convention delegates recommended the first Congress consider. Still other Virginians called for a second continent-wide convention. They wanted another opportunity for delegates to debate the alterations discussed in all the states and negotiate for an improved Constitution.

This became a major obstacle for the Anti-Federalists: Exactly what changes did they think needed to be made? Even the three Philadelphia delegates who refused to sign the Constitution did not agree about *why* they opposed the new plan. As one savvy writer pointed out, "If they had been the sole persons employed to frame a constitution, some two of them, would have rejected almost every other objection, stated by the third."[50] A bill of rights was an especially popular proposal, but exactly what should it contain? And how should changes be made? In a new convention? By the Confederation Congress? Through some yet undefined process of amending the Constitution before ratification? Richard Henry Lee and others offered ideas, but Anti-Federalists did not unite around any consensus plan. They found it much easier to state what they found objectionable in the Constitution than explain which kind of government they wanted instead. The unhappy implication of the Anti-Federalist position on ratification was that the country would continue to operate under the problematic Articles, at least for the short term. Their inability to offer an alternative to the Constitution left Anti-Federalists open to charges, even from skeptics of the federal design, that they were divisive and weakening the union to the breaking point.

In January 1788, James Madison saw in this fractured opposition cause for optimism. "It appears to me," he told Edmund Randolph, "that the ground taken by the opponents in different quarters, forbids any hope of concord among them."[51] There was no such ambiguity within the Federalist agenda, Madison knew. It was crystal clear: ratify the Constitution.

But within a month, Madison's friend Edward Carrington wrote with a bleaker assessment of the quickly changing scene. Though Virginians talked about many, sometimes contradictory revisions—disagreeing over exactly what needed to be changed and how those changes might be achieved— the general idea of "previous" or conditional amendments was fast gaining ground. Carrington predicted that, given the hold this idea had on citizens in the early spring of 1788, "the direct adoption of the Constitution cannot be well expected should less than Nine States have adopted when our Convention comes to sit."[52]

The more Virginians talked about previous amendments and a second convention, the more Federalists feared all would be lost. Pursuing either idea, Madison kept insisting, "will be fatal." Anti-Federalists' unwavering demands struck men like Madison as antithetical to agreeing to *any* changes to the union of states—and certainly the opposite of what prevailed in Philadelphia. There, compromise was the watchword. Madison confided to a friend that the final agreement to the Constitution in Philadelphia was accomplished through concessions made by the delegates that turned on "their ignorance of the opinions & confidence in the liberality of their respective constituents." The months since September had laid bare that falsity. In other words, too many leading men knew too much about their constituents' settled opinions ever again to agree to the Constitution. It was the 1787 plan or nothing.[53]

Federalists insisted that a second convention was "utterly irreconcilable . . . with the dictates of prudence and safety." Anti-Federalists countered that arguing "a bad government must be established for fear of anarchy, is really saying that we must kill ourselves for fear of dying."[54]

Though they were never as fractured as the opposition to ratification, Federalists faced their own, internal struggles. James Madison was immovable on the question of ratification, but he avoided the hyperbolic accusations leveled by many of his allies. While other Federalists condemned the motivations and character of the critics of the Constitution, he was able to see the divisions among Americans dispassionately. They were, he wrote a friend, "intelligent people, equally divided, and equally earnest." Madison was practical and analytical about the divisions. "What" he reasoned, "is the proper conclusion from all this?—that unanimity is not to be expected in any great political question." The perfect, Madison understood, should not be the enemy of the good. And the Constitution should not be judged against some "theory, which each individual may frame in his own mind." Instead, it should be compared "with the system which it is meant to take the place of, and with any other which there may be a probability of obtaining."[55]

George Washington held a darker view and took criticisms of the Constitution much more personally. He believed the opposition was led by parochial and petty men who manipulated uneducated voters by fabricating dangerous consequences to ratification, while hiding their real, self-serving, power-hungry motivations for opposing the Constitution.[56]

Through the spirited public debates, Federalists saw that their divisions ran deeper than simply how to view the opposition. A good number of men who supported ratification did so with much less zeal than either Washington or Madison. Paul Carrington, the chief justice of the Virginia General Court, was typical. He told his brother that he "dislikes the Constitution, but dreads the consequences of a disunion" even more. He reluctantly decided to support ratification. Bishop James Madison told his namesake cousin that his efforts at defending the Constitution "have well nigh worked a Conversion." But a question lingered in his mind, as it did with many voters: "Is it, in reality practicable?"[57]

The search for a "practicable" way out of Virginians' complicated divisions inspired some very creative proposals, including in a broadside published in December in Richmond. The anonymous author, identified only as "A True Friend," started from a point of near universal agreement: American exceptionalism. The United States, he insisted, "cannot be pertinently compared to any thing, which has hitherto existed on earth." There was no example in the history of the world to guide the Americans in deciding whether to reject or accept the Constitution. At first, readers likely thought him an opponent of the Constitution, for "True Friend" reminded advocates of ratification that *"the liberties and the rights of the people have been always encroached on, and finally destroyed by those, whom they had entrusted with the powers of government."* That fear of centralized government destroying citizens' rights would have been music to the Anti-Federalists' ears. But then, the writer pivoted. The critics of the Constitution should want "good order and mutual confidence established at home, and your credit and reputation flourishing among the nations abroad." Here the essayist parroted Federalist arguments about the economic and international strength the Constitution would bring to the floundering American Republic. Surely, he reasoned, no good patriot could dispute either of these two "cardinal points": a better plan of government was required and citizens' rights had to be protected. Unlike many writers, "True Friend" believed that members of the "contending parties" all had the country's best interest at heart. Compromise, then, was both required and possible.

"True Friend" offered a two-part plan that he believed would build the stability Federalists required and preserve the liberty Anti-Federalists refused to surrender. First, Americans should ratify the Constitution only for a short period of time, somewhere between eight and twelve years. The author pointed out that just a decade before, the Articles of Confederation had been "universally admired" and now Americans found it inadequate. By returning in a decade or so for another constitutional convention, Americans could use their time and experience to "become expert in the intricate and complicated science of legislation" and judge whether the federal government served their best interests. Second, no state should ratify the Constitution before the addition of a bill of rights. "What man of upright intentions," he asked, "will dare to say, that free men giving up such extensive prerogatives to their rulers, as the new federal constitution requires, should not at the same time put them in mind of the rights, which constitute them such?"[58]

As the spring elections drew closer, such suggestions of compromise ran in short supply. Strident advocates of ratification and of rejection derided in the pages of Virginia's newspapers the patriotism, motives, and even the good sense of their opponents. In mid-March a supposedly "Impartial Citizen" delivered in the *Petersburg Virginia Gazette* a damning rebuke of Anti-Federalists. He proclaimed that any reasonable man who undertook a close examination of both the Constitution and the writings of the critics would reach an inevitable conclusion: that the objections "are dictated entirely by the most implacable hatred to every idea of confederation, or by the grossest and most stupid ignorance."[59] So much for reasoned debate among "impartial" citizens.

In truth, neither side was inclined toward conciliation. For their part, Federalists thought the Constitution itself was the ultimate compromise. The Anti-Federalists, they believed, acted on the same parochial interests that undermined the confederation government. Their inflexibility offered the best evidence of the necessity of a design of government that militated against such stubborn provincialism—which threatened the very existence republican government.

Opponents to ratification countered that the mortal danger came not from them but from the powers embedded in the Constitution. And it was the Federalists who were being obstinate, demanding only a yes or no vote and insisting rejection meant disunion. Anti-Federalists also continued to claim that the Constitution would "enslave" citizens. This proved a compelling political tactic if also a cruel hypocrisy given Virginians' long history with the actual enslavement of African Americans. Then, in mid-February, Anti-Federalist writers moved—for the first time—from using slavery as a rhetorical device to condemning the Constitution for sanctioning slaveholding.

The Constitution advanced slavery in a number of concrete ways, including through a strong federal fugitive slave law and sanctioning the international slave trade. The very structure of representation depended on slavery: representation in the House, the only part of the government directly elected by voters, was apportioned to reward slaveholders. The infamous three-fifths compromise not only gave southern slave states greater influence within the US government by counting every five slaves as three people; it also implicitly endorsed slaveholders' denial of black equality by counting African Americans as less than full persons.[60]

In Virginia, Anti-Federalists leveled the first public rebuke of slavery's place in the Constitution in the pages of the *Virginia Independent Chronicle*. The anonymous author tried to appeal to the state's Quakers, many of whom shared their faith's moral objection to slavery and found repugnant the provision allowing the international trafficking of Africans to endure for twenty more years. Two weeks later a Kentucky writer similarly condemned the "shocking absurdity" that "such an execrable trade, should be radically woven into, and become an essential part of our national constitution."[61]

White Americans knew that racial slavery could not be reconciled with their republican values. The first antislavery society in the Western world was founded in Philadelphia in 1775. Inspired by the American Revolution, the New England and Mid-Atlantic states moved in the 1770s and 1780s toward creating gradual emancipation programs. Though they certainly were not racial liberals in the modern sense, many citizens in these regions ended their involvement in the international slave trade, disavowed slaveholding, and pushed their representatives to pass laws emancipating men and women held in bondage. The process was slow, unfolding over generations, with African Americans freed upon reaching age eighteen or twenty-one. And some of these states coupled gradual emancipation with laws disfranchising black men. Other Americans, including Quakers, took a stronger stand: they rejected slavery as immoral and expelled slaveholders from their churches. It was, in fact, mostly Quakers who founded the antislavery society in Phila-delphia. Some evangelical churches, especially the Baptists and Methodists, agreed with the Quakers, condemning slavery as un-Christian and welcom-ing African American converts.

Other white Americans, including many planters from Virginia, wanted to close the international slave trade but not end slavery. This was a financial position: Chesapeake slaves reproduced through natural increase, so slave-holders did not need to import bondspersons from Africa. International traf-ficking undercut their ability to sell their own slaves in the Deep South and West. South Carolina leaders, meanwhile, wanted no criticisms of and no impediments to either the international trade or the institution. They were the ones who, in Philadelphia, insisted most stridently that the Constitution protect slavery.

Despite this range of opinion—and despite how the Revolution unleashed a widespread idealization of liberty and equality—the Constitution protected racial slavery. And though they often wrung their hands about owning slaves, Virginia's political leaders never seriously discussed ending slavery in the Old Dominion. They stayed their dreadful course. By their own acknowledgment, their slave ownership violated their most treasured republican values.

Critics of the Constitution struck a nerve, then, when they leveled a moral condemnation of slavery's centrality to the federal plan. In some states, this became a hotly debated issue and the source of serious opposition to the Con-stitution. But not in Virginia. Too many men on both sides of the ratification contest depended on slavery for their livelihood and identity. Slavery did, however, raise an electoral problem for Federalists: the issue ran the risk of costing them support among key niche voters in pivotal counties, especially in the West. And the last thing advocates for the Constitution needed in early 1788 was another reason for Kentucky voters to oppose ratification.

Events unfolded in rapid pace in the last weeks of February. In the Kentucky counties, the seeds Patrick Henry sowed in the fall bore fruit. From his ear-liest commentary on the Constitution, Henry had warned residents of the westernmost region of the state that the federal design put their profits, fu-ture, and safety in jeopardy. Federalists, he maintained, wanted them to sac-rifice their local rights and interests to a distant government, likely to be con-trolled by northeasterners. Many citizens in those counties heartily agreed with Patrick Henry. Harry Innes, a prominent Kentucky judge and strident defender of western rights, announced on 20 February, as voters prepared to go to court day, "Our interests and the interests of the Eastern States are so diametrically opposite to each other that there cannot be a ray of hope left to the Western Country to suppose that when once that interest clashes we shall have justice done us." His paramount concern was commercial access to the Mississippi River, and he felt certain—a conviction widely shared among political leaders in Kentucky—that if "Congress hath this sole power & a majority have the right of deciding on those grand questions we cannot expect to enjoy the navigation of the Mississippi." Such power, he predicted, would doom Kentucky.[62]

On the eve of elections, many of Kentucky's leading politicians stood with Harry Innes and publicly opposed the Constitution. On 29 February, a group of powerful Kentucky residents signed an open letter condemning the authority granted Congress to regulate commerce with foreign countries as a fatal blow to "the happiness & greatness of the Western Country." If ratification occurred, they predicted, Kentuckians would lose access to the Mississippi River. When that happened, migration would slow, land values drop, and wealth evaporate. If economic fears did not mobilize voters, perhaps racist ones would: ultimately, the signers warned, white residents left in disappearing communities would fall prey "to the ravages of the Merciless Savages."[63] By the 1780s, white Virginians had nearly two centuries of experience appropriating land from Native American nations and then complaining bitterly when they resisted those violations and encroachments. This sort of fear-mongering about Indian retaliation was as old as Virginia itself.

That same week, Virginia's Confederation Congress delegation submitted to Congress a petition to approve a "compact" between the state of Virginia and its Kentucky district to make Kentucky a separate state. This had long been an ambition of Kentuckians, and the timing of the petition was no accident. Congress, perhaps wanting to see the outcome of the ratification process, stalled. But back home, the move added more fuel to the fire. Fearing the loss of their bid for statehood and their access to the Mississippi River, Kentucky leaders grew ever more suspicious of centralized power and the federal design.[64]

Federalists worried about how much localism was driving Anti-Federalism in the western regions of Virginia, but they also took heart in the continental scene. In December and January five states ratified, and except for Pennsylvania, without too much lingering controversy. Massachusetts was highly contentious and close and forwarded requested amendments. Still, it did ratify in early February, bringing the number of supporting states to six. New Hampshire convened on 13 February, and Maryland and South Carolina would meet in April and May, respectively. If all went smoothly, Federalists calculated, Virginians would find their hands forced by the time they gathered in June; they would have to ratify or risk being marginalized, because the required nine states would already be committed to the Constitution.

In a widely reprinted March essay from the *Virginia Independent Chronicle*, readers were reminded that six states had already ratified, including Massachusetts, Virginia's closest partner in the Revolution, and Pennsylvania, the second most populous state (after Virginia). That meant that "a majority of the free people of America" had already voted in favor of the Constitution.[65]

But inside those numbers was cause for concern. The vote in Massachusetts had been razor thin: 187-168. And that occurred only because Federalists promised amendments after ratification. Furthermore, as with the Electoral College today, the popular vote did not decide the question: states, not voters, were what mattered.

Then came more bad news for Federalists: New Hampshire delegates suddenly adjourned after just a week of debate. Seeing no path to ratification, Federalists at New Hampshire's convention postponed further discussions until mid-June—after Virginia.[66]

The news stunned Virginia Federalists. A frustrated George Washington wrote Henry Knox: "The conduct of the State of New Hampshire has baffled all calculation." Before "this untoward event," Washington had felt fairly confident about the outcome of the Virginia elections. "What will be the result *now*," he told Knox, "is difficult for me to say."[67]

The timing of the New Hampshire adjournment strengthened the hand of opponents to ratification. Even Washington conceded that Anti-Federalists could now honestly tell voters that the Constitution was "not so generally approved of in other States as they had been taught to believe." Maryland, Virginia's closest neighbor, was meeting soon, too, and Washington was deeply interested in the prospects of the Constitution there. Maryland ratifying would, Washington hoped, "have a very considerable influence upon the decision in Virginia." But any advantage out of Maryland would have to wait. Maryland's convention opened in April, too late to influence the Virginia delegate elections.[68]

As men headed off to the March elections, Federalists' prospects seemed darker than ever. New Hampshire was forced to postpone. The influence of the Pennsylvania dissenters kept growing. Massachusetts had barely ratified at all. Rhode Island would certainly reject the Constitution. And Virginians were still so deeply divided that no one could predict the election outcome. Maybe time was not the best friend of the Federalists after all.

At the end of February 1788, the Constitution was, as one man aptly put it, "the only subject in conversation among all kinds of persons." As to the outcome of the elections and the ratification question, "God only knows."[69] Meanwhile, and to the great frustration of Virginia Federalists, the most formidable defender of the Constitution remained far from home.

James Madison stayed in New York throughout the winter of 1787–88, serving in the Confederation Congress and working feverishly for ratification in New York, including collaborating with John Jay and Alexander Hamilton on the Federalist Papers. Though designed to influence New Yorkers, Madison saw the potential of the essays beyond that state. Even before his first contribution (Federalist no. 10) appeared in print, Madison sent Washington copies of several essays. He recommended that Washington get them "into the hand of some of your confidential correspondents in Richmond who would have them reprinted there." Madison could not reach out to newspaper editors without risking his reputation. His authorship, he explained, precluded "interesting myself directly in the republication elsewhere." Discrete promotion was another matter.[70]

Federalists on the ground in Virginia wanted Madison to come home, not just send theoretical treatises. As winter dragged on, Madison's allies grew increasingly worried about his absence. "You must come in," Edmund Randolph wrote in January (now squarely in the Federalist camp). Opposition was growing in Orange County, Randolph warned, and Madison needed to ensure his election to the ratification convention. Edmund Pendleton agreed. He strongly urged Madison to return to Orange County as quickly as possible, "lest some designing men may endeavour to avail themselves of yr. Absence." Virginia's strongest Federalists saw Madison as "the only man in this State who can effectually combat the influence of Mason & Henry." Though he lacked Patrick Henry's speaking skill and political savvy, a determined James Madison was an awesome force. His friends repeatedly warned him that failing to secure a seat at the convention could deal the Constitution a mortal blow.[71]

These warnings weighed heavy on Madison. At the conclusion of the Philadelphia meeting, he had thought it inappropriate for the framers of the Constitution to participate in state conventions; it was unseemly to lobby for the plan they designed. The shifting political climate changed his mind. Many men who attended the Philadelphia Convention—including some strong critics of the Constitution—served as state delegates. And Madison could not shake his fear that Virginia might vote no "from a misconception of the plan." In late February 1788, Madison told Washington, "I have made up my determination on the subject" of ensuring ratification by serving in the Richmond convention.[72]

First, though, he had to get elected in Orange County, which was no guarantee. For gentlemen of Madison's rank, campaigning for office was a fairly new thing. The very language of public service in the eighteenth century was revealing: candidates "stood" for election, they did not yet "run." A man of Madison's experience and wealth and reputation should have been a shoo-in. But times were changing. County elections in particular had become festive competitions, with candidates compelled to court voters with whiskey and barbecue. In late March, Madison was chagrined to find himself in this unfamiliar, uncomfortable situation: "obliged to mount for the first time in my life, the rostrum before a large body of the people, and to launch into a harangue of some length."[73]

Election Day in Orange County fell on 24 March, and it was unseasonably cold and windy when Madison took to the political stage. He was uncomfortable in the cold and, even more, in asking for power from freeholders of modest means and little education. But he had to because in his long absence Orange County had become, as he put it, "tainted with antifederalism." Madison spoke to voters for almost two hours to win the seat that just a few months before he said he did not want and should not hold.[74]

The very day of Madison's election, Rhode Island held a statewide referendum on the Constitution. Citizens roundly rejected the federal plan.

Since court days ran throughout March, suspense built all month. As the returns filtered in, newspapers printed running totals for the two sides. Men gossiped in letters about vote tallies and representatives' views. Though they calculated slightly differently, everyone thought the results frighteningly close.

The influence of independent-minded farmers and shopkeepers especially worried the self-styled gentlemen Federalists. "I do not like the complexion of many of those elected," grumbled one Fredericksburg planter. "The involved & worthless antifederalists have taken so much pains to poison & prejudice the lower order of People, that I am greatly apprehensive a majority of those will be returned." Edward Carrington was similarly distressed that several counties on the south side of the James River chose "weak & bad men." They would, he predicted "be the tools of Mr. H[enry]." In a phrase repeated by several Federalists, Carrington complained that "the passions instead of Reason of the people" held sway.[75]

All month rumors and speculation ran back and forth: the Federalists were ahead by a handful of delegates, the Anti-Federalists were prevailing by a slim margin, the Federalists were falling behind, the Anti-Federalists were losing key counties. The men in the Kentucky counties were less well known in tidewater circles, and those county results came in slower. Many predictions were qualified because of the unknown results from the western elections.

The unpredictability of Virginia's elections spread across the continent and must have confused newspaper readers in other states. On 11 April, the *Maryland Journal* congratulated opponents of the Constitution for prevailing in the Virginia elections. Virginia, they happily reported, was poised to reject the federal plan. The next day the *Philadelphia Federal Gazette* insisted that the outcome in Virginia's elections favored Federalists, so "Virginia will shortly become one of the brightest pillars of the federal edifice." Four days after that, the *Philadelphia Independent Gazetteer* informed readers that the Anti-Federalists had carried the elections. Virginia would shortly "reject a measure" certain to "endanger those liberties for which America gloriously contended, during an eight year war."[76]

By late April, all the county election results were known and the names of the delegates circulating in newspapers. But rather than clarifying, this knowledge was frustrating. Even the best vote counters found the results too close to call. The regional split so long predicted was now evident, but it was more complicated than Virginians anticipated. The Kentucky delegates seemed more divided than Anti-Federalists had hoped. Other regions of the state elected men less committed to the Constitution than Federalists expected. And that was not the only divide. The convention, Edward Carrington regretfully informed Thomas Jefferson, "contains many obscure characters whom you would know nothing of." On the other hand, nearly all the key players in Virginia politics won seats. James Monroe also corresponded with Jefferson, and he reported that "few men of any distinction have fail'd taking their part." On one thing Carrington and Monroe could agree: "The principal partisans on both sides are elected."[77]

Seven months into their statewide, consuming debates, Virginians found themselves no closer to a final decision. The elections would not dictate the outcome of the June convention. "The real sense of the people of this State," James Madison saw, "cannot be easily ascertained." George Mason reached the same conclusion. Voters were sending to Richmond representatives "so equally divided upon the Subject, that no Man can, at present, form any certain Judgment of the Issue."[78]

George Washington knew one thing for certain: "The plot thickens fast."[79]

Summer 1788, Debating in Richmond

> Our affairs in the Convention are suspended by a hair: I really cannot tell you on
> which side the scale will turn: the difference I am satisfied . . . will be exceedingly
> small indeed.
>
> *William Grayson, 9 June 1788*

AS IT TURNED OUT, the March elections produced no clear outcome except to confirm that Virginians were deadlocked on the question of
ratification. In the wake of the elections, divisions actually worsened. In their
frustration and fear, Virginians sometimes turned to vicious, inflammatory
language. In late May, as delegates from across the state readied for the Virginia Ratification Convention, a Norfolk newspaper favoring the Federalists
insisted that failing to ratify would spark a civil war. The blood would be on
representatives' hands: grieving mothers would rightly blame them for "the
loss of their slaughtered husbands, the rapes of their daughters, and the man-
gled bodies of their sons." At the same time, Federalist writers condemned
Anti-Federalists for "dealing out their vile Declamations against the Constitution . . . That their Sons will be pressed into the Army: that their Daughters

will be ravished—and that every Species of personal Insult and Abuse will be offered them at Pleasure, without the possibility of Redress." On the eve of the Richmond convention, advocates on both sides might have paused to ask themselves the rhetorical question they only posed to their opponents: "What will not wicked and unprincipled Men do and say to effect their infernal Purposes?"[1]

In 1788 Richmond was a small town of some two thousand residents. It had been the capital of Virginia for only eight years—and only as a strategic fallback when British forces imperiled the historic hub of the state, Williamsburg. In anticipation of witnessing history at the June convention, people "in greater numbers than had ever been know before" poured into town "from every quarter." The unprecedented onslaught of travelers overwhelmed tavern keepers. To accommodate all the delegates and spectators, stagecoach operators changed their schedules, and extra coaches ran from Williamsburg and Fredericksburg. May brought an unseasonable drought to the Old Dominion. The rivers were low and creek beds nearly dry, but what troubled farmers made travel on horseback easier than usual. Carriages rattled along the dusty roads into town, joined by "cavalcades of horsemen." Richmonders could track the riders coming in by the clouds of dust their horses kicked up.[2]

Not unlike the innkeepers, Governor Edmund Randolph struggled to find a space adequate to the size of the convention: 170 men were elected to participate and hundreds came to watch. The now-iconic Virginia State Capitol was still under construction that summer. It would have been an inspired place for the convention: Thomas Jefferson designed the glorious building, and Patrick Henry oversaw the laying of the cornerstone. But it was not yet complete.

The representatives instead convened on Monday morning, 2 June, in the chamber of the House of Delegates. Immediately they saw that it could not hold the crowds. So the delegates agreed to move the next morning to the largest building in Richmond: the New Academy. Sitting on Shockoe Hill, it was, Frederick County delegate Alexander White recalled, "a Spacious and Airy Building sufficiently large to accommodate all the Members—and all those who desire to be Spectators." The grand space—regrettably, long since destroyed—was actually used as a theater. A more fitting setting they could not have found.[3]

On that first day, delegates tended to necessary business: appointing a

Edmund Pendleton. Portrait by Thomas Sully. Virginia Historical Society

chaplain and secretary and naming Edmund Pendleton president of the convention. Pendleton was in his late sixties, but he seemed older. A fall from a horse in 1777 left him with a dislocated hip. He never fully recovered and needed crutches the rest of his life. But as his body grew weak, his mind remained strong. A member of the first and second Continental Congresses, Pendleton was president of the Virginia Convention in 1776, the body that adopted the first state constitution and called on Congress to declare independence. His fellow revolutionaries elected him first speaker of the newly created Virginia House of Delegates that year. Widely admired for his keen legal mind and his unfailing defense of the rule of law, Pendleton served in the late 1770s as chief justice of the Chancery Court and the Appeals Court—in essence the head of Virginia's judiciary. He had no children of his own, but many admiring protégés, including several men elected to the Virginia Rati-

D E B A T E S

AND OTHER

P R O C E E D I N G S

O F T H E

C O N V E N T I O N

O F

V I R G I N I A,.

Convened at *Richmond*, on *Monday* the 2d day of
June, 1788, for the purpofe of deliberating on the
Conftitution recommended by the **Grand Federal**
Convention.

TO WHICH IS PREFIXED,

T H E

'EDERAL CONSTITUTION.

•

● ⬦

P E T E R S B U R G:

PRINTED BY

HUNTER AND PRENTIS.

M,DCC,LXXXVIII.

Frontispiece of David Robertson's notes on the Virginia Ratification Convention, published 1788. Virginians unable to get to Richmond were eager to learn about the convention proceedings, and printers sped to get transcripts to curious readers.

fication Convention. Even his political rivals respected Pendleton's rock-solid integrity and trusted that his judgment was always reasoned and fair-minded.

Convention delegates also appointed a committee to consider disputed elections. Ordinarily, this would have been a dry formality. But since everyone present anticipated the vote on ratification would be exceedingly close, they also knew that outcomes of contested elections might decide the final tally. Procedural matters, then, took on great political weight. The elections committee worked throughout the whole convention trying to sort out contested returns and thus who could actually vote when the question was called.[4]

After a brief scrap, delegates agreed to permit David Robertson, a native of Scotland working as an attorney in Petersburg, to take notes, which would be published as the proceedings unfolded. This marked the first time in Virginia history when legislative debates were recorded. Robertson's transcription had its flaws. He sometimes found himself searching for a seat far from the speakers and distracted by excited spectators. Some men spoke so quietly that he could not hear them; others bored him, and he quit taking notes. A few delegates complained that Robertson was biased, but James Madison insisted his "general intelligence & intentional fidelity" was above reproach. His notes certainly served the intended purpose: bringing the debates in Richmond into the homes of anxious Virginians eager to know about the proceedings but unable to get to the New Academy.[5]

Edmund Pendleton gave the only address on the first day of the convention, reminding the delegates that they had been entrusted by "a Great People, the Citizens of Virginia" to decide a momentous question. "The trust is *Sacred & Important*," he said, and required representatives to "calmly reason With each other, as Friends," to treat one another with "*Candor, temper, &* mutual *Forbearance*."[6] No one disagreed. But everyone also knew that the debates would be adversarial. This was not Philadelphia, after all. Men arrived in Philadelphia unsure of what they wanted and intending to reason together. The purpose in Richmond was not to reach consensus on a complex plan but rather to decide a single question: Should Virginia support the Constitution? Great numbers of delegates arrived already firmly committed to an answer.

After Pendleton concluded and on George Mason's motion, the delegates voted to adjourn and meet the next morning at eleven o'clock on Shockoe Hill, to begin their work in earnest.

As they looked around the room that June day, delegates saw old friends and new rivals, men who had stood shoulder to shoulder in the bleakest days of the Revolutionary War and ripped one another to shreds in newspapers over the past eight months. The convention brought together a who's who of Virginians; nearly every major political player in the state served as a delegate. Dozens of talented and experienced men gathered, some with their names already being etched in marble for their contributions to the Revolution. Because of the prominence of Virginia leaders, their convention "presented as proud a galaxy of genius, worth, and public service as had ever shone in the councils of a single State." Or, as a leading historian of the Revolution often remarked, "From time to time, reality surpasses any drama we could reasonably believe. It did so in the Old Dominion in 1788."[7]

James Madison had initially thought it inappropriate to participate in Richmond because of his role in the Philadelphia Convention, but he got over his objections, as did most of the rest of Virginia's delegation to the 1787 gathering. In fact, virtually all of the politically seasoned scions of Virginia's first families took a seat. There was only a handful of conspicuous absences—nearly all by their own choice. Most prominently, George Washington declined to participate because he knew he was the likely first president should the Constitution pass. Thomas Jefferson was in Paris. James McClurg, a delegate to the Philadelphia Convention, and Richard Henry Lee, a leader in the Confederation Congress, both declined to participate in the state convention for reasons they never explained. Lieutenant Governor Beverley Randolph was the only leading Virginian who wanted to serve but failed to get elected.

Governor Edmund Randolph, a quintessential politician with grand ambitions, represented Henrico County. George Wythe, who had trained many of Virginia's greatest legal minds during his tenure at William & Mary, served alongside several of his students, including James Monroe and John Marshall. Although almost as old as Edmund Pendleton, Wythe "moved with a brisk and graceful step" and his "erect stature presented a pleasing image of a fresh and healthy old man." He was bald on the top of his head but wore a long gray ponytail in the back.[8] Men admired his intellect and forthrightness. Wythe's former students Marshall and Monroe had known one another since they were boyhood schoolmates; both served with distinction in the Revolutionary War under General Washington. Now they took opposing sides. Marshall stood with James Madison in championing the achievements they believed the Constitution would promote in the fledgling American Republic. Monroe shared the misgivings of George Mason and feared that Americans were ceding their liberty to a distant, unaccountable government.

Though firm in his views, George Mason left Gunston Hall reluctantly, as he always did. Just before he headed out, Mason sat down to write his old friend Thomas Jefferson, currently serving as US ambassador to France. Mason's son, John, was sailing to Europe to join a trading business in Bordeaux, and Mason wanted Jefferson to welcome the young man when he stopped over in Paris. "Any good Offices which you may do the said House, or any Advice, which you may be pleased to give my Son," Mason wrote, "I shall esteem as the highest Mark of your Friendship." Almost as an afterthought, Mason discussed the upcoming convention. It was, he told Jefferson, "tedious to enumerate all the Objections" he had to the federal design. Jefferson, Mason knew, shared his fierce defense of liberty and could see for himself the flaws. Mason did mention three paramount concerns: the dangers of the new standing army, the power Congress held to determine state elections, and the corruption nearly guaranteed to afflict high-ranking federal officials. All three reflected Mason's antagonism to centralized authority: too much power concentrated in too few hands was too dangerous to abide.[9]

The letter captured Mason's priorities: family first, then politics. Even as Mason prepared to fulfill his duty by attending the Richmond convention, he worried about his son's financial prospects. Throughout Mason's life, that desire to advance his children kept him close to home, physically and emotionally. Philadelphia was his only trip outside the state. In 1787–88, his strong allegiance to the Old Dominion made him particularly skittish about ceding Virginia's sovereignty to what he saw as a powerful, consolidated government.

These famous men gathered alongside up-and-coming, rough-around-the-edges delegates from backcountry counties who, imbibing the spirit of the revolutionary age, thought themselves every other citizen's equal. They took their duty to reason through the proposed government just as seriously as the more politically experienced self-styled gentlemen in the convention.

For all the talent assembled, the spotlight shone on three men: James Madison, who led with intellectual precision and indefatigable resolve the Federalist delegates; Patrick Henry, who even his most disparaging enemies had to concede was unmatched in his oratorical and political skills; and George Mason, the architect of Virginia's founding documents and perhaps the only man in the state with a mind to rival Madison's. Madison's intellectual gifts notwithstanding, he was a most unlikely leader: small, sickly, and soft-spoken. He missed the 9 June session because of a "bilious attack." He managed to return the next day despite feeling, he said, "extremely feeble." For their part, Henry and Mason formed a wobbly partnership ill-equipped to marshal the disparate and unpredictable Anti-Federalist delegates.[10]

Though cloistered in the theater on Shockoe Hill, delegates never forgot about events and men outside those walls. They continued to monitor other states, especially the South Carolinians, who convened in early May. Federalists had cause for optimism that the elite-dominated convention in Charleston would ratify by a resounding majority, while Anti-Federalists held out hope that South Carolina would follow New Hampshire and adjourn until after Virginians had their say. On the second day of the convention, Federalists got the news they'd hoped for: South Carolina voted yes. Anti-Federalists admitted they felt "alarmed" but also insisted "we do not despond" at eight states having ratified.[11]

George Washington and Thomas Jefferson cast shadows from afar. Jefferson, though four thousand miles away from Richmond, was still influential in the debates. For months in advance of the convention, men corresponded with him, seeking his opinion about the Constitution and trying to convince him of their point of view. Once the convention started, partisans on both sides invoked Jefferson's name to garner support.[12] In fact, Jefferson wrote different things to different men, generally taking a middle path on the Constitution, favoring ratification *and* significant revisions. George Washington's views, conversely, were unambiguous and well known, which gave an advantage to Federalists. Throughout the convention Washington remained in steady contact with James Madison as well as his nephew Bushrod Washington, who represented Westmoreland County. He also coordinated letter-writing networks across the country, making sure his allies knew about events in other states, especially when the news helped the Federalist cause.

Throughout the Richmond convention, George Washington remained vexed by the inability of Federalists to turn popular opinion and delegate votes their way. He was certain the Federalists were right and believed "the good sense of this Country will prevail against the local views of designing characters and the arrogant opinions" of critics. Still, it frustrated him that his side failed to "produce a cessation of opposition." The problem, he concluded, lay not with the federal design but with men like George Mason and Patrick Henry, who, he complained, used "every species of address & artifice . . . to create Jealousies & excite alarms," especially among nonelites. James Breckinridge reached the same conclusion. He said Patrick Henry's "eloquence and oratory" made him "better adapted to carry his point & lead the ignorant people astray than any other person upon earth." Meanwhile, Breckinridge regretted, James Madison's "plain, ingenious, & elegant reasoning" seemed "entirely thrown away and lost among such men."[13]

Many delegates kept up their correspondence with neighbors and friends

during the month of June, so public opinion continued to influence representatives' views and vice versa. Not surprisingly, James Madison numbered
among the most prolific letter-writers. He penned at least twenty-eight letters during the convention, sending eight to Alexander Hamilton and a half-
dozen to George Washington. After guiding the conversation each day and coordinating speeches for the next session, he rushed back to his boardinghouse
to write to his close allies throughout the country. Delegates received letters,
too, so they were able to gauge and gather opinion across the states. Even as
they put their extensive networks to steady use during the convention, Federalists complained about "Malcontents" from Pennsylvania and New York
feeding information to Virginia Anti-Federalists.[14]

Across the country that June Americans fixated on Virginia. As one New
Yorker put it, "All Eyes here are looking with Hope or fear towards Virga." In
Richmond, there was "nothing but debate and altercation in all companies"
once the convention started. And throughout Virginia the Constitution absorbed "the whole attention of all ranks and degrees of people."[15]

Knowing all of this made delegates think a lot about their place in history
and how future generations of Americans would judge their conduct. In the
1770s, many Americans believed that the break from England and creation of
the American Republic marked a turning point in human history. "The cause
of America," Thomas Paine declared, "is in a great measure the cause of all
mankind." Now, the radical, history-making propositions of the Declaration
of Independence—that men were naturally equal and free, that just governments reflected the will of citizens, that people could govern themselves—
were being put to the test by the Virginians meeting in Richmond. On that
point, men otherwise disputing every nuance of the Constitution could agree.
"Let no future historian," Edmund Randolph warned the delegates, "inform
posterity that they wanted wisdom and virtue" when it came time to choose
a government.[16]

Everyone was, then, understandably nervous once the debates com-
menced. "We are," Patrick Henry warned, "wandering on the great ocean of
human affairs. I see no landmark to guide us. We are running we know not
whither."[17]

As he took to the stage in that Richmond theater, each actor knew his part
and used the drama of language to captivate the audience. Leaders on both
sides had rehearsed their lines for months, and now they tried to stage the

convention to their advantage. They had an overflowing audience, too: "Every seat was filled, while hundreds of respectable persons remained standing in the passages and at the doors."[18]

George Mason made the first move on 3 June. His raven hair had long since turned white, but he'd lost none of his ferocity to age. With his "black eyes fairly flashing forth the flame that burned in his bosom," Mason called on delegates to work "clause by clause" through every part of the Constitution so that they could "fully and freely investigate this important subject."[19] Mason had planned this tactic well in advance of the convention with Richard Henry Lee. Lee understood the Anti-Federalists needed an approach to counter the better-organized, more-united Federalists. Immersed in a national network of Anti-Federalists, Lee knew that in some states, including Pennsylvania, Federalists had shaped the outcome of the vote by setting the parameters of debate. "I believe," he warned Mason, "you will find entrapping questions proposed at first as a ground-work of proceeding, which will hamper, confine, and narrow all attempts to proper investigation." Lee urged Mason to push for "a thorough, particular, and careful examination . . . into all its parts." Their plan centered on keeping Federalists from calling for piecemeal votes on particular sections of the Constitution. That way, Anti-Federalists thought they could control the momentum of the conversation. Close scrutiny of every part of the plan culminating in a single vote allowed for the maximum number of objections to the Constitution. And, going clause by clause would help Mason see the particular agendas of undecided delegates and chart the best strategy to gain their votes.[20]

To Mason's surprise, Federalists unanimously agreed. They too saw a tactical advantage to the approach Mason proposed. James Madison was confident of his ability to defend the specific parts of the Constitution: staying on track fit his strengths perfectly. So, as they had months before when setting the timing of the convention, partisans on each side believed they won a strategic advantage by agreeing to work systematically though the Constitution. With that crucial point settled, the delegates decided to adjourn for the day and get a fresh start on the proposed government the next morning.

But before the first sentence could be read on 4 June, Patrick Henry decided to reframe the debate by challenging the legitimacy of the whole enterprise. By the summer of 1788, Henry was fifty-three, and the trials of his life made him show his age. His shoulders were slightly stooped and he needed glasses. When he got exercised, which was often, he tugged on the wig that covered his long-bald head. But his voice had lost none of its magisterial force. As one observer marveled, Henry displayed "an astonishing resource of Genius and abilities."[21]

Before they did anything else, Henry moved that the delegates enter into their official record the document calling the Philadelphia Convention. Here he picked up on a point that Richard Henry Lee had made in the Confederation Congress ten months before and that Anti-Federalists had hammered all fall and winter. The men in Philadelphia violated their sole charge and the only lawful purpose of that gathering: to revise the Articles of Confederation. Today, Americans call that meeting the "Constitutional Convention," but the term is historically flawed. The government of the United States, the Confederation Congress, called the Philadelphia Convention for a specific, clearly articulated reason: "for the sole and express purpose of revising the Articles of Confederation." Patrick Henry intended to underscore from the outset that the delegates in Philadelphia had grossly overstepped that charge.[22]

Edmund Pendleton immediately dropped any pretense of impartiality and countered with a dismissal that could be read as a concession: "We are not to consider whether the Federal Convention exceeded their powers." After all, insisted Pendleton, the Confederation Congress had sent the Constitution to the states, and the voters in Virginia had "sent us hither to determine whether this Government be a proper one or not." All of that, he argued, rendered moot any questions about the ethics of the Philadelphia delegates' conduct.[23]

This was the first of many tussles between Henry and Pendleton. The two men never got along very well, though they shared a common background. Neither man was born to a rich family; each rose through the ranks of Virginia society through talent and hard work, as self-made eighteenth-century men. But Henry retained more of the trappings of his humble beginnings; he seldom wore fancy clothes and liked hunting and making music with his neighbors in rural Virginia. Pendleton loved elegance, in his clothes, language, carriage, and friends. He was more intellectual than Henry and in 1787–88 adopted a more national outlook. For his part, Henry nursed a long-held grudge against Pendleton. As a young man just starting his legal career, he sought Pendleton's aid, but Pendleton rebuffed him. Though they had this personal history, their conflict in Richmond centered on principle. Each man believed that his opinion about the Constitution was the only virtuous one and essential for the survival of republican government in Virginia.[24]

Despite the counter from Pendleton, Henry had made his point: to challenge the validity of the entire federal plan by revealing its extralegal origins. With his objection written into the record, Henry withdrew his motion.

As he returned to his seat, Henry surely felt in command of the debates. But his chief opponent, James Madison, saw in the morning's proceedings an opening for Federalists. "Henry & Mason," Madison wrote Washington that evening, "made a lame figure & appeared to take different & awkward ground." Henry's motion contradicted Mason's strategy, and the Federalists, Madison reported, "are a good deal elated by the existing prospect."[25]

The clerk finally read the preamble to the Constitution and the beginning two sections of Article I. George Nicholas spoke first. From outside appearances, Nicholas seemed a poor counter to the ever-captivating Patrick Henry. Nicholas was short and pudgy, and though only thirty-five, completely bald. Whereas Henry's eyes sparkled and mesmerized, Nicholas's hid under a low brow. While Henry's voice soared, Nicholas's was flat. Nicholas, though, had qualities essential to succeed in late eighteenth-century politics: he knew everything about every part of Virginia's recent legislative history and could instantly muster his command of law and philosophy to make finely honed arguments. Nicholas descended from one of Virginia's most prestigious families: a grandson of Robert "King" Carter, he enjoyed all the benefits of a first-rate education and tremendous wealth. He and his brothers were extraordinarily influential in Virginia. One of the Nicholas brothers became a prominent judge, another a congressman, and a third a governor. Men found George Nicholas "utterly fearless." Without any advantages of style, the substance of his ideas held his audience in rapt attention.[26]

In advance of the convention, Nicholas clearly studied Anti-Federalist writings and knew that one widespread criticism centered on the power granted Congress to alter the time and place of elections. As Federalists would do repeatedly in the coming weeks, he countered the critics even before they spoke. Nicholas insisted that "the possible abuse here complained of, never can happen as long as the people of the United States are virtuous." Nicholas then turned to another highly controversial matter: the number of representatives. For nearly a year Anti-Federalists had insisted that one man could not possibly represent thirty thousand under the federal design; the government was too distant and centralized. Critics also pointed out that the number was a minimum, and they speculated that it might grow exponentially. Nothing, they repeatedly warned, would keep Congress from settling on ten or even twenty times that ratio. That was representation in word only, they complained, and a recipe for corruption. Nicholas preemptively dismissed this speculation, too, and, in a gross miscalculation, said "I conceive there will be always one for every thirty thousand." (According to the 2010 census, the average population size of a congressional district is 710,767. Virginia, with just over 8 million residents and 11 members of the House of Representatives, is slightly above the national average.)[27]

George Nicholas, continuing to anticipate his opponents' objections, then turned to defending the two-year terms and absence of term limits for members of the House of Representatives. Annual elections and strict term limits were mandated in Virginia and the Confederation Congress, so the exclusion of those regulations from the Constitution troubled Virginians. Nicholas insisted the structural innovations would not cause corruption and assured the delegates that representatives "will become watchful guardians of the interest of the people." Nicholas worked meticulously through the first two sections of Article I. He showed at every turn a remarkable command of Anti-Federalist ideas and always stayed on point. Underlying his speech was confidence in the character of American citizens and the structure of the proposed government. Together, he believed, virtuous citizens operating within the balanced federal design rendered Anti-Federalists' doubts baseless.[28]

Patrick Henry saw things differently, and in rebutting Nicholas took a different tack. He pronounced himself "the servant of the people of this Commonwealth" and a guardian of "their rights, liberty, and happiness."[29]

As they tried to persuade the handful of wavering delegates who would ultimately decide the outcome of the convention, each man played to his strength. Nicholas laid out detailed rebuttals to very specific Anti-Federalist criticisms of the Constitution, whereas Henry used soaring rhetoric to challenge the heart of the proposed government. He started his condemnation with the first three words. "What right had they to say, *We, the People*," Henry demanded. "States are the characteristics, and the soul of a confederation." The framers, Henry believed, had destroyed the sovereign states and created "one great consolidated National Government." Undeterred by Edmund Pendleton's challenge to his first motion about the charge to the Philadelphia delegates, Henry doubled back. Not only was the Constitution wrong from its opening phrase; it was fruit from a poisonous tree. The Philadelphia delegates had no right to propose this radically different government: "That they exceeded their power is perfectly clear." Henry included George Washington among the men who needed to account for their actions. "On this great occasion," he insisted, "I would demand the cause of their conduct."[30]

When Patrick Henry yielded the floor, Edmund Randolph rose. Characteristically, he vacillated. He first explained that he had refused to sign the Constitution in Philadelphia because he thought the demand for an up-or-down vote "too hard an alternative to the citizens of America."[31] Without ever saying it, Randolph rejected Henry's criticism of the Philadelphia Convention by signaling that the time for that question had long since passed. Whatever the history, the federal plan was now before Virginia. It was not perfect, he allowed, and so delegates needed to decide *when* and *how* to make necessary changes. As to precisely what changes he favored, Randolph evaded. He would explain his substantive objections to the Constitution, he said, in due course.

To the question of whether to pursue previous (conditional) or subsequent (requested) amendments, Randolph ultimately depicted Virginians as victims of timing. Scheduling their convention so late and after so many other states had ratified made amendments before ratification impossible, he concluded, "without inevitable ruin to the Union." Forced into a corner, Randolph claimed he now saw only two choices: ratify unconditionally or destroy the republic.[32]

Though he was the last person who wanted to hand Patrick Henry any more power, Edmund Randolph could not stop himself from taking Henry's bait. Directly responding to the condemnation of the opening words of the preamble, Randolph answered, "Why not? The Government is for the people." Perhaps it was a good answer, but offering it validated Henry's strategy.[33]

George Mason, who'd taken to calling Edmund Randolph "young Arnold"— a damning link to Benedict Arnold, the greatest traitor of the Revolution— spoke next. Mason had little of Randolph's political savvy and none of his concern about other men's opinions. Whereas Randolph courted popularity, Mason was true to himself alone, come what may. After leaving Philadelphia he proudly owned his minority status and accepted the loss of his decades-long friendship with George Washington. "I would not," he told his son, "forfeit the approbation of my own mind for the approbation of any man, or all the men upon earth."[34]

Mason remained razor focused on the substantive issues under consideration. The language in Article I made clear, he began, that "it is a National

Government, and no longer a confederation." Delegates should never lose sight of that fact, he argued, or what it meant for Virginia. Mason's speech on 4 June offered a brilliant response to George Nicholas. He showcased an astute understanding of the Constitution and its ideological and political implications. His critique was focused, precise, and compelling.[35]

Mason moved adeptly from the practical to the philosophical, criticizing the threat of concurrent tax powers before reminding delegates that history showed that a government with authority over so vast a territory inevitably destroyed citizens' liberty. Mocking George Nicholas's "eulogium in favor of this system" and "the encomiums he has been pleased to bestow upon it," Mason insisted that sixty-five representatives "cannot possibly know the situation and circumstances of all the inhabitants of this immense continent." "It would," he predicted, "be impossible to have a full and adequate representation in the General Government; it would be too expensive and too unwieldy."[36]

Mason held traditional, localistic ideas about representation. Representatives, Mason maintained, "ought to mix with the people, think as they think, feel as they feel, ought to be perfectly amenable to them, and thoroughly acquainted with their interest and condition." That could not happen under the federal design. Mason also mocked the assertion that the 1:30,000 model would be honored over time. What, he cautioned, could the people do if Congress decided one man could represent 200,000? "The worthy Gentleman" (meaning George Nicholas) "tells us, we have no reason to fear; but," Mason declared, "I always fear for the rights of the people." On that score, he and Patrick Henry were in lockstep.[37]

The Federalists' optimism struck Mason as naïve. Nicholas, he reminded the audience, believed that only the most virtuous men on the continent would be elected to Congress. But Mason was a realist: "This, like all other assemblies, will be composed of some bad and some good men; and considering the natural lust of power so inherent in man, I fear the thirst of power will prevail to oppress the people."[38]

By the time Mason finished and Edmund Pendleton recognized James Madison, the day had slipped away. As Madison listened to the speakers he must have felt a sense of déjà vu: he heard again many of the same arguments the Philadelphia delegates engaged in the summer before. There was little time left that day for him to reply, though. As he would often do, Madison reminded the delegates to stay on task and "reconcile our proceedings to the resolution we have taken." As the time was late, the convention adjourned until eleven o'clock the next morning.[39]

When the delegates reconvened on 5 June, Patrick Henry continued to set the parameters of the debates. He knew the circumstances favored him: he needed only to raise more criticisms than the Federalists could successfully counter. So he led a hard-hitting, relentless assault on the federal plan. In doing so, he proved that old axiom, "the tallest nail gets the hammer." Edmund Pendleton opened by circling back to Henry's comments the day before. He derided Henry's claim that "the public mind was at ease" before the Philadelphia Convention. Pendleton ran through the list of troubles that everyone in the room knew faced the young republic: "Our General Government was totally inadequate to the purpose of its institution; our commerce decayed; our finances deranged; public and private credit destroyed." If Americans felt sanguine in 1787, Pendleton lectured, it surely could not be attributed to "being in a happy and easy situation." Instead, "it must have been an inactive unaccountable stupor."[40]

Distracted from the substantive matter of defending Article I of the Constitution, Pendleton essentially tailored his speech to rebut Henry. He also revealed his principal concern: economics. Again and again, Pendleton and other Federalists pointed out the financial decay under the Articles, the international implications of failing to pay foreign creditors, and the economic advantages of the Constitution. Sometimes it seemed as if the two sides debated across, not against one another, with the Anti-Federalists defending citizens' rights and the Federalist preoccupied with financial turmoil.

Seeing the same Anti-Federalist division Madison intuited in the opening speeches, Pendleton then pivoted from refuting Patrick Henry to courting George Mason. He agreed with Mason's reasoning about the scope of government. But he disagreed that the Constitution created a consolidated government. The Federal government, he claimed, "does not intermeddle with the local particular affairs of the States."[41]

Pendleton also took up Mason's anxieties over representation. The Constitution said only that the number of representatives should not exceed one for every thirty thousand citizens. But Anti-Federalists needlessly worried that the number might change. Pendleton dismissed this fear: "If Virginia sends in that proportion, I ask, where is the power in Congress to reject them?" Surely states might send too many representatives, so the Constitution needed to protect against that. But, Pendleton, asked, "Can it be doubted, that they will send the number they are intitled to?"[42]

Henry "Light-Horse Harry" Lee III followed Pendleton. Lee descended from one of Virginia's leading families and was keenly aware of the need to carry on that legacy. A Princeton graduate and Revolutionary War hero, Lee was nearly six feet tall and classically handsome. He was only thirty-two that summer, with three young children at home with their mother, his second cousin, Matilda Lee. (Virginians had a narrow incest taboo in the eighteenth century; cousin marriages were quite common in elite families.) Lee's most famous son would not be born for another twenty years. That boy, Robert, would eventually lead the effort to destroy the republic his father helped build. But in 1788 that lay in the distant future.[43]

Henry Lee, at odds with his kinsman Richard Henry Lee, pilloried Patrick Henry. "Instead of proceeding to investigate the merits of the new plan of Government," he charged, Patrick Henry "informed us of horrors which he felt, of apprehensions in his mind, which make him tremblingly fearful of the fate of the Commonwealth." Rather than reasoned, as men should be, Henry appeared emotional—or, Lee implied, feminine. "I trust," he chided, "he is come to judge and not to alarm." Lee also upbraided Patrick Henry for questioning the character of the framers of the Constitution, strategically casting George Washington as emblematic of the men whose conduct Henry questioned.[44]

Lee then played one of the Federalists' strongest cards: he depicted the Articles of Confederation—which everyone knew had fundamental flaws—as the only alternative to ratification. Lee blasted the "imbecility of the confederation" and derided it as a "defective system which never can make us happy at home, nor respectable abroad."[45] He seized an advantage offered by a central Anti-Federalist weakness: the lack of a consensus plan. If ratification failed, the confederation government would be all that remained to bind the states together. Few saw that as a viable, or even plausible, way forward.

By now Patrick Henry, who preferred to sidestep this specter hanging over the convention, had heard enough from Henry Lee. He rose to defend the Anti-Federalist cause and himself, starting with Lee's aspersions on his manhood. If anyone was unmanly, Patrick Henry implied, it was Edmund Randolph, who seemed willing to passively let other states cast Virginia's vote on the most important question ever posed to the United States. Virginians must, Henry proclaimed, exercise "that manly fortitude that ought to characterize republicans." So what if eight states ratified? "I declare that if twelve States and an half had adopted it, I would with manly firmness, and in spite of an erring world, reject it."[46]

Then Patrick Henry zeroed in on Henry Lee's zeal to be "respectable abroad." "You are not to inquire how your trade may be increased, nor how you are to become a great and powerful people," Henry lectured, "but how your liberties can be secured."[47]

As to Lee's blanket condemnation of the Articles of Confederation, Henry reminded the delegates that the confederation government "carried us through a long and dangerous war," and secured victory over the most powerful empire in the world. Now, Patrick Henry pointed out, men who had prevailed in that great contest were being asked to sign away everything they fought for. Whatever the flaws of the Articles, surely citizens should pause before embracing the Constitution. "Here," he warned them, "is a revolution as radical as that which separated us from Great Britain."[48]

Henry then charged the Constitution with "a fatal ambiguity" of language that put citizens' rights in grave jeopardy. A master at self-effacing, moving rhetoric, Patrick Henry was not short on genius that June. "I am not well versed in history," he said, "but I will submit to your recollection, whether liberty has been destroyed most often by the licentiousness of the people, or by the tyranny of rulers?"[49]

Jumping ahead to Section 8 to highlight one of the most controversial innovations in the Constitution, Henry pointed out that in exchange for their dearly bought liberties, citizens would fund a national standing army. He struck a nerve with his outrage over the creation of an army under the command of a powerful chief executive. This, he proclaimed, was an "extremely ridiculous" and dangerous reversal of republican values. "This acquisition will trample on your fallen liberty," he warned.[50]

As he spoke, Patrick Henry moved brilliantly from indignant to inspiring to fearful to anguished, and he spoke confidently about nuanced details of the federal plan as well as the broad sweep of political philosophy and history. He carried many men with him during his long address that day. "Whither," he pined, "is the spirit of America gone? Whither is the genius of America fled?"[51]

Henry's dedication was unshakable all month long. One day as he spoke one of his sons suddenly appeared in the chamber. Henry's wife was pregnant, so he knew the news from home was important. Without missing a beat, he motioned a friend to take the young man outside. The friend shortly brought back the news that Mrs. Henry "had been safely delivered of a son, and that mother and child were doing fine."[52]

Patrick Henry's problem was that he never knew when to stop. He spoke nearly the whole day on 5 June—six hours by one man's calculation. He railed on, as minutes turned to hours, with specific criticisms giving way to generalities. Sometimes he buried his best points in streams of repetitive rhetoric.

Some of Patrick Henry's most vivid language—and the most often quoted over time—was likely lost on listeners as the words spilled out of him, pell-mell. Just after he proclaimed the government under the Constitution "incompatible with the genius of republicanism" and before he insisted "This Government is not a Virginian but an American Government," Henry acknowledged, "I fear I tire the patience of the Committee." But he could not, would not, stop: "I beg to be indulged with a few more observations," he said at one point and then proceeded to talk as long again as he already had. Veering off track of the day's subject, which was the structure of Congress, he condemned the office of the president, absence of a bill of rights, and creation of a standing army. He questioned the size of the planned federal city, the reach of the judiciary, and the legitimacy of ratification in the Pennsylvania state convention. He asserted, with no specific elaboration, that "Your President may easily become King."[53]

David Robertson grew weary of transcribing and instead made comments that captured the problem of talking too much: "Here Mr. Henry strongly and pathetically expatiated on the probability of the President's enslaving America, and the horrid consequences that must result."[54]

Delegates must have been astounded when, near the close of the day he had monopolized, Patrick Henry insisted, "yet I have not said the one hundred thousandth part of what I have on my mind." An exasperated Edmund Randolph said what many others must have thought: "If we go on in this irregular manner, contrary to our resolution, instead of three or six weeks, it will take us six months to decide the question."[55]

When the convention finally adjourned that afternoon, Federalists left the New Academy frustrated, but many Anti-Federalists felt inspired. James Madison wryly acknowledged that in giving his critics no time to reply to his marathon speech, Patrick Henry emboldened his allies. The opponents to ratification seemed "much revived" by his operatic performance.[56]

Not to be outdone by Patrick Henry, Governor Edmund Randolph led off the debates on 6 June, spending a lot of time saying nothing. He proclaimed his patriotism and recounted his long years of service, which had been, he said, "the unwearied study of my life." Surely no one in the hall believed him when he declared "ambition and popularity are no objects to me." In fact, Randolph's life had been a study in the quest for fame.[57]

Eventually—and to no one's surprise—Randolph announced his intention to vote for ratification. Trying to counter Patrick Henry's rambling but affecting performance the day before, he seized on a powerful warning: "Our rejection must dissolve the Union; and that dissolution will destroy our political happiness."[58]

Randolph knew he could never rival Henry's oratorical talents, but he was determined to undermine the substance of his arguments. Complaining that Henry had raised "arguments out of order" and "promiscuously debated" them, Randolph did the same, inadvertently validating Henry's efforts to control the debates. Randolph rejected Henry's predictions about the federal courts and congressional powers. He also took Henry to task for challenging the patriotism of men who disagreed with him about the Constitution: "Is it not possible that men may differ in sentiments, and still be honest?" Suspicion, he conceded, had its place in republican government. But, he reasoned, "it ought not to be extended to a degree which is degrading and humiliating to human nature."[59]

Governor Randolph revealed the perspective of many Federalists by enumerating the fiscal and foreign dangers Americans faced if they rejected the Constitution. "Cast your eyes to your seaports," he urged, "see how commerce languishes."[60] Profits, the Anti-Federalists repeatedly insisted, should not be the paramount concern of true patriots. Nor should liberty-loving Americans obsess over power in the international arena. But Randolph understood how to read a room, and he intuited that his emphasis on national security and fiscal strength could influence swing voters. He and others hammered the deepening losses to foreign trade and heightened risks of invasion that Americans should expect if they failed to ratify. The delegates knew from the Revolution how quickly fiscal turmoil and military occupation could destabilize politics and imperil liberty.

Randolph refuted George Mason, too, by willfully mischaracterizing his objections to the Constitution. Randolph acted as if Mason lobbied for an independent Virginia and played on the apprehension of some delegates by pointing out the state's precarious position: open to invasion from sea and bordered by three states, two of which had ratified. Those neighboring states would, Randolph ominously predicted, "if disunited from us, be our bitterest enemies." Virginians could then expect their own state to splinter, with the Northern Neck likely seceding to join Maryland. Courting the Kentucky delegates, Randolph then called on men to "cast your eyes to the Western Country, that is inhabited by cruel savages, your natural enemies." Knowing well the fears of the room full of planters, he emphasized the vulnerability of whites, warning about potential slave uprisings. Virginia, he insisted, needed unity with its sister states in order to thrive and perhaps even survive, especially given "that species of population" Virginians held in bondage. He also stoked fears about invasions from Spain, France, the Dutch, and the British.[61]

Between predicting international invasions, an economic freefall, violent collisions with neighboring states, and slave uprisings, Randolph reminded Virginians of the security promised by ratification. "We are unsafe without the Union," he insisted, "in Union alone safety consists."[62] Some of his language was doubtless exaggerated for effect. But to veterans of the Revolution, such warnings probably did not seem so far-fetched. They'd seen their darkest fears realized just a decade before, at the hands of their own mother country.

Like Henry Lee, Edmund Randolph drew a bleak picture of what awaited Americans if they continued under the Articles, even for the short term. Borrowing Lee's exact language, he dismissed the "imbecility" of the Articles and thought it miraculous that the government had survived the Revolutionary War. The Confederation Congress was, he proclaimed, "contemptible in the eyes of foreign nations" and "too despicable to be regarded" by European countries. The Constitution offered a fresh start, the opportunity to avoid further humiliation in the international arena. Again, Randolph cast the current state of affairs in the harshest light. (His opponents, meanwhile, did precisely the same thing with their predictions of tyranny under the Constitution.)[63]

As he held forth, Randolph, like Patrick Henry, knew he was talking too long. "I have tired the patience of this House," he acknowledged. But still he continued.[64]

Finally, exhausting himself as well as the patience of his opponents, Randolph headed to a close by praising the union of states as "the rock of our salvation." "I believe," he declared, "that as sure as there is a God in Heaven, our safety, our political happiness and existence, depend on the Union of the States." Without ratification, Virginia and the other states should expect "unspeakable calamities" including "discord, faction, turbulence, war, and bloodshed."[65]

Governor Randolph ended with a ringing call to history, as moving today as it must have been in 1788: "Let it not be recorded of Americans, that after having performed the most gallant exploits, after having overcome the most astonishing difficulties, and after having gained the admiration of the world by their incomparable valor and policy, they lost their acquired reputation, their national consequence and happiness, by their own indiscretion." "Catch the present moment," he pleaded, "seize it with avidity and eagerness—for it may be lost—never to be regained."[66]

James Madison then gave his first substantive speech before the delegates. No one was more meticulously prepared. In addition to his long study in advance of the Philadelphia Convention, he took copious notes of every question and conversation at that gathering. In the months since, especially with the Federalist Papers, he had reasoned through every minute detail of the Constitution.

Madison was too short to see over many other men in the theater and too quiet to be heard by all the audience. David Robertson was forced to note periodically that Madison "spoke so low that his exordium could not be heard distinctly." But it is clear from what Robertson did record that Madison was nothing short of masterful. In the first place, he treated every delegate, no matter how critical of the Constitution, with respect. Unlike many of his allies, Madison said he knew his opponents were men of "truth, honor, candour, and rectitude of motives," no less than the friends of the Constitution. Although he had left Philadelphia unhappy with key elements in the final design, on the question of ratification Madison never wavered. He was, a French diplomat in Richmond during the convention marveled, "always clear, precise and consistent in his reasoning, and always methodical." Years later John Marshall was asked to rank the debating skills of the revolutionary generation. "If it includes persuasion by convincing," he replied, "Mr. Madison was the most eloquent man I ever heard."[67]

Before rebutting Patrick Henry's claims, James Madison signaled his frustration with Henry's tactics: "I hope that Gentlemen, in displaying their abilities, on this occasion, instead of giving opinions, and making assertions, will condescend to prove and demonstrate, by a fair and regular discussion." "Let us," he urged, "not rest satisfied with general assertions of dangers, without examination." He then specifically asked Henry to define "the dangers which this system is supposed to be replete with."[68]

Madison was disappointed by Henry's histrionics: "I must confess, I have not been able to find his usual consistency, in the Gentleman's arguments on this occasion." But he did not linger over such matters, preferring to answer specific Anti-Federalist objections, always hoping they would take no offense. "I wish," he said at one point, "as seldom as possible to contradict the assertions of Gentlemen." But contradict he did, with his signature and often overwhelming rigor of thought. To Henry's claim that the federal government's power to tax would destroy the sovereignty and ultimately the survival of Virginia, Madison offered a persuasive response. "If the General Government were wholly independent of the Governments of the particular States, then indeed usurpation might be expected to the fullest extent: But, Sir, on whom does this General Government depend? It derives its authority from those Governments, and from the same sources from which their authority is derived."[69]

That day, Madison made the first affirmative case for the Constitution by pointing out its exceptionality. This move fit perfectly with Americans' sense of their special place in history. The federal design, he explained, was unprecedented: "We cannot find one express example in the experience of the world: —It stands by itself." The government was partly federal, partly consolidated, but not entirely either. The happy result, he concluded, would be that the new government would escape both "the evils of absolute consolidation, as well as of a mere confederacy."[70]

The similarly thorough George Nicholas followed Madison, and he too criticized Patrick Henry for abandoning the delegates' plans to consider the Constitution clause by clause. "To my surprize," he began, "the debates have taken a different turn." Nicholas saw no choice but to respond to Henry's sweeping condemnation in kind, and he did not show Madison's restraint. Henry's argument, he said, "appears to me inconclusive and inaccurate."[71]

Nicholas scoffed at Henry's warning that taxpayers would face "two sets of collectors, who, he tells us, will oppress us with impunity." He insisted the federal tax power would not be burdensome or abused, and he predicted the actual amount of taxes citizens paid would not increase at all, only be balanced between state and federal collectors. Nicholas also countered Henry's speculation about the number of representatives.[72] The audience could see the significance of this issue by the way the delegates lingered over it day after day. They could see, too, in George Nicholas's point-by-point counter to Patrick Henry, that, while the object of withering criticism he was controlling the debates.

The day had been long—Governor Randolph spoke for three hours himself—and the arguments intense. George Nicholas closed by asserting that the opponents to the Constitution had been misled into seeing dangers that simply did not exist. "On a fair and candid investigation," he maintained, "very few would oppose it."[73] Henry and Mason and their side had no time to respond, for with that, the delegates adjourned. But even Nicholas knew that his last words of the day were just wishful thinking.

Francis Corbin spoke first on 7 June. He was only twenty-nine and, though brilliantly educated, lacked any experience from the Revolution. Sent abroad as a very young man, he was studying at Cambridge when the conflict with England turned violent. His rich family remained loyal to George III; Virginia was no place for their son, at least until peace was secured. He returned home after the close of the war to a family fortune. Young Corbin began his address to the convention describing his deference to the talented men who had preceded him: "It is with great difficulty I prevail on myself to enter into the debate, when I consider the great abilities of those Gentlemen who have already spoken." "I shall offer my observations," he continued, "with diffident respect, but with firmness and independence." Despite that prologue, Corbin rather quickly got over his supposed diffidence and confronted Patrick Henry, whose lifetime of experience included serving as a wartime governor of Virginia while Corbin's family protected their profits and kept him abroad. Corbin's speech sometimes veered toward reproach and even ridicule. "Objections should be founded on just and real grounds," he declared, "and ought not to be urged out of mere obstinacy!" He later called Henry's objections to a standing army "absurd" and mocked his "wild and frantic" opposition to ratification.[74] So much for deference!

Henry, who must have loathed everything about Corbin, bided his time. Instead of immediately rebutting the young man, he encouraged Governor Randolph, who had spoken for three hours the day before, to continue where he left off. Relishing his command of events and the chance to dig the governor for his change of heart, Henry said he wished to learn "every thing that

Gentlemen could urge in defence of that system, which [in Philadelphia] appeared to him so defective."[75]

Unable either to see Henry's strategy or to control his own defensiveness, Randolph obliged. He tried to stay on topic, though, and started by rejecting Anti-Federalists' skepticism about the ethics and accountability of members of Congress. Echoing George Nicholas's confidence in the federal structure, Randolph asked, "Will not the people choose men of integrity? What laws can they make that will not operate on themselves and friends, as well as on the rest of the people? Will the people re-elect the same men to repeat oppressive legislation? Will the people commit suicide against themselves?" Supporters of the Constitution, he explained, believed that the structure of Congress would allow only the most virtuous leaders to hold power. And even if some did incline toward corruption, how would such men ever act on that ambition? "If they should be liable to lapse from virtue, yet would not one man be found out of a multitude to guard the interest of the people?" asked Randolph. Should the entire House of Representatives fall victim to corruption, the people's interest would still be protected by senators, "distinguished for their wisdom, not elevated by popular favor, but chosen by a select body of intelligent men." In order for the Anti-Federalists' fears to come to fruition, Randolph explained, sixty-five representative and twenty-six senators would have to "be suddenly changed from upright men to monsters: Ninety-one persons selected for superior qualities are to compose this pandemonium of iniquity."[76]

Borrowing James Madison's brilliant reasoning in Federalist no. 10, Edmund Randolph explained to his fellow Virginians why corruption was likelier on the state than the federal level: "Greater talents, and a more extensive reputation will be necessary, to procure an election for the Federal, than for the State representation."[77]

When Randolph yielded the floor, James Madison rose. Relying on notes based on his studies as far back as 1786 and rehearsed in the Federalist Papers, Madison delivered a detailed lecture on comparative confederacies. At several points he either confused or bored David Robertson, who took to editorializing about Madison's comments rather than transcribing them. "Here Mr. Madison quoted sundry passages," Robertson noted, and "Here Mr. Madison then recapitulated many instances." Though characteristically dispassionate, James Madison made no bones about the necessity of a stronger union: "A Government which relies on thirteen independent sovereignties, for the means of its existence, is a solecism in theory, and a mere nullity in practice."[78]

Perhaps sensing he was losing the crowd, Madison decided to invoke George Washington. Madison reminded the delegates that at the close of the Revolutionary War Washington "publicly testified his disapprobation of the present system, and suggested that some alteration was necessary to render it adequate to the security of our happiness." Evidently some men in the room bristled, because Madison immediately said he did not "introduce that great name to bias any Gentleman" but simply as "a respectable witness to prove that the Articles of Confederation were inadequate, and that we must resort to something else."[79]

James Madison agreed with Patrick Henry that "national splendor and glory are not our objects." But, he insisted, respectability abroad would determine security at home, and at present the confederation government "is so notoriously feeble, that foreign nations are unwilling to form any treaties with us." In Madison's view, Americans' dire present trumped any prediction about the future.[80]

When Madison was done, Patrick Henry at last spoke. Having the last word two days before had worked so well he decided to try it again. Edmund Randolph was the first object of his ire: "It seems to me very strange and unaccountable, that that which was the object of his execration, should now receive his encomiums." As to promises of a bright future, "assertions and declarations, do not satisfy me," he said. "I must be convinced, Sir."[81]

Henry raised compelling doubts about the sanguine predictions of the defenders of the planned Congress with a single question. The best and brightest had been sent to Philadelphia to revise the Articles, and citizens' trust had been met with a radical new plan. "Will the ten men you are to send to Congress," Henry asked, "be more worthy than those seven were?"[82]

As the day drew to a close, Patrick Henry raised the troublesome issue of the "necessary and proper" clause. Though not widely discussed in Virginia before the convention, the vague language and implied congressional powers in the clause made it a hot topic during the formal debates. To some men, Henry included, it symbolized the fatal flaws in the Constitution. There was too much power concentrated in the hands of federal officials, too few specific checks on that power, and too few guarantees of states' rights and citizens' liberty. Who was to say what might become "necessary" and "proper" for Congress to pursue its vast powers? In later sessions James Madison insisted that the clause "gives no supplementary power: It only enables them to execute the delegated powers." Edmund Pendleton agreed: "I understand that clause as not going a single step beyond the delegated powers." Henry and Mason, however, saw the "necessary and proper" clause as among the most insidious parts of the Constitution. The "implication is dangerous," Henry insisted, "because it is unbounded." Since it was late on Saturday afternoon, Henry promised his audience that he would speak further about the matter on another day.[83] No one doubted him. With that, the first fitful, fascinating week of debates drew to a close.

Over the next three weeks, enthralled spectators who continued to vie for precious seats in the crowded galleries witnessed clashes of personality and will unsurpassed in Virginia's history. Debate topics varied from day to day as speeches spun from interrogations of specific sentences in the Constitution to soaring rhetoric about liberty to unfounded screeds assailing other men's motivations to philosophical considerations of government and law— sometimes from the same speaker on a single day. Delegates debated at one moment what the Constitution would mean for specific constituents in particular regions of Virginia and in the next the international implications of the federal design.

Men played to their strengths and played up their opponents' shortcomings. Since many of the leading men in the convention knew one another very well, it was not difficult, for example, for George Mason to goad Edmund Randolph about his vanity and waffling, or for George Nicholas to needle Patrick Henry about his lifelong dedication to getting rich off land.

The debates were often tense, then, and sometimes personal. On several occasions men got so exercised that their colleagues feared they might come to blows. Rumors flew after one especially vicious exchange between Edmund Randolph and Patrick Henry that they might fight a duel—the macabre and often deadly way men sometimes settled political disputes in the eighteenth century.[84]

Each side warned that failure to adopt its position might throw Virginia into civic convulsions. In the last week of the debates, George Mason said that he "dreaded popular resistance" to the "adoption of a system so replete with defects." Henry Lee was aghast: "Such speeches within these walls, from a character so venerable and estimable, easily progress into overt acts, among the less thinking and the vicious." Undeterred by Lee, Patrick Henry predicted the very next day that "the interval between this and bloodshed, is but a mo-ment." Edmund Randolph matched him step for step. At one point he said if ratification did not occur, "the dogs of war will break loose, and anarchy and discord will complete the ruin of this country."[85]

Federalists claimed that Anti-Federalists wanted to derail the Constitution in order to force separate confederacies, with New England and the Mid-Atlantic going their own ways and Virginia leading a southern confederation. Breaking apart the union of states was not the stated intention or secret plan of Anti-Federalists. Raising the specter of disunion proved a good political move, however, for it fit with the Federalists' vision of their opponents as consumed with their own power and parochial interests.

At the same time, it was—and is—hard to make out exactly the full thoughts of some leading Anti-Federalists, starting with Patrick Henry. If pressed, Patrick Henry insisted that he agreed with Edmund Randolph about the necessity of preserving the union. But he also said that, when compared to a single consolidated government, he thought "small Confederacies are little evils." It is difficult to imagine that a man of his savvy would not see both the peril and the unpopularity of severing ties with the other states. Virginians often discussed the pervasiveness of "ideas of the necessity of preserving the union." Henry perhaps hoped to use fear among other states of a Virginia-led southern confederacy to his advantage, by moving their convention delegates toward demanding fundamental change to the Constitution. In any event, his rivals in Richmond used fears of disunion as an effective tool against him.[86]

It was not just the leaders who blasted one another, either. Berkeley County's Adam Stephen rebuked Patrick Henry for trying to frighten men "by his bugbears and hobgoblings." Stephen said that if Henry found the Constitution so intolerable, he should "go and live among the Indians." Green Clay of Kentucky took to the floor to denounce Henry Lee for being "deficient in common decency."[87]

Richmonders worried that this coarse rhetoric might spill over into their city. Some charged the delegates with "inflaming the minds of the People." Their vitriol risked provoking residents "to put a stop to their proceedings by force." Federalists in particular charged critics of the Constitution with spreading "their interest without doors, to induce others to oppose the sys-tem."[88]

Despite the anxiety and invective—including not-so-subtle whispers of treason—the Richmond convention was defined by a remarkable degree of civility. Sometimes it was grudging, but the delegates, audience, and Virgin ians "out of doors" respected the right to strenuously disagree. The formal debates, James Madison concluded, were "conducted generally with great or- der, propriety & respect of either party to the other." Spectators agreed. James Breckinridge told his brother that he found the debates "exceed, if possible my expectations; they have been elaborate, elegant, eloquent, & consequently entertaining and instructive."[89]

Whenever debate threatened to spin out of control, men found a way back to order and perspective. In one great example, after Governor Randolph's incendiary prediction "that every calamity is to attend us, and that we shall be ruined and disunited forever, unless we adopt this Constitution," William Grayson broke the tension with humor. "Pennsylvania and Maryland are to fall upon us from the North, like the Goths and Vandals of old," Grayson paro- died Randolph. "The Indians are to invade us with numerous armies on our rear." Not content to mock Randolph's actual predictions, Grayson sarcasti- cally added: "And the Carolinians from the South, mounted on alligators, I presume, are to come and destroy our corn fields and eat up our little chil- dren!"[90]

The delegates' dedication could not keep them from getting frustrated by the often meandering debates. Eight days in, George Nicholas voiced a wide- spread aggravation: "We have hardly begun to discuss the question regularly." Instead of proceeding clause by clause, "gentlemen alarm us by declamation, without reason or argument." James Madison agreed. "Vague discourses and mere sports of fancy" he complained, "are very improper on this interest- ing occasion." It was past time to "come to the point."[91] Clearly, Federalists wanted to shut down Patrick Henry. But there was another factor at play: they suspected Anti-Federalists were prolonging the debates in hopes of forcing an adjournment—which would be perceived as a rejection of the Constitution.

In fact, staying on point was exceedingly difficult. Looking at any one is- sue almost automatically raised others. Particular questions about the Con- stitution led to larger structural and philosophical considerations. A case in point was the creation of the federal city. Seldom discussed before the formal debates, the federal city sparked fresh controversy in Richmond and raised a myriad of other questions. Anti-Federalists' opposition to centralized power drove their skepticism about the proposed permanent seat of government. William Grayson worried because Congress controlled the ten square mile area that would house the federal government. What, he asked, would keep congressmen from granting exclusive trading power to merchants living in the district? It was possible, he warned, that "the whole commerce of the United States may be exclusively carried on by the merchants residing within the seat of Government." George Mason feared the federal city would ignore the laws of the surrounding states and thus "become the sanctuary of the blackest crimes." James Madison rejected such speculation as too silly to discuss. But Anti-Federalists were not persuaded. The federal city raised in their minds troubling concerns about state sovereignty, trade policy, regional rivalries, and the corruption inherent in centralized power.[92]

Critics of the Constitution pointed to the Senate as another invitation to corruption in the proposed federal city, especially in light of senators serving six years with no term limits. Senators, Anti-Federalists warned, "will fix themselves in the federal town, and become citizens of that town more than of our State." They also predicted that senators and representatives would abuse the power granted them to set their own pay, building personal empires at the expense of citizens' interests. "This," Madison tried to assure delegates, "is a power which cannot be abused without rousing universal attention and indignation." Furthermore, Madison noted, in the past representatives had often "reduced their own wages lower rather than augmented them." John Tyler then speculated that congressmen might set their salaries so low that only rich men could afford to serve, "by which the Government might terminate in an Aristocracy." Madison seized on these contradictory fears to point out the inconsistency of Anti-Federalist arguments: "Some Gentlemen object because they may make their wages too high—Others object to it, because they may make them too low!"[93]

Delegates also fiercely debated the larger concerns associated with the offices of president and vice president. Anti-Federalists predicted that the presidency would "be an elective Monarchy," with men holding the position as a lifetime sinecure. How, they asked, would a man with such power ever be turned out of office? The vice presidency seemed both dangerous and unnecessary. By serving as president of the Senate, the vice president would give his state an unfair advantage. The position dangerously blurred the necessary lines between executive and legislative branches.[94]

A further dangerous intermixing of executive and legislative branches came, James Monroe added, in disputed presidential elections. According to the Constitution, if electors failed to produce a majority decision, the House of Representatives would choose, with each state delegation casting one vote. Monroe linked this to a recurrent Anti-Federalist fear: the marginalization of southern states. Monroe detailed several scenarios by which the northeastern states would nearly always elect the president. When that happened, the manufacturing and commercial states would dominate the agricultural ones.[95]

James Madison grew exasperated with the ceaseless conjecture, which invariably ended in disaster. Even so, he understood having a clear plan played to his advantage. "It is observable," he said after listening at length, "that none of the Honorable Members objecting to this, pointed out the right mode of election."[96] Madison would repeat this point many times: critics challenged the Constitution without offering a better alternative.

George Washington proved a great help against criticisms of the executive branch because many Virginians thought he would become the first president. It was difficult for men to harbor calamitous thoughts about presidential corruption when they already imagined the most respected man in America in that office. William Grayson tried to get delegates to look beyond the hero at Mount Vernon. "We do not fear while he lives," Grayson acknowledged. "But who," he asked, besides Washington, "can concentrate the confidence and affections of all Americans?"[97]

Even Washington's stellar reputation could not defuse the controversy over the creation of a standing army. The troubles predicted if Americans adopted a consolidated government with a powerful chief executive commanding a permanent army did not strike most delegates as paranoia. Rather, it seemed frighteningly familiar, given their recent history with Great Britain. On the issue of a standing army, Anti-Federalists upheld the traditional republican attitude. "I abominate and detest the idea of a Government, where there is a standing army," announced George Mason. They were, he reminded the audience, antithetical to liberty: "Once a standing army is established, in any country, the people lose their liberty." Because history was the best teacher of this lesson, Mason challenged the delegates to "recollect the history of most nations of the world. What havoc, desolation, and destruction, have been perpetrated by standing armies?" The federal army would also supersede the state militias. "Are we at last brought to such a humiliating and debasing degradation," Patrick Henry beseeched the delegates, "that we cannot be trusted with arms for our own defence?"[98]

Federalists did not contradict the position that a standing army was antithetical to republican government. Even Madison conceded "that a standing army is one of the greatest mischiefs that can possibly happen." But, he promised, federal oversight of an army would not destroy state militias: "The power is concurrent, and not exclusive." Madison also insisted the federal military was only for defense. "The best way to avoid danger," he argued, "is to be in a capacity to withstand it."[99]

Anti-Federalists found this highly dubious. How could the best path to peace lie in preparing for war? "If you be in constant preparation for war, on such airy and imaginary grounds, as the mere possibility of danger," Patrick Henry reasoned, "your government must be military, which will be inconsistent with the enjoyment of liberty."[100]

Federalists faced their most formidable challenge when the convention turned to tax powers—long an incendiary issue. This had been contentious in Philadelphia, too, but delegates there eventually agreed that the inability to tax crippled the confederation government and that a change was essential. Requisitions had failed time and again; the government, they decided, needed to be able to compel funds from the states. Delegates in the states that ratified before Virginia reluctantly conceded that point, too. In Richmond, John Marshall challenged Anti-Federalists "to produce a single instance where requisitions on the several individual States composing a confederacy, have been honestly complied with." None existed. Defenders of the Constitution also promised taxes would not increase under the Constitution. Any new federal costs, they predicted, would be offset by decreasing state expenses.[101]

Critics were, to say the least, unconvinced. "Instead of amusing ourselves with a diminution of our taxes," George Mason proclaimed, "we may rest assured that they will be increased." But Anti-Federalist objections were not simply about resenting paying taxes. Giving tax power to the federal government would leave the states impotent and at the mercy of federal legislators. "In my opinion," William Grayson reasoned, "the State which gives up the power of taxation has nothing more to give." Moreover, George Mason added, "the ruinous exercise of that power" would be held "by those who know not our situation"—in other words, those New England merchants that southern planters dreaded. Discussing tax powers returned delegates to the fraught issue of sovereignty and thus the fate of Virginia under the Constitution.[102]

Like taxation powers—and for the same underlying reason—access to the Mississippi River consumed a great deal of time during the Richmond debates. Delegates spent two days, 12–13 June, exhaustively discussing the free navigation of the Mississippi. But the subject—and the courting of Kentucky votes—bled into many other conversations. From the first week to the last, Patrick Henry and William Grayson stoked Kentuckians' apprehensions about losing access to the Mississippi River. They missed no chance to remind delegates that under the federal government they should expect powerful northeastern states "to give away this river" to the Spanish. "Every advantage is taken," Madison ruefully wrote Washington, "to work on the local prejudices of particular sets of members."[103]

Federalists countered by arguing that the best chance of negotiating effectively with Spain lay in adopting "an efficient firm Government."[104] Local interests, Federalists argued, could actually be better advanced through a stronger, united government. Hour after hour they debated, jockeying for those Kentucky votes. The topic exhausted David Robertson, who yet again took to describing the "desultory conversation" about the Mississippi River rather than writing down everything men said. But the issue of access to the Mississippi persisted because of the larger philosophical and political questions it raised, especially about sovereignty and the local and regional interests of Virginians.

Profound disagreements over the foundations of republican government ran through the delegates' conversations all month long. What was the nature of representation? How could citizens ensure the necessary powers of government while protecting personal liberties? As proud Virginians, they worried especially about where sovereignty would reside, and what authority would remain for Virginia if the Constitution passed. How would state and federal powers be balanced? There were elemental questions about the Constitution, too. Exactly what kind of government was this? Was it consolidated, national, federal, or something else?

Underlying many of these questions about the American Republic were Virginians' noxious dealings with racial slavery. Federalists slyly warned that without the Constitution social turmoil—coded as slave rebellions—could erupt. They defended states' skimpy representation in the House with the three-fifths compromise, which ensured Virginia and all the slave states greater congressional influence. Federalists also tried to link ratification to the successful extension of slavery into the West, but Anti-Federalists had a counter. The power of northern states under the Constitution, Anti-Federalists warned, posed a grave threat to slaveholders' "peace and tranquility."[105]

Throughout the Revolution, white Virginians had used warnings about their own "enslavement" as a powerful political tool. Now, Anti-Federalists said that white men risked being "enslaved" by the federal government. No one exploited this rhetorical move with greater effect than Patrick Henry. One spectator, upon hearing "the fervid description which Henry gave of the slavery of the people wrought by a Federal executive at the head of his armed hosts," was so captivated that he "involuntarily felt his wrists to assure himself that the fetters were not already pressing his flesh."[106]

But even as each side used racialized fears to court votes, they shared a general consensus about the future of slavery. On the morning of 17 June, debates began with a reading of Section 9, Article 1, which allowed the continuation of the international slave trade for twenty years. George Mason, a slaveholder himself, began by condemning this "fatal section, which has created more dangers than any other." The international slave trade, he proclaimed, "is diabolical in itself, and disgraceful to mankind." In the next breath, he blasted the Constitution for failing to secure "the property of the slaves we have already." The Philadelphia delegates, he complained, "have done what they ought not to have done, and have left undone what they ought to have done."[107]

Mason drew a line familiar to eighteenth-century Virginians: condemning the international slave trade while defending domestic slavery. The former, international human trafficking, was not in Virginia's financial interests; the state had a surplus of slaves. Many slaveholders also thought the international trade immoral. But that was quite different from believing in emancipation or racial liberalism. To end slavery was to destroy the foundation of elite Virginians' wealth, power, and self-identity. At the same time, leading Virginians almost universally agreed that slavery was antithetical to their republican values. Thomas Jefferson called slavery a "moral and political depravity." "I will not, I cannot justify it," Patrick Henry insisted.[108]

So, when George Mason blasted the international trade, James Madison offered no challenge, only explaining: "I should conceive this clause to be impolitic, if it were one of those things which could be excluded without encountering greater evils." South Carolinians at the Philadelphia Convention, he explained, refused to support the Constitution unless it protected the international trade. To coax Virginia slaveholding delegates to his side, he pointed out "another clause secures us that property which we now possess."

That was the fugitive slave clause. Lauding that part of the Constitution as "better security than any that now exists," Madison reminded the audience that under the Articles of Confederation "if any slave elopes to any of those States where slaves are free, he becomes emancipated by their laws." The Constitution, Madison assured delegates, would not undermine their livelihood or disturb their racial order.[109] Virginians on both sides of the constitutional question might lament their lifelong immersion in a brutal labor system that could not be reconciled with their political views. But they all agreed that government—whatever form it took—should not threaten that hypocrisy.

Few days passed without delegates debating the nature of representation in the federal government, for that core issue touched on so many others. Anti-Federalists worried about distant, entrenched leaders abandoning their local allegiances and falling into self-interested corruption. This was especially dangerous given the tremendous powers granted Congress under the Constitution. "It seems to have been a rule with the Gentlemen on the other side," William Grayson scoffed, "to argue for the excellency of human nature, in order to induce us to grant away . . . the rights and liberties of our country."[110] In fact, Federalists felt confident that the structure of government would produce virtuous leaders—so long as the people upheld republican principles. At the heart of Madison's vision for the federal government lay the idea of a "filtration of talent"—that if citizens exercised their rights responsibly, only the most capable and virtuous men could secure power in the federal government.

Madison dismissed predictions that representatives "will do every mischief they possibly can, and that they will omit to do every good which they are authorised to do." But, he continued, he also did not "place unlimited confidence in them." Instead, he proclaimed, "I go on this great republican principle, that the people will have virtue and intelligence to select men of virtue and wisdom." Republican government always reflected the character of the people, Madison believed. Virtuous citizens elected virtuous leaders; a corrupt citizenry could never do so. "To suppose that any form of Government will secure liberty or happiness without any virtue in the people," Madison insisted, "is a chimerical idea."[111]

The Constitution also turned on its head the common perception of the scope of republics. Eighteenth-century understanding held that a republic had to be small enough for voters to hold their leaders to account and homogeneous enough for all citizens to share common interests. The Constitution created a republic larger than any nation in Europe. Madison believed that the scope of the American Republic would be its greatest asset: the diversity of constituencies and perspectives would ensure that the best interests of the whole country would prevail over petty, local prejudices. Federalists found this a brilliant and persuasive argument, a solution to the problems of the Articles of Confederation and the way to save the revolutionaries' republican experiment.[112]

Opponents to ratification challenged Madison's theories on multiple fronts. Patrick Henry declared that Madison's claim about a republic working on as vast a scale as the United States "contradicts all the experience of the world." James Monroe pointed out the high stakes if Madison was wrong. Delegates were wagering a precious legacy: "The freedom of mankind has found an asylum here, which it could find no where else."[113]

Patrick Henry also considered the whole proposition of filtering talent upward to federal offices ludicrous: "If, Sir, the diminution of numbers be an augmentation of merit, perfection must centre on one." Even if Madison was right, James Monroe allowed, and "gentlemen of influence and character, men of distinguished talents, of eminent virtue, and great endowments, will compose the General Government," that posed another problem. "In what a situation will the different States be, when all the talents and abilities of the country will be against them?" he asked.[114]

Henry Lee dismissed this all as a stunning lack of faith in voters and duly elected representatives. "Would the people be so lost to honour and virtue," Lee scoffed, "as to select men who would willingly associate with the most abandoned characters?" Patrick Henry had an immediate response: "However cautious you may be in the selection of your Representatives," he warned, "it will be dangerous to trust them with such unbounded powers."[115]

Disagreements over representation could not be separated from competing ideas about sovereignty. Everyone at the New Academy would have agreed with James Monroe when he called on delegates "to act as shall appear for the best advantage of our common country." But what country? Many men in Richmond thought of Virginia as their country. Thus Patrick Henry asked, "What is to become of your country?" and immediately answered: "The Virginian Government is but a name" under the proposed Constitution.[116] Other men who had long operated on the continental stage—led by James Madison—thought of the United States as their country.

Men dedicated to retaining traditional state powers saw abundant cause for concern in the Constitution. The judiciary, for example, seemed to wholly swallow state courts. "I am greatly mistaken," Mason said, "if there be any limitation whatsoever, with respect to the nature or jurisdiction of these Courts."[117]

Delegates with a more national outlook dismissed such traditional ideas about state power as local prejudice. From Patrick Henry's "harangues," Henry Lee complained, "one would have thought that the love of an American was in some degree criminal; as being incompatible with a proper degree of affection for a Virginian." "The people of America, Sir, are one people," he continued. "I love the people of the North . . . because I fought with them as my countrymen, and because I consider them as such."[118]

Federalists also discounted Anti-Federalist speculation about the federal government encroaching on state prerogatives as so much ungrounded fear. Madison believed that "the State Governments, and not the General Government, will preponderate" once the Constitution was ratified.[119] "The powers of the General Government relate to external objects," he explained, "and are but a few." Meanwhile, "the powers of the States relate to those great objects which immediately concern the prosperity of the people." Overall, Madison predicted a harmonious sharing of duties between the states and the federal government.[120]

Patrick Henry vehemently disagreed. "This Government will operate like an ambuscade," he insisted. "It will destroy the State Governments, and swallow the liberties of the people."[121]

This issue came up again and again as men worked through the federal plan. James Monroe gave an especially moving speech during the second week of the convention. Monroe always listened to be persuaded, and he openly acknowledged the benefits he saw in the Constitution; he was not a reflexive opponent. Ultimately, though, he found the notion of concurrent powers, particularly the power to tax, unprecedented and unworkable. The "necessary and proper" clause alone could extinguish any real balance of power between the states and the federal government, he predicted. Monroe made the matter deeply personal: "Consult the human heart. Does it not prove, that where two parties, or bodies, seek the same object, there must be a struggle?"[122]

Perhaps without even knowing it, Monroe described the central struggle in the Virginia convention. Two parties sought the same object: the survival of their most deeply held political ideals. Their precious, fragile republic, both sides agreed, was "a new, and interesting spectacle to the eyes of mankind." Monroe eloquently captured delegates' perception of American exceptionalism. Twelve centuries of European history, he said, had been marked by efforts of "the people, to extricate themselves from the oppression of their rulers." In America, by contrast, the challenge was "to establish the dominion of law over licentiousness." The Revolution "put the entire Government in the hands of one order of people only—the freemen." Now, those freemen had to choose what kind of government to adopt for themselves and posterity.[123]

Monroe concluded that the Constitution "is a dangerous Government, and calculated to secure neither the interests, nor the rights of our countrymen." The plan, he cautioned, would not protect "the best hopes and prospects of a free people." "We have struggled long to bring about this revolution," he reminded his fellow patriots, "by which we enjoy our present freedom and security." "Why then," he wanted to know, "this wild precipitation?"[124]

Monroe's friend John Marshall started from the same convictions but reached the opposite conclusion. "The friends of the Constitution," he insisted, "are as tenacious of liberty as its enemies. They wish to give no power that will endanger it. They wish to give the Government powers to secure and protect it." "I differ in opinion from the worthy Gentleman," Marshall said, referring to his friend James Monroe. "I think the virtue and talents of the members of the General Government will tend to the security, instead of the destruction of our liberty."[125]

In the winter of 1787–88, James Madison had seen three groups emerging in Virginia: citizens strongly supporting the Constitution without any changes (like himself); men who favored the Constitution but still wished to see modest changes, particularly regarding state powers and citizen rights; and individuals (like Patrick Henry) who fundamentally objected to the Constitution. As the Richmond convention unfolded, however, fewer men stood squarely behind the idea that the Constitution, utterly unchanged, would fulfill the Revolution. Throughout the month of June, Anti-Federalists lobbied hard for changes to protect state governments and the rights of citizens.

"Grant us amendments like these," George Mason promised, "and we will cheerfully with our hands and hearts unite with those who advocate it." "But," he immediately added, "in its present form we never can accede to it."[126]

Gradually, even strident Federalists began to concede that some changes might be in order. Perhaps, they admitted, the plan could benefit from some clarification about the balance of power between the federal and state governments or regarding citizens' rights.[127]

But under no circumstance, Federalists maintained, should any change be a condition of Virginia ratifying. Repeating language from a March newspaper essay, Francis Corbin called on delegates to "go hand in hand with Massachusetts." Ratify the Constitution, he urged, "and then propose amendments of a general nature." Federalists felt sanguine about accomplishing any necessary revisions to the new government after ratification. "When experience shall shew us any inconveniences," John Marshall assured the audience, "we can then correct them." George Nicholas was even more optimistic: "If you recommend alterations after ratifying, the friendship of the adopting States to the Union, and the desire of several of them to have amendments, will lead them to gratify every reasonable proposal."[128]

Anti-Federalists found this preposterous—"delusive and fallacious" George Mason said. They offered many vivid metaphors to make their point. "You agree to bind yourselves hand and foot—For the sake of what?" Patrick Henry asked. "Of being unbound. You go into a dungeon—For what? To get out." Following the Federalists' logic, Mason mockingly suggested, "we should cheerfully burn ourselves to death in hopes of a joyful and happy resurrection!" But perhaps the best line came from the audience. One spectator said that the opponents to ratifying unconditionally "do not think it prudent to mount a fiery high-blooded Steed without a bridle."[129]

Anti-Federalists wanted numerous structural changes to the federal design, but they were most successful in pushing for a bill of rights: written guarantees of citizens' rights, including freedom of speech, assembly, religion, and the press. Interestingly, the defense of freedom of religion marked one of the rare times Virginians raised the topic of religion in their formal debates—or in the months before, for that matter. Aside from disagreeing over whether the Constitution might undermine state laws guaranteeing religious freedom, matters of church and faith were rarely mentioned and seemed to matter little to Virginians' conversations about the Constitution. Even the issue of freedom of religion was about freedom more than religion.

The absence of a bill of rights worried many men around the room. James Monroe spoke for many delegates when he proclaimed, "I am a decided and warm friend to a *Bill of Rights*—the polar star, and great support of American liberty." "The necessity of amendments is universally admitted," Patrick Henry declared. "Reason, self-preservation, and every idea of propriety, powerfully urge us to secure the dearest rights of human nature."[130]

On this score, history was squarely on the Anti-Federalists' side. When Virginians, led by George Mason, adopted their constitution in 1776, they ensured specific individual rights that the state government could never violate. Mason's Declaration of Rights became a model for other states and a centerpiece of American constitutionalism. Now, Virginians were being asked to sign on to a government bereft of guaranteed rights and to be administered mostly by strangers who shared little in common with Virginians and perhaps "at a distance of 1000 miles from us." For Virginians to uphold their state constitution and consent to the absence of a bill of rights in the powerful federal government was, Anti-Federalists concluded, "a conduct of unexampled absurdity."[131]

In Philadelphia, the decision not to include a bill of rights in the Constitution had been remarkably hasty (and, in retrospect, flawed). George Mason raised the issue, but the delegates decided not to pursue it. Some were fatigued and ready to get home. Others feared further negotiating might undo their fragile near-consensus on the Constitution. And many felt confident that the federal government was so limited in its scope that it could not infringe on rights guaranteed by states: a federal bill of rights would be redundant. In several state conventions, and now in Virginia, this proved to be the framers' biggest mistake.[132]

During the long ratification process, citizens in many states made clear they wanted a bill of rights added to the Constitution. Federalists in state conventions, including in Virginia, found themselves pushed toward this change. Unwilling to give much ground, James Madison and George Nicholas continued to insist that Americans' rights were not in jeopardy. But they did reluctantly acknowledge that "it was proper for the Convention to have inserted a Bill of Rights."[133]

What was *not* proper, they contended, was making a bill of rights "the condition of our accession to the Union."[134] On the ropes over protecting citizens' liberties, Federalists still tried to claim the high ground of reason and practicality. Previous (or conditional) amendments, Edmund Pendleton reasoned, were disrespectful to the sister states. Virginians should, he urged, follow the example set by Massachusetts and propose amendments to be debated in the first federal Congress. This was the "conciliatory and friendly" approach. The Constitution provided explicit guidelines for making amendments, Federalists pointed out, and Virginians could avail themselves of that process at the proper time. When Patrick Henry produced a list of amendments for Virginians to debate and then demand as a condition of ratifying, Edmund Randolph discounted them as "fraught with perhaps, more defects than the Constitution itself." James Madison agreed. Members of the Virginia convention had already discussed forty changes, and Henry's proposal contained twenty more. What would happen, Madison asked, if every state did the same?[135]

Federalists also countered demands for a bill of rights with an argument that simultaneously upheld the union and tilted toward fear-mongering. Patrick Henry's position, George Wythe likewise cautioned, invited "the extreme danger of dissolving the Union." "If you reject the Constitution and say, that you must have alterations as the previous condition of adoption," George Nicholas warned, "you sacrifice the Union, and all the valuable parts of it." Hoping to move uncommitted delegates, Governor Randolph urged men to be practical. "I do not reverence the Constitution," he said. But eight states had ratified, leaving Virginia with only two options: ratify or "hazard a breach of the Union." "Nothing but the fear of inevitable destruction," Randolph insisted, "would lead me to vote for the Constitution in spite of the objections I have to it."[136]

As the days sped by, both sides grew increasingly anxious, and with good reason. Their shared experiment with republican government was just a decade old and perhaps about to come undone. Federalists were sure they had the right plan but feared the salvation of the Revolution slipping from their hands because of their opponents' self-interestedness. Anti-Federalists thought their dearly bought freedoms were on the verge of being sacrificed to exactly the kind of corrupting power they'd fought in Great Britain.

It fell to the undecided delegates to determine who was right. Should they hold out for conditional amendments to ensure their liberty? Or would doing that risk the collapse of the union? Which way should they vote? The answer was elusive but the stakes obvious: "If a wrong step be now made, the Republic may be lost forever."[137]

Summer 1788, Deciding the Question and the Future

If I shall be in the minority, I shall have those painful sensations, which arise from a conviction of being overpowered in a good cause. Yet I will be a peaceable citizen!

Patrick Henry, 25 June 1788

EVERY MEMBER OF THE Virginia Ratification Convention arrived early on Tuesday, 24 June. They had considered nearly every clause of the Constitution, so they knew a vote would happen soon. "The decision was still uncertain," Archibald Stuart recalled, "and every mind and every heart was filled with anxiety." Patrick Henry's stunning "storm" speech captured Virginians' imagination that day. Henry's voice, begging delegates to see their duty to the happiness of all mankind, rose with the ferocity of a gathering thunderstorm. Observers marveled that he seemed "as if he had indeed the faculty of calling up spirits from the vasty deep." At the very instant the violent storm shook the whole building, Henry's voice rang out over the wind and rain and thunder. "In point of sublimity," Stuart insisted, that speech "has never been surpassed in any age or country of the world."[1]

The drama may have gone to Patrick Henry, but the most revealing speech that day came from the previously silent John Dawson. A twenty-seven-year-old Harvard graduate and lawyer, Dawson represented Spotsylvania County, alongside his good friend James Monroe. He and Monroe were related to one another, too, in the way eighteenth-century elite Virginians often were: Dawson's stepfather, Judge Joseph Jones, was Monroe's uncle and guardian (Monroe lost his father when he was a teenager). Dawson was also a close friend and frequent correspondent of James Madison. His speech showed his respect for both friends and the precise reasoning behind his vote.

Capturing the lingering vestiges of political deference as well as the civic duty required of citizens in a republic, Dawson began by explaining why he had, until that moment, said nothing: it arose "from a satisfactory impression of the inferiority of my talents, and from a wish to acquire every information which might assist my judgment in forming a decision on a question of such magnitude." (Most delegates followed this pattern and did not address the convention.) Dawson spoke up now, he continued, "not from any apprehension that my opinions will have weight, but in order to discharge that duty which I owe to myself, and to those I have the honor to represent."[2]

Dawson understood the problems with the Articles of Confederation and the results: "The seeds of civil dissension" and "political confusion" had, he regretted, "pervaded the States." In 1787 he had consequently welcomed the idea of changing the Articles through the Philadelphia meeting, all the more so when he realized "the very respectable characters who formed that body." In fact, the reputations of the men who designed the Constitution—including his good friend James Madison—almost persuaded him to reflexively support the document they produced. *Almost.* "But when I came to investigate it impartially, on the immutable principles of government, and to exercise reason," Dawson said, he was brought up short. "I was convinced," he told the crowded hall, "of this important, though melancholy truth, 'that the greatest of men may err,' and that their errors are sometimes of the greatest magnitude." "With the diffidence of a young politician, but with the firmness of a republican," he concluded that the Constitution would endanger "the liberties of America, in general; the property of Virginia in particular."[3]

Dawson also rejected the implication often made by Federalists that the critics of the Constitution were "enemies of the Union." He was, he asserted, "a warm friend to a firm, federal, energetic Government." But he feared the states turning into a single, consolidated government. "When that event shall happen," he proclaimed, "I shall consider the history of American liberty as short as it has been brilliant." Dawson considered the Constitution, echoing popular Anti-Federalist language, "incompatible with republican liberty."[4]

Dawson then offered a very precise and forceful review of the key elements of the Constitution, including the power to tax, the establishment of the federal judiciary, and the centrally controlled military to argue that, in fact, the result was "one consolidated government." And, he predicted, that government would quickly become unwieldy, expensive, and corrupt.[5]

Clearly, Dawson had paid close attention and taken good notes over the preceding three weeks, for he criticized Federalists' dismissal of the Mississippi River rights debates as "a pretext for scuffling for votes." In Dawson's opinion, that issue was of paramount importance in its own right and revealed the overreaching powers of the federal government generally. Linking himself to Patrick Henry, whom he praised as a "truly patriotic friend . . . whose name shall ever be hallowed in the temple of liberty," Dawson said that he shared Henry's distress over the "ambiguous terms in which all rights are secured to the people." He could not help noticing that the ambiguity of citizens' rights stood in sharp contrast to "the clear and comprehensive language used, when power is granted to Congress."[6]

"I am so far an enthusiast in favor of liberty," Dawson said, as he drew to a close, "that I never will trust the sacred deposit to other hands, nor will I exchange it for any earthly consideration." For that reason, he announced, he intended to vote against ratification of the Constitution in its current, unamended form.[7]

James Madison tried to answer John Dawson's many criticisms as precisely as he could. He even conceded some shortcomings in the Constitution and accepted the idea of amending after ratification. But he insisted he would never consent to previous amendments "because they are pregnant with dreadful dangers." He was emphatic about the perils of following Dawson's path. "It is a most awful thing that depends on our decision," Madison warned. Either Americans would stand together to secure "their common liberty and happiness" or "every thing is to be put in confusion and disorder!" It was an uncharacteristically emotional speech from a decidedly reasoned and dispassionate man: "I beg that Gentlemen in deliberating on this subject, would consider the alternative." Throughout the convention, Madison had resolved to "choose rather to indulge my hopes than fears." But as he struggled to answer his friend's objections, perhaps the steel-spined Madison wavered just a bit.[8]

Wednesday morning, 25 June, was even more tense. Before the church bells chimed ten o'clock, every member had already taken his seat. A thousand spectators overflowed the hall that day, "with minds agitated by contending and opposite opinions."[9] It was time for the Virginians to vote. Given Patrick Henry's earth-shaking speech from the day before, Federalists feared that, should he lose, Henry might walk out of the convention and take his many supporters with him. Even if the Federalists won the vote, they might lose the cause. Who knew what might happen if Patrick Henry took his ringing defense of liberty "out of doors." The General Assembly of Virginia would perhaps side with Henry, given his influence and Assembly members' Anti-Federalist leanings. And the citizens of Virginia were every bit as closely divided as the convention delegates. Great numbers continued to regard the Constitution with skepticism and disdain. Ominous thoughts crossed men's minds that June morning. If Henry walked out, the vote might appear illegitimate, and what would the winners do then? Would they reassess the vote and negotiate conditional amendments with Henry's faction? Or would they defend their decision, come what may? Could the great state of Virginia fracture or even devolve into a civil war?

By late June, even James Madison recognized the value of making some changes to the Constitution. "It has never been denied by the friends of the paper on the table," he allowed, "that it has defects." Gone were the fawning paeans. The division among the delegates now was mostly over whether the amendments Virginians wanted should be previous or subsequent, required before ratification or proposed afterward. On this topic, nothing new was left to be said. But who spoke up was very interesting. Madison, who'd maintained for a year that changes were unnecessary, now promised "how easy it will be to obtain subsequent amendments."[10] (Soon, he would be in the US Congress and eating those words.)

Benjamin Harrison contradicted Madison: amendments, he insisted, had to come before ratification. Siding with Mason and Henry, Harrison also balked at the tremendous powers granted federal officials, including the president. Like most delegates, he'd left a young family at home. He had no way of knowing that one of those children, fifteen-year-old William, would one day hold the executive powers he now found intolerable. Nor could Benjamin Harrison have even imagined that his son's grandson, named in his honor, would become a president in the government he rejected, too. James Monroe, a future president himself, agreed with Harrison about amendments. He predicted that if Virginians failed to insist on amendments now, the Constitution would "never be amended, not even when experience shall have proved its defects." Monroe said he stood with Harrison in voting no on the Constitution.[11]

Realizing this would be the last day of debates, several men who sat silent all month followed the example John Dawson set the day before. They addressed the crowd with eloquence and force, revealing their perceptions of the long debates. These delegates spoke to the future, too, hoping to claim their place in Virginia's history.

The leaders on both sides yielded most of the time on 25 June to these men, including James Innes. Innes was the sitting attorney general of Virginia and was widely respected for his keen legal mind. If his judicial duties had not kept him from attending all of the convention, he likely would have taken a leading role in the debates. Innes exerted quite a physical presence. He was, his contemporaries said, one of the largest men they knew: over six feet tall and so heavy he "could not ride an ordinary horse, or sit in a common chair."[12] His brother Harry, a prominent judge in Kentucky, had authored a widely circulated rebuke of the Constitution, in which he argued the liberty and happiness of western county residents would be destroyed by the federal government. Westerners' interests, Harry Innes charged, would fall victim to domination by the northern states. James Innes, however, announced his intention to vote for ratification because he believed that all the Anti-Federalists' concerns had been "satisfactorily answered by the friends of the Constitution." In response to the reasoned explanations given by Federalists, he chided, "horrors have been called up, chimeras suggested, and every terrific and melancholy idea adduced" to prevent ratification. He said he was sorry to see men—though he did not say it, including his own brother—stir up "a general spirit of jealousy with respect to our Northern brethren." As Innes reminded delegates, "it was not a *Virginian, Carolinian* or *Pennsylvanian*, but the glorious name of an *American*" that allowed the patriots to triumph over Britain. "Does not our existence as a nation depend on our Union?" he asked.[13]

John Tyler, a forty-one-year-old lawyer and judge representing Charles City County, followed Innes, and he held the exact opposite view on ratification.

When he considered what the Constitution would allow the government to do, he said, "I tremble at it." He began with a foundational problem: "The Constitution is expressed in indefinite terms,—in terms, which the Gentlemen who composed it, do not all concur in the meaning of." "If the able Members who composed it, cannot agree on the construction of it," Tyler asked, "shall I be thought rash or wrong to pass censure on its ambiguity?" As did many Virginians, Tyler considered it "a degrading situation" that the most powerful state in the union had, according to the advocates for ratification, "no right to propose amendments." But mostly, Tyler objected to the federal government's reach: the Constitution "contains a variety of powers too dangerous to be vested in any set of men whatsoever." "I cannot but dread its operation," he proclaimed. He would vote no.[14]

Tyler was also explicit about why he spoke up. Like many men in the room, he intended "to hand down to posterity" a clear record of his conduct. He wanted to be certain that his name got recorded in the "nay" column and "that it may be known that my opposition arose from a full persuasion and conviction, of its being dangerous to the liberties of my country."[15] Tyler's personal "posterity" eventually included a namesake, born in 1790. In 1841, when Benjamin Harrison's son, President William Henry Harrison, died in office, his vice president, John Tyler, became the first man to succeed to the presidency without being elected.

Zachariah Johnston responded to Tyler's substantive objections, pointing out "the strained construction which has been put, by the Gentlemen on the other side, on every word and syllable, in endeavouring to prove oppressions which can never possibly happen." Johnston was unpersuaded by the Anti-Federalists' pessimistic reading of the Constitution. Certainly the Constitution might have defects. But, he pointed out, "the annals of mankind do not shew us one example of a perfect Constitution." "My judgment," he concluded, "is convinced of the safety and propriety of this system."[16]

When every man who wished to speak was done, all eyes turned back to Patrick Henry. He began his closing speech with a robust defense of previous rather than subsequent amendments. He urged Virginians to stand with him "in a manly, firm and resolute manner" and demand changes before ratification.[17]

Even as he spoke, Patrick Henry knew that he'd come close but would fall short. From the outset, leaders on both sides nervously counted votes. At the end of the first week of debates, Bushrod Washington wrote his famous uncle that any prediction "must be founded on conjecture." The next week James Madison felt even more uneasy. "The issue of it is more doubtful than was apprehended when I last wrote," he told a friend. "The majority on either side will be small & at present the event is as ticklish as can be conceived."[18]

Patrick Henry and the Anti-Federalists expected the mounting weight of daily criticisms to sway enough undecided delegates to defeat ratification, and early on Federalists like James Madison and Bushrod Washington feared they might be right. But three weeks in, Henry sensed that he was not moving as many men as he'd hoped. With hints of desperation, he begged delegates to "recollect what they are about to do." Anti-Federalists also doubled down on their criticisms, with Henry taking the lead in blasting every part of the Constitution as worse than the last. In typical language, he railed against the judiciary as "a more fatal defect than any we have yet considered." He'd said the same thing before about other clauses and would repeat it again later. Federalists used this to their advantage, challenging wavering delegates to find any part of the Constitution that Patrick Henry—a stand-in in Federalist rhetoric for opponents of ratification—would accept. "No part," they insisted, "if he had his way, would be agreed to."[19] By painting Henry as willfully captious, advocates for ratification attempted to discredit all Anti-Federalist criticisms. Was this really the unbending model good republican citizens wanted to follow? If nothing of value came from the Philadelphia meeting, what hope was there for a second convention? If there was no room for compromise, how could any governmental design be adopted?

As Patrick Henry studied the undecided delegates in late June, he began to accept the math. Henry's last words were poignant, reflecting his understanding that he would lose the vote. Like many men around the room, his thoughts turned to the future: about what would become of Virginia under the Constitution and about his own place in history. In particular, Henry seemed to ponder how to use his considerable influence and what future generations might draw from his conduct at that crucial hour. With all that in mind, Henry thanked the convention for the "patience and polite attention with which I have been heard" and apologized for "having taken up more time than came to my share."[20]

Then, Patrick Henry offered a way to start to heal Virginia's deep divisions and, with it, a powerful lesson about constitutionalism and republican government. It must have been painful to face defeat in that democratic forum, where so often he had prevailed. And he doubtless found it awkward to back-track on his steadfast positions of the prior weeks. But Patrick Henry was not so unbending after all; the common good, he decided, was paramount. The words he spoke captured the example he and the Anti-Federalists set for generations of Americans to come. "If I shall be in the minority," he said, "I shall have those painful sensations, which arise from a conviction of being overpowered in a good cause. Yet I will be a peaceable citizen!" "I wish not to go to violence," Henry continued, "but will wait with hopes that the spirit which predominated in the revolution, is not yet gone." He vowed to work within the bounds of the law to see the federal government "changed so as to be compatible with the safety, liberty and happiness of the people."[21]

How lovely it would have been if those were the last words spoken be-fore Edmund Pendleton called the question. Spencer Roane marveled at the character his father-in-law showed in the face of imminent defeat. The virtue Patrick Henry demonstrated in submitting to the will of the majority left a profound and lasting legacy for America, Roane believed. And Henry's eloquence "would almost disgrace Cicero and Demosthenes." Even Henry's strongest opponents shared Roane's viewpoint. When George Washington heard what he'd done, he wrote several friends to trumpet Patrick Henry's integrity and virtuous example: "Mr. Henry it seems having declared that, though he cannot be *reconciled* to the Government in its *present* form, and will give it every *constitutional* opposition in his power; yet, that he will sub-mit to it peaceably; as every good citizen he thinks ought; and by precept and example will endeavour, within the sphere of his action, to inculcate the like principles into others."[22]

But Patrick Henry did not get the last word, for Edmund Randolph was thinking about the future, too, especially his reputation. Unable to let Hen-ry's moving call lead into the vote, the governor could not resist: "One part-ing word I humbly supplicate." His last remarks (hardly humble) consisted of a defense of his changing attitudes toward the Constitution. Randolph's speech had none of the magnanimity and grace that characterized Henry's final address. It was small and self-serving: "Lest however some future an-nalist should in the spirit of party vengeance, deign to mention my name, let him recite these truths,—that I went to the Federal Convention, with the strongest affection for the Union; that I acted there in full conformity with this affection; that I refused to subscribe; because I had, as I still have, objections to the Constitution, and wished a free inquiry into its merits; and that the accession of eight States reduced our deliberations to the single question of Union or no Union."[23]

And then, suddenly at last, it was time to vote. George Wythe proposed a resolution to ratify, but Patrick Henry countered with a list of structural amendments and a bill of rights. Anti-Federalists wanted a vote on those changes before the final vote on ratification, and Federalists obliged. Henry's motion was defeated, 88 to 80. (Two delegates were absent.) That left only one question: the one posed to all Americans by the Philadelphia Convention.

The members of the Virginia Ratification Convention voted by roll call, and the name of each man and whether he say "aye" or "nay" was dutifully recorded for everyone in Virginia and, in time, all posterity to know. They proceeded alphabetically, by county. When they got to Northumberland, the vote was tied at 60. When Randolph County's representatives voted, the convention found itself tied again, at 69. Though called by county, for the first time in Virginia's history, representatives voted as individuals, not as members of a larger county or state delegation. In the first county, Accomack, Edmund Custis voted no, and George Parker voted yes.[24]

When the last vote was cast, the tally stood at 89-79, in favor of ratification. (David Patteson, from Chesterfield County, voted first with the Anti-Federalists, then switched his vote, reluctantly siding with the Federalists when he saw amendments were impossible.)[25] Five votes swung in the opposite direction would have turned the fate of Virginia and the United States. Instead, by a stunningly narrow margin, Virginia—the most important, largest, and most populous state—ratified the Constitution and made the federal government possible.

As fast as he could and at the behest of the convention, printer Augustine Davis published as a broadside the outcome and the final resolution endorsing ratification. Within the week, seven Virginia papers did the same. By mid-July half a dozen out-of-state papers, including in Pennsylvania, New York, and Massachusetts, published excerpts from the day's debates and the ratification resolution.[26]

Inside the New Academy, defeated Anti-Federalists followed Patrick Henry's example. The result was "distressing & awful to great Numbers of very respectable Members." James Madison saw the "keen feeling of their disappointment." But opponents to ratification conducted themselves as quintessential republican citizens. "An acquiescence of the minority can not be in the

Virginia Constitution Ratification Poster. In this 1988 poster commemorating the two-hundredth anniversary of ratification in Virginia, Edmund Randolph stands behind James Madison, who is slaying a shark marked "tyranny." George Mason holds onto Patrick Henry as he tries to lift up a common man. Credit: Picture History least doubted," Madison proudly reported. In fact, outvoted Anti-Federalists quickly "declared themselves firmly attached to the Union, and generously offered their influence in support of the new system."[27]

Federalists acted no less respectfully. There was no rejoicing on their side. "The business was closed with due decorum & solemnity," Madison said. His close friend and erstwhile opponent James Monroe agreed: the vote "was accompanied with no circumstances on the part of the victorious that mark extra exultation." The citizens of Richmond showed remarkable respect for the defeated Anti-Federalists, too. "Either wise enough, or polite enough," one newspaper reported, they refrained from holding parades and public celebrations upon hearing the final outcome.[28]

Why did it turn out this way? The divisions in Virginia between Federalists and Anti-Federalists were too complicated to easily categorize. Traditional explanations offered by historians looking at other states or at national patterns don't really fit.[29] Virginians did not clearly split along generational lines, by how much they were immersed in commercial pursuits, or according to education or past military service. Class divisions were often invoked in the newspapers but not really born out in the final vote. Region definitely mattered, but not as consistently as observers had predicted in March. Ten of the fourteen Kentucky delegates voted against ratification: a large majority but certainly not a consensus. And the Northern Neck of Virginia went strongly Federalist but it was also home to George Mason and William Grayson. There is, then, no convincing way to "map" the Federalist/Anti-Federalist divide in the Old Dominion.

There was, in fact, much that virtually all the delegates at the Virginia Ratification Convention agreed upon from the outset. The Articles were inadequate to meet the country's long-term challenges. Some constitutional changes were necessary. Individual rights were of vital concern. Virginia's future, its influence, its economy, and its racial order, had to be protected. A single consolidated government and a standing army were dangerous. The only acceptable form of government was republican: administered by virtuous, educated citizens seeking to reason together to achieve the common good. By the end of their debates, the delegates had also mostly decided the Constitution warranted important changes, especially regarding citizens' rights.[30]

Of course, on certain specific matters, delegates found no middle ground whatsoever—on the number of representatives in the House, for example, or the length of terms in the Senate. But many of their divisions were nuanced and some were much narrower than the debates suggested. Which changes were essential for stability and which threatened liberty? How should they balance power between the states and central government? How best could they protect citizens' rights? How dire was the current political situation? What choice would secure a bright future?

The partisans, who were evenly divided, knew their answers and how they would vote. The outcome was ultimately determined by a handful of uncommitted delegates who, on 25 June, had to choose a side. They could hold out for amendments, which might jeopardize the union of states, or they could swallow their reservations and vote for the Constitution.

How then to explain their choices and the final vote? James Innes and Zachariah Johnston offer insight. The advocates for ratification had a year's experience answering questions about the Constitution. Starting in Philadelphia, they puzzled through the subtle meanings and speculated about the implications of every part of the federal design. Not everyone was persuaded by their logic, not by a long shot. But the Federalists were almost never caught off guard: every criticism Anti-Federalists leveled brought a detailed reply. The Federalists formed a united front, too, with a single and specific goal: ratify. Their arguments cohered, and they were extremely, some would say cunningly, organized. The newspaper editors sided disproportionately with the Federalists and used their papers to help build enthusiasm for the Constitution. Anti-Federalists raised a long list of powerful and troubling questions about the federal plan, but they were not unified, either in their objections to the Constitution or in their strategy during the debates. They did not agree on what needed to be changed or when. Raising doubts, it turned out, was not enough after all. Aside from some groundwork on amendments, Anti-Federalists offered no specific alternative plan to the Constitution. The Anti-Federalists seemed to play more on men's fears rather than their hopes, and this was a hopeful age. Men still had the audacity to believe they could, as Thomas Paine called them to do in 1776, "begin the world over again." By the spring of 1788, Federalists had momentum on their side nationally. The timing of the Virginia convention worked to their favor, as did the ever-looming presence of George Washington. His endorsement quieted some men's fears about the dangers posed by the Constitution. And the Federalists' remarkable success in convincing convention delegates that the only choice was voting yes or no shaped the outcome, too, as did their persistent warnings about the union fracturing into separate confederacies. In the end, eight Virginia delegates disregarded the clear wishes of their constituents, and two others ignored specific directions to cast their votes in favor of ratification.

Perhaps the most important factor that led to a Federalist victory can be seen in what happened after the vote. Delegates did not go home. Instead, they stayed to work together on amendments to send to the first Congress. On 26–27 June, Federalists modeled the promises they'd made all month about how the new government would work. Many seemed eager to forge some consensus and send a clear message of mutual respect and cooperation—to fulfill in Richmond the republican ideal of reasoning together to achieve the common good. And some were genuinely convinced by the Anti-Federalists about the necessity of guaranteeing citizens' rights. As it turned out, the decision in Philadelphia not to include a bill of rights—a major misstep because of the controversy and opposition that choice provoked—might have actually worked to the Federalists' long-term advantage. The promise of amendments gave them a fallback position and negotiating tool.[31]

Most members of the Virginia convention enjoyed much-deserved rest on 26 June. Delegates did not convene until noon and met only briefly to attend to practical matters: finalizing the wording of their ratification form and paying the doorkeeper, sergeant-at-arms, and other staff. Meanwhile, twenty members, eleven Federalists and nine Anti-Federalists, had no respite. They set to work preparing amendments. George Wythe chaired the group, which intentionally included all the leaders who'd so vehemently disagreed all month: George Mason, Edmund Randolph, Patrick Henry, James Madison, George Nicholas, James Monroe, William Grayson, and John Marshall. Madison was skeptical of the outcome. He wrote both Alexander Hamilton and George Washington that some of the requested amendments were "highly objectionable." But, he confided to Washington, the move to debate them "could not be parried." Patrick Henry was no happier with the results. He thought the whole thing a cynical move on the Federalists' part to lull the opposition. Still, Henry and Madison worked together, as good citizens should.[32]

The committee started from a draft that a group of men led by George Mason had crafted earlier in the month. They followed the example of Massachusetts and South Carolina; both states ratified and formally requested amendments. In the end, Virginia's committee on amendments agreed to forward to the full convention a list of twenty guarantees in a bill of rights and another twenty structural changes. They attached to those amendments a statement directing Virginia's representatives in the first Congress to pursue the changes, according to the guidelines in the Constitution. On 27 June, delegates reconvened and passed Wythe's committee's proposals, including the charge to the state's first senators and representatives: "to exert all their influenceanduseallreasonableandlegalmethodstoobtainaRATIFICATIONoftheforegoing alterations and provisions."[33]

Mindful of their wide influence, delegates then ordered copies of their final resolution and requested amendments to be sent to all the other state legislatures. Never forgetting about history, they also directed the journal of all their proceedings alongside a copy of their ratification form and the requested amendments "to be entered in a well bound book" and deposited in Virginia's state archives.[34]

Only then was their work done. Edmund Pendleton was slow to rise, adjusting his crutches as he started to speak. He called on the delegates, Federalists and Anti-Federalists alike, to take pride in how they had conducted themselves, "to forget the heats of discussion, and remember that each had only done what he deemed to be his duty to his country." "We are brothers, we are Virginians," he reminded everyone. "Our common object is the good of our country." If the men around the room let "our rivalry be who can serve his country with greatest zeal" then, Pendleton believed, "the future would be fortunate and glorious." With that, the Virginia Ratification Convention adjourned for the last time.[35]

Spectators gradually drifted away from the New Academy, and delegates said their last goodbyes. Most were weary and ready to be on their way. They called for their horses and carriages and "were before sunset some miles on their way homeward."[36] As they left Richmond, delegates must have remained apprehensive about what would happen next. Whose fears and whose hopes would come to fruition in the next months and years? What place would Virginia hold in the new United States government? What would become of the convention's proposed amendments? Most delegates were slaveholders, and many owned vast plantations. With all these questions in mind, they made their way home not only to their wives and children but also to the African American men and women and boys and girls they held in perpetual bondage.

At least there was no questioning that part of the future. The Constitution, the Virginians knew, safeguarded that long and terrible tradition.

Not everyone left Richmond right away, however, and not everyone followed Edmund Pendleton's last counsel. Friday evening, as most delegates headed home, George Mason invited a group of Anti-Federalists to discuss drafting an address to give to their constituents, explaining the outcome of the convention. Mason arrived at the gathering with a draft address, the contents of which have never been found. But what he wrote and said was apparently so provocative that Benjamin Harrison, John Tyler, and Patrick Henry—certainly no friends of the federal system—all recoiled.

Since Mason's address is lost to history, we can only speculate about its contents. The men who heard it, perhaps out of respect for Mason or discretion regarding their own presence, never revealed exactly what Mason proposed. But that it was inflammatory cannot be doubted. An anonymous eyewitness to the meeting said George Mason's ideas aimed "to irritate, rather than to quiet the public mind." When Mason finished, "a number of that respectable body immediately withdrew, others for some time either remained in silence, or, in general terms recommended temper and moderation."[37]

Eventually, Benjamin Harrison got up and "in a firm and manly stile opposed not only the address which had been read, but earnestly recommended an adjournment without taking farther steps in the business." Harrison insisted that since the Constitution "had been adopted by a majority of their countrymen it became their duty to submit as good citizens."[38]

Mason read the group's reaction and withdrew his proposal, and the meeting abruptly ended. Within the week, however, a story about that night appeared in the *Virginia Herald*. By the end of July, nine newspapers across the country, including in New York, Massachusetts, and Connecticut, reported on the incident.[39]

The press coverage indicated that George Mason failed to exercise the virtue and self-sacrifice required of good citizens, to say nothing of the restraint expected of southern gentlemen. To be revealed—and reviled—this way damaged Mason's reputation in Virginia and, in time, in history. The story in the *Massachusetts Centinel* charged Mason with trying to promote "a fiery, irritating manifesto" and praised his fellow Anti-Federalists, who, "seeing the serpent in the grass, exposed it, and prevented any thing of the sort taking place." In a Pennsylvania paper, the "good people" of Virginia were likewise praised for being "perfectly reconciled to the determination of its convention." Mason, however, "wished to excite some confusion by a publication addressed to those who were averse to the new government, but he was warmly opposed by the antifederalists, and compelled to relinquish his design."[40]

Even Patrick Henry kept his distance. Years later, friends of Henry insisted that when he heard Mason's plan, Henry proclaimed "he had done his duty strenuously, in opposing the Constitution, in the *proper place*,—and with all the powers he possessed. The question had been fully discussed and settled," and the Anti-Federalists had lost. Their duty as "true and faithful republicans" seemed clear to Patrick Henry, and so, he told everyone, "they had all better go home!"[41]

News about Virginia's ratification of the Constitution flew from Richmond as fast as horses and riders could go. Though they avoided celebrating in Richmond, Federalists couldn't wait to share the outcome of the convention. They were especially eager to get word to their allies in New York and New Hampshire, where delegates were also debating ratification that June. In fact, Federalist leaders in those three states had, at the suggestion of Alexander Hamilton, hired riders to be ready to carry news from their respective conventions. Hamilton told James Madison he would gladly pay the costs if Madison found horses and men in Richmond.[42]

The news left Richmond right away, but it turned out to be only partly right. Virginians believed that theirs was the crucial ninth state to ratify, that with their support the Constitution officially moved from a plan to the law. But they were wrong. That distinction, unbeknownst to the Virginians, went to the small state of New Hampshire.

New Hampshire ratified the Constitution at one o'clock on the afternoon of 21 June. John Langdon, who was both the Federalist in charge of hiring express riders in New Hampshire and the president of the state's convention, immediately wrote his friend Alexander Hamilton, and the horse and rider he hired sped away. Langdon's news reached Hamilton in Poughkeepsie, New York, where the New York Ratification Convention was meeting, seventy-one hours later, at noon on 24 June. At two o'clock in the morning on 25 June a rider left Poughkeepsie bound for New York City, to notify the Confederation Congress. The Confederation Congress received that rider's information at noon on 25 June. When the leaders of the current government of the United States officially recognized that a new government had been created, the Virginians had not yet started their roll call vote. Within the hour, yet another rider left New York City and headed south toward Virginia. He made Philadelphia on 26 June and Baltimore the next day. As the delegates in Richmond concluded the last of their business and made their way home, the express rider crossed the state line into Virginia.[43]

Sometime before dawn on 28 June, the rider from New York City arrived in Alexandria. There he shared the news from New Hampshire and, by chance, met another rider: the one who had left Richmond for New York. In the middle of the night, as the 27th turned to the 28th, these two men were the first to verify, in the town of Alexandria, that both states had ratified the Constitution.

George Washington was actually in Alexandria that very night. He'd gone up from Mount Vernon to celebrate the news of Virginia's ratification at John Wise's tavern. According to a local paper, "the General was met some miles out of town by a party of gentlemen on horseback, and escorted to the tavern." Upon arriving, Washington was greeted by a discharge of cannon. Sometime that night, the revelers at Wise's tavern got the word that New Hampshire had ratified, too, which added to their glee. "This flood of good news," Washington told a relative, "gave, as you will readily conceive, abundant cause for rejoicing." Alexandria was a Federalist town, and the celebration ran for four days. Residents shot off guns and cannon and watched fireworks fill the night skies. They toasted and feasted together all weekend, and on Monday they continued the merriment with another party. This one, Washington added, included "fiddling & Dancing, for the amusement, & benefit of the Ladies."[44]

The folks in Alexandria would have known that, although New Hampshire technically made it official, Virginia made it real. When representatives in the largest and most important state endorsed the Constitution, they gave Americans a new government and a new start.

Alexandria was hardly alone in the days-long revelry. Eager to move forward and gratified for some clarity about their government, most Virginians seemed to want to come together. Towns and cities throughout the state celebrated the resolution of the yearlong ratification contest. As soon as city leaders in Norfolk heard the news, they fired nine cannon, followed by fireworks. In Winchester, citizens threw a parade, capped off with a nine-cannon salute, a bonfire, and, of course, many toasts, including to Washington, Lafayette, and Franklin, as well as to veterans and all "Patrons of Freedom." Across the Chesapeake, Virginians drank toasts in honor of the Constitution,

Revolutionary War heroes, the American economy, the virtuous citizens of the American Republic—nearly anything they could think of that sounded patriotic. In many Virginia towns, the revelry bled right into the Fourth of July.[45]

Celebrations also ran up the eastern seaboard as fast as the horsemen who carried the news: Alexandria to Baltimore to Philadelphia to New York. The express rider made New York City just before three o'clock in the morning on 2 July, but that hour did not slow the revelry. "The bells of the city were set a ringing immediately," the newspapers reported, and ten cannon—for they already knew about New Hampshire—were set off at five o'clock.[46]

Couriers raced from New York City to Boston, hoping to reach the town by the Fourth of July. Levi Pease's stagecoach arrived first, at five o'clock on the afternoon of 4 July. Pease rushed the letters he carried to Governor John Hancock, who immediately told the townspeople. Boston residents were nearing the end of their Independence Day celebration, but then they heard the news from Virginia. The bells of Boston, the newspaper reported, "were set to ringing, and the guns to firing again, without any mercy." Bostonians lit candles and paraded through the streets amid fireworks and huzzas.[47]

Within three weeks, word of Virginia ratifying reached every corner of the country, from Portland, Maine, to Savannah, Georgia, to Fort Harmar in the Northwest Territory.

As they paraded and toasted, many Americans seemed grateful to put the partisan turmoil of the past year behind them. It helped that ratification rather quickly got linked to the Fourth of July. In newspapers and private letters, supporters of the Constitution generally sought reconciliation and affirmed Anti-Federalists' civic virtue. One Winchester paper, for example, praised the "magnanimity and disinterested patriotism" that characterized all the Virginia convention delegates and expressed confidence that "the minority will reconcile themselves" to the Constitution "with their usual love of their country." At the combined Fourth of July and ratification celebration in Portsmouth, "The joyful spirit of Republicanism pervaded every breast" and "the utmost harmony and good order was preserved through the day."[48]

Efforts to come together as a unified group continued apace all summer. Formerly divided Virginians joined in this zeal for harmony; honoring all the framers of the Constitution, advocates and critics alike, offered them a way to build that desired sense of unity. One orator, who later published his speech in a Norfolk newspaper, called on Virginians to "embrace this and every future opportunity to entwine the wreath of praise around the venerable brow of the framers of this government." Those framers included the critics of the Constitution, "among whom," the orator proclaimed, "were many great and good men distinguished by learning and integrity." He went so far as to argue that "the virtue which prompted the exertions of the opposers, will induce them to support and guard, as a sacred deposit, this system." If they stood together, he declared, Americans held "the brightest prospect of erecting an empire of justice and morality, which has ever been exhibited on the political theatre of the world."[49]

But as George Mason revealed before ever leaving Richmond, not every Anti-Federalist was so eager to drop principles for promises of harmony. Richard Henry Lee for one was shocked at the final vote in Richmond and at the future Americans had chosen, by their own free will. " 'Tis really astonishing," he wrote a friend, "that the same people who have just emerged from a long & cruel war in defence of liberty, should now agree to fix an elective despotism upon themselves & their posterity!"[50]

Not every newspaper conflated Independence Day with ratification either. Editors of the *Virginia Gazette and Independent Chronicle*, for example, printed an "Obituary for Constitutional Liberty" upon hearing about the Richmond vote. "Just departed this life in the bloom of Youth, our much admired and dearlybelovedFriend,CONSTUTUTIONALLIBERTY," thepaperproclaimed.Theeulogylamentedhow "the enemy . . . turned their cannon on him, no less than 89 heavy brass pieces, incessantly playing upon his flanks and center" while 79 of his "brother officers" looked on with "anguish, pity, rage, fear, terror, fury."

Thepaperevenprovidedanepitaph: "Hereliestheblessedbodyofour CONSTITUTIONALLIBERTY in hopes of glorious resurrection." The funeral procession leading to the burial of liberty, the eulogy said, included "Public integrity, Virtue, Friendship, and every domestic smile." Trial by jury, freedom of the press, and freedom of religion numbered among the pall bearers. And "the solemn scene was closed by the Goddess Liberty shedding tears for the loss of her departed Hero."[51]

Tellingly, even such hyperbolic language did not spark among Virginians any uprising to resist ratification. Anti-Federalists made a critical choice in the summer of 1788. They accepted defeat over the vote but refused to surrender their commitment to reconciling the Constitution to their republican values. Like Patrick Henry, they resolved to change the new government "so as to be compatible with the safety, liberty and happiness of the people." Over the coming months and years, Virginians worked consistently and imaginatively to rein in federal powers and protect citizens' liberty—but always within the political system and the bounds of law. They would not "go to violence" in pursuit of their vision of the American Republic.[52]

Even as he celebrated his triumph, James Madison understood that struggles over the Constitution would not end any time soon. "My conjecture," he told Alexander Hamilton, "is that exertions will be made . . . in the task of regularly undermining the government." But such opposition, he also understood, would respect the laws established by the Constitution. Madison was thus relieved to write Thomas Jefferson that "it may be safely concluded that no irregular opposition to the System will follow" in the state of Virginia.[53] And none did.

The Fourth of July 1788 was a joyful time at Mount Vernon. George Washington returned from the celebrations at Alexandria gratified to see another trial behind him. Congratulations poured in all week, from all over the country. Some writers added to their well wishes the hope of soon seeing Washington "at the head of the American Government."[54]

For now, though, the citizen and planter George Washington tended to his many business interests: coordinating navigation improvements on the Potomac River, negotiating the price of shingles to renovate parts of his prized estate, and, as he did nearly every day, riding out to check on his various plantations. On the Fourth it rained off and on nearly all day. It was, Washington recorded in his diary, too wet to make much progress on reaping the rye, so "the People"—the scores of African Americans forced to work in his fields—spent the day weeding peas and carrots. The Fourth merited no celebration in their quarters of Mount Vernon, for they remained excluded from the republic that their labor built and enslaved by the celebrated "father" of a country ostensibly conceived in liberty.[55]

George Washington had urged James Madison to spend a few days of well-earned leisure at Mount Vernon, and a happy if exhausted Madison arrived on the afternoon of the Fourth. The two friends shared several gratifying days of visiting with doubtless not a little preparation for the future. Soon, they knew, it would be time to make their plans for the American Republic a reality.

Madison stayed at Mount Vernon until 7 July, when he headed back to New York. John Jay and Alexander Hamilton were still fighting for ratification in that state. News of Virginia's support buoyed their cause at the deeply divided Poughkeepsie convention. "The constitution constantly gains advocates among the People," Jay assured Washington, "and its Enemies in the Convention seem to be much embarrassed." Virginia's choice put terrific pressure on New York delegates. That pressure soon split the Anti-Federalist majority into two factions: those willing to accept requested amendments and those determined to hold out for conditional amendments. George Washington predicted that New York would soon fall in line behind Virginia. Practicality made that inevitable: "The point in debate has, at least, shifted from policy to expediency." It took several more weeks to convince the majority to accept the idea of recommending amendments, but the force of Virginia swayed just enough New York delegates to that point of view. On 26 July, New York became the eleventh state to ratify, though by a very slim margin: 30-27.[56]

As the summer weeks passed along, George Washington remained heartened by the "spirit of harmony" that seemed to continue "among the large and respectable minority." But, like James Madison, he was also clear-eyed. Both men knew that opponents to the Constitution, though peaceful, were not persuaded. They did not seem likely to relent in their principled pursuit of citizens' liberties.[57]

When Washington reflected on Virginia's momentous summer of 1788 in a letter to Thomas Jefferson, he wrote: "It is nearly impossible for any body who has not been on the Spot to conceive (from any description) what the delicacy and danger of our situation have been." He knew he could not fully capture the drama Jefferson had missed. "Though the peril is not passed entirely," he added, "thank God! The prospect is somewhat brightening."[58]

As he looked toward America's future, inextricably bound up with his own, George Washington knew unprecedented challenges lay ahead. Still, he felt confident that both he and the United States were ready to meet those trials. "By folly & misconduct (proceeding from a variety of causes) we may now & then get bewildered," he knew, "but I hope, and trust, that there is good sense and virtue enough left to bring us back into the right way before we shall be entirely lost."[59]

epilogue

The preservation of the sacred fire of liberty, and the destiny of the republican model of government, are justly considered as deeply, perhaps as finally staked, on the experiment entrusted to the hands of the American people.

President George Washington, 30 April 1789

CRITICS OF THE CONSTITUTION may have lost the ratification vote in June, but the struggle over the character of the American Republic was far from over. Virginia's state legislature reconvened on 20 October 1788, and Patrick Henry lost no time in following through on his pledge to see the federal government "changed so as to be compatible with the safety, liberty and happiness of the people."[1] Former Anti-Federalists still dominated the House of Delegates, and under Henry's firm guidance they made the most of the rich opportunities before them. State legislators needed to appoint two senators and map out congressional districts for the ten Virginians to be popularly elected to the House of Representatives. Henry wanted to advantage the opponents to strong federal powers, and he was particularly determined to thwart his archrival, James Madison.

Former Federalists wanted James Madison in the first Congress, preferably in the more powerful Senate. But Patrick Henry would not hear of it. When Madison's name was raised as a possible Senate candidate, Henry openly condemned the idea. Madison opposed amendments, Henry proclaimed, which put him at odds with the great majority of Virginians and disqualified him from getting the appointment. The Virginia legislature chose instead Richard Henry Lee and William Grayson—two stronger opponents to federal powers they could not have found. Lee lobbied with his friends in the legislature for the Senate appointment expressly so that he could ensure the passage of Virginia's requested amendments. Once chosen, he confirmed his priorities. "I assure you," he wrote Patrick Henry from New York City (the temporary home of the federal government), that passing amendments to protect civil liberties was "the sole reason that could have influenced me to come here."[2]

Not satisfied with denying James Madison a place in the Senate, Patrick Henry worked to keep Madison out of the House of Representatives, too. Before the term "gerrymandering" was even invented, Henry made sure the state legislature drew districts that helped candidates who shared his views—especially in the part of Virginia where Madison would have to campaign.

Finally, Patrick Henry pushed the Virginia legislature to pass a formal request for a second Constitutional Convention to debate amendments. In sum, he did everything he could to ensure that ideas advanced by Anti-Federalists —about state powers, decentralized authority, and citizens' rights—remained at the forefront of US politics.[3]

James Madison, of course, wanted to serve in the new federal government he had essentially designed. To do so, however, he found he had to hit the campaign trail in the winter of 1788–89. Not only had Patrick Henry drawn the congressional district lines to Madison's disadvantage, but he also convinced James Monroe to challenge Madison in the fifth district. Madison eventually prevailed over Henry's designs and defeated Monroe, but only after he made a campaign promise to pursue a federal bill of rights if elected.[4]

True to his word, Madison did just that, despite the fact that, nationwide, strong supporters of the Constitution carried a majority of congressional elections, and there was little political enthusiasm in the first Congress for debating amendments—certainly not early in the first session. The work before the Congress seemed endless: establish procedures and rules for themselves, approve a system for generating revenue, create a cabinet for the president, figure out how to pay war debts, select a permanent location for the federal city, and pass a litany of laws "necessary and proper" to their constitutional duties. Now, James Madison wanted to add the divisive and time-consuming matter of amendments. Despite opposition from varied corners, Madison used his considerable political clout to push for amendments to the Constitution, many along the lines offered up by the Virginia Ratification Convention in June 1788.

The result of Madison's efforts met with disdain in many quarters. George Mason called the twelve amendments drafted in Congress "a farce." Mason lived for four years after the summer of 1788. During that time he refused every position offered him in the federal government and never indicated that he gave the Constitution his blessing—even after the passage of the Bill of Rights.[5] Other former Anti-Federalists made a different choice: to serve in the federal government to advance their vision of the new United States.

Richard Henry Lee accepted a US Senate appointment, though he ultimately shared Mason's disappointment over the amendments passed under James Madison's leadership. He told Patrick Henry that the proposed twelve amendments sent to the states for debate in late September 1789 fell "far short of the wishes of our convention." As Lee had predicted all along, the whole idea of subsequent amendments turned out to be "little better than putting oneself to death first, in expectation that the doctor, who wished our destruction, would afterwards restore us to life."[6]

When Lee and William Grayson sent the text of the proposed amendments to the House of Delegates in 1789, they included an effusive apology for not being able to do more to secure the meaningful changes to the Constitution that so many Virginians desired. It was impossible, they wrote, not to feel "apprehensive for civil liberty."[7]

As Congress's amendments worked their way through the long ratification process—ten states needed to approve each proposed change for the amendments to become law—the idea of a second Constitutional Convention lost steam. The first two proposed amendments, altering the number of representatives in Congress and prohibiting pay raises for congressmen before the next election cycle, ultimately fell short. So, what had been the third proposed amendment from Congress—freedom of religion, of speech, of the press, to assemble, and to petition government—moved up to first. Ratification of these ten amendments took nearly two years. The Bill of Rights became law in late 1791, after a contentious and polarized debate in the crucial tenth state: where else but Virginia.[8]

Often forgotten when modern-day Americans look with reverence to the Bill of Rights is the fact that their most treasured liberties were revisions forced by critics of the original design of the Constitution.

The fears Virginians often voiced during the long ratification contest that the Constitution would allow northern domination of southern interests turned out to be entirely misplaced. It was a Virginia dynasty of power that emerged in the early national era. To no one's surprise, George Washington became the unanimous choice for first president of the United States, and he accepted the call to service. When he retired after two terms, his vice president, John Adams, succeeded him for a single term, before being defeated by Thomas Jefferson in the nation's first contested presidential election. James Madison followed Jefferson, and James Monroe followed Madison. Four of the first five presidents, then, leading the nation for thirty-two of its first thirty-six years, hailed from the Old Dominion.

It was not only within the executive branch that the Virginians held more than their share of power. James Madison played the central role in shaping the traditions of Congress. Edmund Randolph was the first attorney general. John Marshall took the lead in defining the federal judiciary, and he still remains the longest-serving Supreme Court chief justice in US history—a thirty-four-year tenure. Virginians fairly monopolized leadership of the State Department in the early national era. Thomas Jefferson, Edmund Randolph, Charles Lee, John Marshall, James Madison, and James Monroe all held that office. By the 1810s, marvel at the talents of the Virginians turned to envy and frustration. Politicians even floated the idea of a constitutional amendment to "wrest the sovereignty of the union out of the hands" of Virginians.[9]

Exercising all that power was far from easy, however, for these Virginians found themselves, yet again, at the forefront of contending visions of the American Republic. James Madison was George Washington's close friend and most trusted political adviser in the first years of his presidency, and Thomas Jefferson, another firm friend and admirer of Washington, came home from Paris and served as his secretary of state. But during Washington's second term, Madison and Jefferson became political rivals to Washington and launched an opposition movement to counter his leadership. The "Republicans" began openly challenging Washington's "Federalist" policies. (Though the word is the same, the Federalist faction in the 1790s was not connected to the Federalist position on ratification in 1787–88, as Madison's leadership of the Republican faction demonstrates.) Republican leaders also privately gossiped that President Washington had become a doddering old man, manipulated by the machinations of Alexander Hamilton. As an indicator of the shifting loyalties of the 1790s, Madison's former close ally Hamilton became his estranged opponent and Washington's closest adviser. Washington and Madison stopped speaking; Washington retired in 1797, and the two men never communicated again.[10]

Virginians Thomas Jefferson and James Madison thus led the creation of what historians call the first party system: two political factions, the Federalists and the Republicans, fighting for public opinion, power, and principles. The divide centered on a host of questions implicit and unanswered in the Constitution. Where was the line between state and federal authorities? How much power could the president and the Congress justly exercise? What foreign policy should be pursued? How much fiscal authority should the federal government wield? How should revenue be raised? What economic policies should the government adopt?

These debates and controversies centered on constitutional issues—a lasting legacy of 1787–88. Indeed nearly all of the political debates in the early national and antebellum eras were framed in constitutional terms. The high stakes made advocates all the more resolved to prevail. As they tried to convince voters that they had the right answers to important constitutional questions, both Republicans and Federalists disavowed political parties as destructive to republican government. They were not partisans, each side insisted, but, again reminiscent of 1787–88, the only true patriots.[11] To spread that word and their respective agendas, they turned to America's activist press. Partisan newspapermen working as operatives for each side gave their readers a familiar warning: the opposition was plotting to destroy America's future. From the example of the Anti-Federalists during the ratification debates in particular, leaders of the two factions saw a new model of legitimate dissent. Citizens could fiercely disagree about the fundamental nature of their government without inviting anarchy. Federalists and Republicans borrowed from the fiery rhetoric of 1787–88, too. For example, Alexander Hamilton condemned Thomas Jefferson and James Madison for heading up a disloyal campaign "subversive of the principles of good government and dangerous to the union, peace and happiness of the Country." Jefferson blasted Hamilton for advocating policies built on "principles adverse to liberty" and "calculated to undermine and abolish the republic." Such accusations sounded very familiar to veterans of the ratification contest.[12]

As the last members of the founding generation retired from public life and the Virginia dynasty faded away, a new generation of leaders took to the national stage. In the 1820s, southern politicians revived and distorted the states' rights concerns of Anti-Federalists, concentrated now on a new and relentless proslavery ideology. As most of the rest of the Western world rejected slavery, southern states doubled down. Gone were the admissions among eighteenth-century slaveholders that slavery was immoral and irreconcilable with their republican principles; gone was the expectation that slavery would eventually wither away. The southern way of life, many antebellum leaders bragged, was distinct from and superior to the rest of the country *because* of racial slavery. Nothing, they insisted, and certainly not the federal government, would compel them to part with it. For decades proslavery leaders like James Henry Hammond and Edmund Ruffin stoked regional loyalties and threatened disunion. After the election of Abraham Lincoln, they made good on those threats. In 1860–61, southern politicians made the fear of 1787–88—that separate, regional confederacies would destroy the American Republic—their plan. Secessionists set about intentionally creating a southern confederacy, dedicated to protecting one state right: the right to racial slavery. Abandoning the example of the Anti-Federalists, they decided to "go to violence." At least 620,000 men laid down their lives in the resulting Civil War to finally answer questions raised at the very creation of the Constitution: the Union was perpetual and inviolable, slavery could not exist in the American Republic, and the United States would endure.

The ratification debates of 1787–88 marked a new start in American political life in a myriad of ways: a new federal government, a new way of imagining the union of states, a new way of calculating the balance between liberty and power, a new understanding of representation and of sovereignty, and a new constitutional framework for political debates. Today, Americans often look back with longing to the accomplishments of the founding generation and worry that we have somehow betrayed that precious legacy. But a deeper understanding of the messy way the Constitution actually got created reveals, for better or worse, abiding connections between the eighteenth century and the twenty-first. We see it every day: in Americans' chronic frustration with and yet reelection of their senators and representatives, their ideologically selective condemnation of judicial activism, the close divide in the popular vote of most presidential elections; and the contradictory fears about federal overreach and gridlock. Advocates on both ends of the political spectrum are still sure that they alone are standing on the side of justice and virtue and that their opponents are wrecking the country. But that is the genius of the American system, too. Intentionally or not, the founding generation created a Constitution inherently, inevitably contestable. James Madison knew that was all part of the "life and validity" breathed into the federal plan "by the voice of the people, speaking through the several state conventions." The most difficult questions are unanswered—maybe unanswerable—and left for each generation to confront. "We the people" are still trying to form "a more perfect union," still, as Patrick Henry saw so long ago, "wandering on the great ocean of human affairs" and looking for landmarks to guide us.[13] Thankfully, they set for us a model of and mechanism for peacefully resolving our sometimes bitter and seemingly impossible disagreements. Every generation can only do—and must do—what the founding generation did: debate, vote, and decide together the fate of our American Republic.

Acknowledgments

It was a privilege to work again with Robert J. Brugger, as he comes to the close of a tremendous career at Johns Hopkins University Press. I am grateful he suggested I work on a contribution to the Witness to History series and for everything he did to see this book to fruition.

Members of the Missouri Regional Seminar on Early American History offered excellent advice on an early draft of the first chapter. Daniel Mandell, who authored a book in this series, provided invaluable insight, and the conversation at the workshop was inspirational and influential. Todd Estes generously read the entire manuscript and gave me much-needed encouragement and the benefit of his deep expertise. Matt Schoenbachler improves everything I write, and this book bears the mark of his long friendship. Colleagues in the History Department at Saint Louis University thoughtfully read and discussed various parts of the project at various stages. Special thanks go to Luke Yarbrough, Jennifer Popiel, and Torrie Hester. Ivy Farr McIntyre and Idolina Hernandez provided terrific research assistance as well as advice on revisions. Generous funding for the project—and the time to pursue it—came from the College of Arts and Sciences at Saint Louis University.

I am deeply grateful for the close attention of the anonymous reader and the perceptive recommendations offered, as well as for the work of everyone at Johns Hopkins University Press. As always, Dan Smith read and encouraged far more than I deserve. He did not think it at all strange that I spent one June reading the convention debates in "real time." And he never tired of hearing about the Virginians' exploits—or at least he never let it show.

Anyone working on the founding era owes an immeasurable debt to the State Historical Society of Wisconsin and the editorial team that created *The Documentary History of the Ratification of the Constitution*. Their remarkable work enables modern-day readers to access the eighteenth-century debates about the creation of the Constitution, to bear witness to one of the most enthralling, dramatic, and important moments in all of American history.

Notes

Prologue

1. George Lee Turberville to Arthur Lee, 28 October 1787, in John P. Kaminski et al., eds., *The Documentary History of the Ratification of the Constitution*, Virginia, 3 vols. (Madison: State Historical Society of Wisconsin, 1988–93), 1:127 (first quotation). The Virginia materials are consecutively numbered across the three volumes, and hereinafter the volume is not given, only *DHRC* and the page number. Hugh Blair Grigsby, *The History of the Virginia Federal Convention of 1788: with some account of eminent Virginians of that era who were members of the body*, with a biographical sketch of the author and illustrative notes edited by R. A. Brock, 2 vols. (Richmond: Virginia Historical Society, 1890–91), 1:31–32 (second quotation).

2. Bushrod Washington to George Washington, 7 June 1788, *DHRC*, 1581; Theodorick Bland to Arthur Lee, 13 June 1788, *DHRC*, 1617.

3. James Madison, 24 June 1788, *DHRC*, 1500–1501.

4. For James Madison, see Lance Banning, *The Sacred Fire of Liberty: James Madison and the Founding of the Federal Republic* (Ithaca, NY: Cornell University Press, 1995); Drew R. McCoy, *The Last of the Fathers: James Madison and the Republican Legacy* (Cambridge: Cambridge University Press, 1989); Jack N. Rakove, *James Madison and the Creation of the American Republic*, 3rd ed. (New York: Pearson, 2007). For Madison's role in the Constitution, see especially Richard Labunski, *James Madison and the Struggle for the Bill of Rights* (New York: Oxford University Press, 2006); Jack N. Rakove, *Original Meanings: Politics and Ideas in the Making of the Constitution* (New York: Knopf, 1996); Jack Rakove, *Revolutionaries: A New History of the Invention of America* (Boston: Houghton Mifflin Harcourt, 2010), chap. 8.

5. For Patrick Henry, see Richard R. Beeman, *Patrick Henry: A Biography* (New York: McGraw Hill, 1974); Kevin J. Hayes, *The Mind of a Patriot: Patrick Henry and the World of Ideas* (Charlottesville: University of Virginia Press, 2008); Henry Mayer, *A Son of Thunder: Patrick Henry and the American Republic* (New York: Franklin Watts, 1986); David A. McCants, *Patrick Henry, the Orator* (Westport, CT: Greenwood Press, 1990).

6. Patrick Henry, 20 June 1788, *DHRC*, 1425; Patrick Henry, 5 June 1788, *DHRC*, 959; Patrick Henry, 24 June 1788, *DHRC*, 1506. For republicanism, see especially Gordon S. Wood, *The Creation of the American Republic, 1776–1787* (Chapel Hill: University of North Carolina Press, 1969).

7. Patrick Henry, 24 June 1788, *DHRC*, 1506. Henry's son-in-law Spencer Roane had a similar recollection as Stuart, far more graphic than the one recorded by David Robertson. See Spencer Roane Memorandum, undated, in George Morgan, *The True Patrick Henry* (Philadelphia: J. B. Lippincott, 1907), 447.

8. For ratification, see especially Pauline Maier, *Ratification: The People Debate the Constitution, 1787–1788* (New York: Simon & Schuster, 2010); Jürgen Heideking, *The Constitution before the Judgment Seat: The Prehistory and Ratification of the American Constitution, 1787–1791*, ed. John P. Kaminski and Richard Leffler (Charlottesville: University of Virginia Press, 2012).

9. For Washington's influence, see Ron Chernow, *Washington: A Life* (New York: Penguin, 2010); Don Higginbotham, *George Washington: Uniting a Nation* (Lanham, MD: Rowman & Littlefield, 2002); Paul K. Longmore, *The Invention of George Washington* (Berkeley: University of California Press, 1989).

10. The best overview of the Philadelphia Convention is Richard Beeman, *Plain, Honest Men: The Making of the American Constitution* (New York: Random House, 2009). For historiographical debates, see James H. Huston, "The Creation of the Constitution: Scholarship at a Standstill," *Reviews in American History* 12 (1984): 463–77.

11. James Madison in Congress, 6 April 1796, in William T. Hutchinson et al., eds., *The Papers of James Madison, Congressional Series*, 17 vols. (Chicago: University of Chicago Press, 1962–77, vols. 1–10; Charlottesville: University Press of Virginia, 1977–91, vols. 11–17), 16:295–96.

12. See, for example, Saul Cornell, *The Other Founders: Anti-Federalism and the Dissenting Tradition in America, 1788–1828* (Chapel Hill: University of North Carolina Press, 1999); Woody Holton, *Unruly Americans and the Origins of the Constitution* (New York: Hill and Wang, 2007); Jackson Turner Main, *The Anti-Federalists: Critics of the Constitution, 1781–1788* (Chapel Hill: University of North Carolina Press, 1961).

13. "Brutus," *Virginia Journal*, 22 November 1787, *DHRC*, 174.

14. James Madison to Edmund Pendleton, 21 February 1788, *DHRC*, 398.

15. The first volume appeared in 1976, and the project is ongoing.

16. The mammoth papers of George Washington and James Madison are now digitally available through the National Archives at www.founders.archives.gov.

17. David Robertson, *Debates and Other Proceedings of the Convention of Virginia* (Petersburg, VA: Hunter and Prentiss, 1788–89). The debate transcripts are also available through Grigsby, *History of the Virginia Federal Convention*, and *DHRC*. Robertson quoted in *DHRC*, 905.

18. Examples of these debates include Lance Banning, "Virginia: Sectionalism and the General Good," in Michael Allen Gillespie and Michael Lienesch, eds., *Ratifying the Constitution* (Lawrence: University Press of Kansas, 1989), 261–99; Banning, *Sacred Fire of Liberty*, especially 261–64; Richard E. Ellis, "The Persistence of Antifederalism after 1789," in Richard Beeman, Stephen Botein, and Edward C. Carter II, eds., *Beyond Confederation: Origins of the Constitution and American National Identity* (Chapel Hill: University of North Carolina Press, 1987), 299–300; Heideking, *The Constitution before the Judgment Seat*, 271–72; James H. Huston, "Country, Court,

and Constitution: Antifederalism and the Historians," *William and Mary Quarterly* 38 (1981): 337–68; Cecelia M. Kenyon, "Men of Little Faith: The Anti-Federalists on the Nature of Representative Government," *William and Mary Quarterly* 12 (1955): 3–43; Jon Kukla, "A Spectrum of Sentiments: Virginia's Federalists, Antifederalists, and 'Federalists Who Are for Amendments,' 1787–1788," *Virginia Magazine of History and Biography* 96 (1988): 277–96; Maier, *Ratification*, 268–69; Main, *The Anti-Federalists*; Norman Risjord, "Virginians and the Constitution: A Multi-variant Analysis," *William and Mary Quarterly* 31 (1974): 613–32; Robert E. Thomas, "The Virginia Convention of 1788," *Journal of Southern History* 19 (1953): 63–72. Most recently, scholars have considered the larger, international context of ratification, including foreign policy considerations and state formation. See Max M. Edling, *A Revolution in Favor of Government: Origins of the U.S. Constitution and the Making of the American State* (New York: Oxford University Press, 2004); David C. Hendrickson, *Peace Pact: The Lost World of the American Founding* (Lawrence: University Press of Kansas, 2003); Robert W. Smith, "Foreign Affairs and the Ratification of the Constitution in Virginia," *Virginia Magazine of History and Biography* 122 (2014): 41–63.

19. "A Planter," *Virginia Independent Chronicle*, 13 February 1788, *DHRC*, 565.

CHAPTER ONE: Fall 1787, First Reactions

1. George Mason to George Washington, 2 April 1776, in Robert A. Rutland, ed., *The Papers of George Mason, 1725–1792*, 3 vols. (Chapel Hill: University of North Carolina Press, 1970), 1:267; George Washington to Lafayette, 1 February 1784, in W. W. Abbot, ed., *The Papers of George Washington (Confederation Series)*, 6 vols. (Charlottesville: University of Virginia Press, 1992–97), 1:87–88. See also Peter R. Henriques, "An Uneven Friendship: The Relationship between George Washington and George Mason," *Virginia Magazine of History and Biography* 97 (1989): 185–204.

2. George Mason to George Mason Jr., 1 June 1787, *Papers of George Mason*, 3:892–93.

3. George Washington to Lafayette, 7 February 1788, *DHRC*, 355.

4. James Madison, Notes on the Constitutional Convention, 31 August 1787, in Jonathan Elliot, ed., *The Debates in the Several State Conventions, on the Adoption of the Federal Constitution*, 5 vols. (Philadelphia: J. B. Lippincott, 1901), 5:502; James Madison to Thomas Jefferson, 24 October–1 November 1787, *DHRC*, 106. For Mason's Anti-Federalism, see also Peter Wallenstein, "Flawed Keepers of the Flame: The Interpreters of George Mason," *Virginia Magazine of History and Biography* 102 (1994): especially 238–42; Jeff Broadwater, *George Mason, Forgotten Founder* (Chapel Hill: University of North Carolina Press, 2006), especially 206–15; Saul Cornell, *The Other Founders: Anti-Federalism and the Dissenting Tradition in America, 1788–1828* (Chapel Hill: University of North Carolina Press, 1999), chap. 2; Brent Tarter, "George Mason and the Conservation of Liberty," *Virginia Magazine of History and Biography* 99 (1991): 279–304.

5. *DHRC*, xxxvii–xxxix. For matters of sovereignty, see David C. Hendrickson,

Peace Pact: The Lost World of the American Founding (Lawrence: University Press of Kansas, 2003), especially 220–21.

6. Hugh Blair Grigsby, *The History of the Virginia Federal Convention of 1788: with some account of eminent Virginians of that era who were members of the body*, with a biographical sketch of the author and illustrative notes edited by R. A. Brock, 2 vols. (Richmond: Virginia Historical Society, 1890–91), 1:32, n. 36; James M. Elson, ed., *Patrick Henry in His Speeches and Writings and in the Words of His Contemporaries* (Lynchburg, VA: Warwick House Publishers, 2007), 116.

7. For Madison and Washington's relationship, see Stuart Leibiger, *Founding Friendship: George Washington, James Madison, and the Creation of the American Republic* (Charlottesville: University Press of Virginia, 1999).

8. George Washington to David Stuart, 1 July 1787, *Papers of George Washington (Confederation)*, 5:240.

9. James Madison, "Vices of the Political System of the United States," April 1787, in William T. Hutchinson et al., eds., *The Papers of James Madison, Congressional Series*, 17 vols. (Chicago: University of Chicago Press, 1962–77, vols. 1–10; Charlottesville: University Press of Virginia, 1977–91, vols. 11–17), 9:348–58. For Madison's political views and influence, see Lance Banning, *The Sacred Fire of Liberty: James Madison and the Founding of the Federal Republic* (Ithaca, NY: Cornell University Press, 1995); Richard Labunski, *James Madison and the Struggle for the Bill of Rights* (New York: Oxford University Press, 2006); Drew R. McCoy, *The Last of the Fathers: James Madison and the Republican Legacy* (Cambridge: Cambridge University Press, 1989); Jack N. Rakove, *James Madison and the Creation of the American Republic*, 3rd ed. (New York: Pearson, 2007); Jack N. Rakove, *Original Meanings: Politics and Ideas in the Making of the Constitution* (New York: Knopf, 1996), especially chap. 3.

10. For the best overview of the debates in Philadelphia, see Richard Beeman, *Plain, Honest Men: The Making of the American Constitution* (New York: Random House, 2009). For the ideas behind the Constitution, see especially Gordon S. Wood, *The Creation of the American Republic, 1776–1787* (Chapel Hill: University of North Carolina Press, 1969), chaps. 12–13.

11. James Madison to Edmund Pendleton, 20 September 1787, *DHRC*, 13. For the atypicality of this consensus and compromise model, see Hendrickson, *Peace Pact*, 251.

12. James McClurg to James Madison, 5 August 1787, Library of Congress, Manuscript Division.

13. George Mason to John Mason, 13 March 1789, *Papers of George Mason*, 3:1142; George Mason, "Objections to the Constitution of Government Formed by the Convention," *DHRC*, 45 (last quotation).

14. Max Farrand, ed., *The Records of the Federal Convention of 1787*, 4 vols. (repr., New Haven, CT: Yale University Press, 1966), 2:646. For Randolph, see also Kevin R. C. Gutzman, "Edmund Randolph and Virginia Constitutionalism," *Review of Politics* 66 (2004): 469–97; John J. Reardon, *Edmund Randolph: A Biography* (New York: Macmillan, 1975); Banning, *Sacred Fire of Liberty*, 246–63.

15. Grigsby, *History of the Virginia Federal Convention*, 1:83 (on Randolph's appearance); Martin Oster to Comte de la Luzerne, 4 February 1788, *DHRC*, 344; John Randolph quoted in Broadwater, *George Mason*, 229.

16. Madison, Notes on the Constitutional Convention, *DHRC*, 11.

17. *Records of the Federal Convention of 1787*, 2:645–46. For Randolph reflecting the political culture of the era, see William E. Nelson, "Reason and Compromise in the Establishment of the Federal Constitution," *William and Mary Quarterly* 44 (1987): 458–84.

18. Richard Henry Lee to Samuel Adams, 27 October 1787, in Richard H. Lee, ed., *Memoir of the Life of Richard Henry Lee, and His Correspondence with the most distinguished men in America and Europe, illustrative of their characters, and of the events of the American Revolution*, 2 vols. (Philadelphia: H. C. Carey and I. Lea, 1825), 2:82. For the Lee family, see Paul C. Nagel, *The Lees of Virginia: Seven Generations of an American Family* (New York: Oxford University Press, 1990).

19. Richard Henry Lee to Samuel Adams, 27 October 1787, *Memoir of the Life of Richard Henry Lee*, 2:82 (quotation); Beeman, *Plain, Honest Men*, 371.

20. Richard Henry Lee to George Mason, 1 October 1787, *DHRC*, 28.

21. Beeman, *Plain, Honest Men*, 371–73; Rakove, *Original Meanings*, 108–10; Articles of Confederation; Congressional Resolution, 21 February 1787, in *Journals of the Continental Congress, 1774–1789*, 34 vols., ed. Worthington C. Ford et al. (Washington, DC: Government Printing Office, 1904–37), 32:74 (quotation).

22. Richard Henry Lee to George Mason, 1 October 1787, *DHRC*, 28.

23. Richard Henry Lee to George Mason, 1 October 1787, *DHRC*, 29; George Washington to James Madison, 10 October 1787, *DHRC*, 49.

24. Richard Henry Lee to George Mason, 1 October 1787, *DHRC*, 29.

25. For ratification, see especially Pauline Maier, *Ratification: The People Debate the Constitution, 1787–1788* (New York: Simon & Schuster, 2010); Jürgen Heideking, *The Constitution before the Judgment Seat: The Prehistory and Ratification of the American Constitution, 1787–1791*, ed. John P. Kaminski and Richard Leffler (Charlottesville: University of Virginia Press, 2012).

26. George Mason to George Washington, 7 October 1787, *DHRC*, 43; *DHRC*, 16, n. 2.

27. Matthew Maury to James Maury, 10 December 1787, *DHRC*, 228 (regarding Fredericksburg); James Madison to Thomas Jefferson, 24 October–1 November 1787, *DHRC*, 107.

28. Franklin quoted in Beeman, *Plain, Honest Men*, 361; US Constitution, 17 September 1787.

29. James Madison to Thomas Jefferson, 24 October–1 November 1787, *DHRC*, 106.

30. George Mason, "Objections to the Constitution of Government Formed by the Convention," *DHRC*, 43–46. This document was eventually circulated across America. For analysis, see Cornell, *The Other Founders*, chap. 2; Tarter, "George Mason and the Conservation of Liberty."

31. For the influence of these men in particular and Anti-Federalism generally, see Cornell, *The Other Founders*. See also Cecelia M. Kenyon, "Men of Little Faith: The Anti-Federalists on the Nature of Representative Government," *William and Mary Quarterly* 12 (1955): 3–43; Jackson Turner Main, *The Anti-Federalists: Critics of the Constitution, 1781–1788* (Chapel Hill: University of North Carolina Press, 1961).

32. George Washington to Patrick Henry, George Washington to Benjamin Harrison, George Washington to Thomas Nelson Jr., 24 September 1787, *DHRC*, 15. For the importance of such private correspondence in the ratification controversy, see Heideking, *The Constitution before the Judgment Seat*, 94–104.

33. Alexander Donald to Thomas Jefferson, 12 November 1787, *DHRC*, 155.

34. For Virginia's political culture, see especially Richard R. Beeman, *The Old Dominion in the New Nation, 1788–1801* (Lexington: University Press of Kentucky, 1972); Charles Sydnor, *Gentlemen Freeholders: Political Practices in Washington's Virginia* (Chapel Hill: University of North Carolina Press, 1952); Brent Tarter, *The Grandees of Government: The Origins and Persistence of Undemocratic Politics in Virginia* (Charlottesville: University of Virginia Press, 2013). For challenges to elites, see especially Woody Holton, *Unruly Americans and the Origins of the Constitution* (New York: Hill and Wang, 2007).

35. Grigsby, *History of the Virginia Federal Convention*, 1:31–32 (first quotation); "A Ploughman," *Winchester Virginia Gazette*, 19 March 1788, *DHRC*, 509 (second quotation); "Philanthropos," *Virginia Journal*, 6 December 1787, *DHRC*, 209 (third quotation); *Philadelphia Freeman's Journal*, 2 January 1788, *DHRC*, 283 (last quotation).

36. Virginia Declaration of Rights, 1776. Virginia's gentlemen-politicians thought it wise to preserve this colonial tradition and thereby their control over state politics. Their state constitution read: "The right of suffrage in the election of members for both Houses shall remain as exercised at present." The law did allow exceptions of the property requirement for residents of the two largest towns, Williamsburg and Norfolk. Virginia Constitution, 1776.

37. Martha Washington to Fanny Bassett Washington, 25 February 1788, in Joseph E. Fields, ed., *"Worthy Partner": The Papers of Martha Washington* (Westport, CT: Greenwood Press, 1994), 205. For women's participation in informal politics, see Rosemarie Zagarri, *Revolutionary Backlash: Women and Politics in the Early American Republic* (Philadelphia: University of Pennsylvania Press, 2007), especially 68–75. For their direct participation, see Judith Apter Klinghoffer and Lois Elkis, " 'The Petticoat Electors': Women's Suffrage in New Jersey, 1776–1807," *Journal of the Early Republic* 12 (1992): 159–93; Zagarri, *Revolutionary Backlash*, 30–37.

38. For race and the Revolution in Virginia, start with Edmund S. Morgan's field-defining work, *American Slavery, American Freedom: The Ordeal of Colonial Virginia* (New York: W. W. Norton, 1975). See also Michael A. McDonnell, *The Politics of War: Race, Class, and Conflict in Revolutionary Virginia* (Chapel Hill: University of North Carolina Press, 2007); Alan Taylor, *The Internal Enemy: Slavery and War in Virginia, 1772–1832* (New York: W. W. Norton, 2013).

39. Arthur Lee to John Adams, 3 October 1787, *DHRC*, 34 (first quotation); Ben-

jamin Harrison to George Washington, 4 October 1787, *DHRC*, 36 (second quotation). For sectionalism in the debates, see Jack P. Greene, "The Constitution of 1787 and the Question of Southern Distinctiveness," in Greene, *Imperatives, Behaviors, and Identities: Essays in Early American Cultural History* (Charlottesville: University Press of Virginia, 1992), 327–47.

40. George Washington to Edmund Randolph, 8 January 1788, *DHRC*, 286.

41. For the "Political Club" see *DHRC*, 408–10. To avoid redundancy, we will turn to the specific constitutional matters Virginians debated in chapter 4. These issues were pursued fairly systematically in the official convention. But the opinions voiced by representatives during the formal debates in June were far from spontaneous; they had been practiced by citizens for many months.

42. Letter to Editor, *Virginia Independent Chronicle*, 31 October 1787, *DHRC*, 139; "A Planter," *Virginia Independent Chronicle*, 13 February 1788, *DHRC*, 565.

43. Thomas Pleasants Jr. to Stephen Collins, 7 November 1787, *DHRC*, 141 (first quotation); *Winchester Virginia Gazette*, 7 March 1788, *DHRC*, 470 (second quotation).

44. Patrick Henry, 18 January 1773, in William Wirt Henry, *Patrick Henry: Life, Correspondence and Speeches*, 3 vols. (New York: Charles Scribner's Sons, 1891), 1:152; James Madison, 6 June 1787, *Debates in the Several State Conventions*, 5:162; "A Virginian," *Virginia Independent Chronicle*, 13 February 1788, *DHRC*, 367.

45. George Lee Turberville to Arthur Lee, 28 October 1787, *DHRC*, 128 (quotations). See James Madison to George Washington, 20 December 1787, *DHRC*, 254, for altered writings of John Jay, George Mason, and Benjamin Franklin. For the importance of print media during ratification, see Heideking, *The Constitution before the Judgment Seat*, 68–93; Todd Estes, "Perspectives, Points of Emphasis, and Lines of Analysis in the Narrative of the Ratification Debates," *William and Mary Quarterly* 69 (2012): 361–64. For newspapers in the early national era, see Jeffrey L. Pasley, *"The Tyranny of Printers": Newspaper Politics in the Early American Republic* (Charlottesville: University Press of Virginia, 2001).

46. Letter to Editor, *Virginia Independent Chronicle*, 28 November 1787, *DHRC*, 179–80 (first and second quotations); "A True Friend," *Virginia Independent Chronicle*, 14 November 1787, *DHRC*, 163 (last quotation). See also Alexander White, *Winchester Virginia Gazette*, 29 February 1788, *DHRC*, 443.

47. Letter to Editor, *Virginia Independent Chronicle*, 28 November 1787, *DHRC*, 177 (first quotation); Letter to Editor, *Virginia Independent Chronicle*, 31 October 1787, *DHRC*, 139 (second quotation); "Americanus II," *Virginia Independent Chronicle*, 19 December 1787, *DHRC*, 244 (last quotation).

48. Letter to Editor, *Virginia Independent Chronicle*, 31 October 1787, *DHRC*, 139–40 (first quotation); James Breckinridge to John Breckinridge, 31 October 1787, *DHRC*, 136 (second quotation).

49. "A Virginian," *Norfolk and Portsmouth Journal*, 12 March 1788, *DHRC*, 480–81.

50. "A Ploughman," *Winchester Virginia Gazette*, 19 March 1788, *DHRC*, 508.

51. "The Impartial Examiner," *Virginia Independent Chronicle*, 27 February 1788, *DHRC*, 422. For the significance of the military, see Max M. Edling, *A Revolution in*

Favor of Government: Origins of the U.S. Constitution and the Making of the American State (New York: Oxford University Press, 2004), part 2. For understanding conceptions of liberty, see Michal Jan Rozbicki, *Culture and Liberty in the Age of the American Revolution* (Charlottesville: University of Virginia Press, 2011).

52. "A Ploughman," *Winchester Virginia Gazette*, 19 March 1788, *DHRC*, 508–9.

53. James McClurg to James Madison, 31 October 1787, *DHRC*, 137; James Madison to George Washington, 18 November 1787, *DHRC*, 167.

54. George Washington to Bushrod Washington, 10 November 1787, *DHRC*, 153 (first quotation); George Washington to David Stuart, 30 November 1787, *DHRC*, 193 (second quotation). See also George Washington to Alexander Hamilton, 10 November 1787, *DHRC*, 152.

55. George Mason to George Washington, 7 October 1787, *DHRC*, 43.

56. George Washington to James Madison, 10 October 1787, *DHRC*, 49; George Washington to David Stuart, 17 October 1787, *DHRC*, 69 (quotation).

57. George Washington to James Madison, 10 October 1787, *DHRC*, 49; Tobias Lear to John Langdon, 19 October 1787, *DHRC*, 80. Here Lear repeats language George Washington used in his 10 October letter to James Madison. This language was again repeated in George Washington to Tobias Lear, 10 November 1787, *DHRC*, 152.

58. House of Delegates Proceedings and Debates, 25 October 1787, *DHRC*, 113.

59. *DHRC*, 40–42. See also "Brutus," *Virginia Journal*, 22 November 1787, *DHRC*, 174–75.

60. "Philanthropos," *Virginia Journal*, 6 December 1787, *DHRC*, 209–11.

61. George Washington to James Madison, 10 October 1787, *DHRC*, 50. For speculation about Patrick Henry, see also James Madison to Thomas Jefferson, 24 October–1 November 1787, *DHRC*, 106. Rumors, most notably from Henry's enemy Thomas Jefferson, continued even after Henry's death. See Thomas Jefferson to William Wirt, miscellaneous correspondence, *Pennsylvania Magazine of History and Biography* 34 (1910): 385–418.

62. Patrick Henry to George Washington, 19 October 1787, *DHRC*, 79.

CHAPTER TWO: Winter 1787–1788, Jockeying for Power

1. William Wirt, *Sketches of the Life and Character of Patrick Henry* (Philadelphia: James Webster, 1817), 28. The case was the famous "Parson's Cause."

2. David Stuart to George Washington, 16 October 1787, *DHRC*, 67.

3. James Madison to William Short, 24 October 1787, *DHRC*, 109.

4. Proceedings of the House of Delegates, 25 October 1787, *DHRC*, 113.

5. Proceedings of the House of Delegates, 25 October 1787, *DHRC*, 114.

6. Proceedings of the House of Delegates, 25 October 1787, *DHRC*, 114; Resolution of the House of Delegates, 25 October 1787, *DHRC*, 118. For Marshall's life, see Jean Edward Smith, *John Marshall: Definer of a Nation* (New York: Henry Holt, 1996).

7. James Madison to Thomas Jefferson, 9 December 1787, *DHRC*, 226.

8. For Shays's Rebellion, see Leonard L. Richards, *Shays's Rebellion: The American Revolution's Final Battle* (Philadelphia: University of Pennsylvania Press, 2003).

9. Richard Henry Lee to George Mason, 1 October 1787, *DHRC*, 29; Gouverneur Morris quoted in Jack N. Rakove, *Original Meanings: Politics and Ideas in the Making of the Constitution* (New York: Knopf, 1996), 94.

10. George Washington to James Madison, 10 January 1788, *DHRC*, 292; John Breckinridge to James Breckinridge, 25 January 1788, *DHRC*, 321. See also John Dawson to James Madison, 10 November 1787, *DHRC*, 150.

11. James Madison to George Washington, 28 October 1787, *DHRC*, 127. Washington echoed this in a letter to Bushrod Washington, 10 November 1787, *DHRC*, 153.

12. House and Senate Proceedings, 25–31 October 1787, *DHRC*, 116–18.

13. George Washington to David Stuart, 5 November 1787, *DHRC*, 147; John Pierce to George Washington, 12 November 1787, *DHRC*, 156 (last quotation).

14. *DHRC*, 184; Henry Lee to James Madison, 7 December 1787, *DHRC*, 223.

15. *DHRC*, 184; Archibald Stuart to James Madison, 2 December 1787, *DHRC*, 196.

16. George Washington to James Madison, 10 January 1788, *DHRC*, 292.

17. "An Act Concerning the State Convention," 12 December 1787, *DHRC*, 190.

18. Archibald Stuart to James Madison, 2 December 1787, *DHRC*, 196.

19. James Madison to Archibald Stuart, 14 December 1787, *DHRC*, 237–38.

20. James Madison to George Nicholas, 8 April 1788, *DHRC*, 708.

21. John Ferling, *A Leap in the Dark: The Struggle to Create the American Republic* (New York: Oxford University Press, 2003), 264–66; *DHRC*, 156, n. 3.

22. James Madison to George Washington 7 December 1786, Founders Online, National Archives (founders.archives.gov).

23. John Pierce to George Washington, 12 November 1787, *DHRC*, 155–56.

24. *Virginia Independent Chronicle*, 14 November 1787, *DHRC*, 157.

25. "Cato Uticensis," *Virginia Independent Chronicle*, 17 October 1787, *DHRC*, 73–74.

26. "Cato Uticensis," *Virginia Independent Chronicle*, 17 October 1787, *DHRC*, 75. For localism in Virginia politics, see Richard R. Beeman, *The Old Dominion in the New Nation, 1788–1801* (Lexington: University Press of Kentucky, 1972); Brent Tarter, *The Grandees of Government: The Origins and Persistence of Undemocratic Politics in Virginia* (Charlottesville: University of Virginia Press, 2013). And for the influence of localism in the ratification contest, see Lance Banning, "Virginia: Sectionalism and the General Good," in Michael Allen Gillespie and Michael Lienesch, eds., *Ratifying the Constitution* (Lawrence: University Press of Kansas, 1989), 261–99.

27. Harry Innes to John Brown, 7 December 1787, *DHRC*, 222 (first quotation); *Virginia Independent Chronicle*, 14 November 1787, *DHRC*, 158 (second quotation). For the importance of local concerns to Anti-Federalist leaders Patrick Henry and George Mason, see Richard R. Beeman, *Patrick Henry: A Biography* (New York: McGraw Hill, 1974); Peter Wallenstein, "Flawed Keepers of the Flame: The Interpreters of George Mason," *Virginia Magazine of History and Biography* 102 (1994): 229–60.

28. *Virginia Herald*, 11 October 1787, *DHRC*, 52.

29. Letter to Editor, *Virginia Independent Chronicle*, 28 November 1787, *DHRC*, 177. See also Robert W. Smith, "Foreign Affairs and the Ratification of the Constitution in Virginia," *Virginia Magazine of History and Biography* 122 (2014): 41–63.

30. Edward Carrington to James Madison, 10 February 1788, *DHRC*, 359.

31. "An Impartial Citizen," *Petersburg Virginia Gazette*, 28 February 1788, *DHRC*, 431–32.

32. George Washington to Bushrod Washington, 9 November 1787, in W. W. Abbot, ed., *The Papers of George Washington (Confederation Series)*, 6 vols. (Charlottesville: University of Virginia Press, 1992–97), 5:421–22.

33. Miscellaneous entries, George Washington Diary, December 1787, Founders Online, National Archives (founders.archives.gov). For an example of such concerns, see James Madison to Edmund Randolph, 10 January 1788, *DHRC*, 288–91.

34. For Pennsylvania's ratification process, see Pauline Maier, *Ratification: The People Debate the Constitution, 1787–1788* (New York: Simon & Schuster, 2010), chap. 4.

35. *DHRC*, 401.

36. Alexander White, "To the Citizens of Virginia," *Winchester Virginia Gazette*, 22 February 1788, *DHRC*, 402–5.

37. For the Massachusetts convention, see Maier, *Ratification*, chaps. 6–7.

38. After Massachusetts ratified, the church was renamed Federal Street Church.

39. Edward Carrington to James Madison, 10 February 1788, *DHRC*, 360; James Madison quoted in Maier, *Ratification*, 214.

40. Joseph Jones to James Madison, 14 February 1788, *DHRC*, 368. See also Joseph Jones to James Madison, 17 February 1788, *DHRC*, 381.

41. John Hancock quoted in Maier, *Ratification*, 196.

42. George Washington to James Madison, 2 March 1788, *DHRC*, 452; *Virginia Independent Chronicle*, 19 March 1788, *DHRC*, 504.

43. For analysis of the Federalist Papers, see Lance Banning, *The Sacred Fire of Liberty: James Madison and the Founding of the Federal Republic* (Ithaca, NY: Cornell University Press, 1995), chap. 7; Rakove, *Original Meanings*. And for misrepresentations at the time, see Woody Holton, *Unruly Americans and the Origins of the Constitution* (New York: Hill and Wang, 2007), 250–51.

44. *DHRC*, xliii, 653. New York had a larger population than Philadelphia according to the 1790 census. For most of the colonial era, Philadelphia was the largest city.

45. For more about the spread of information and how it changed over time, see Richard D. Brown, *Knowledge Is Power: The Diffusion of Information in Early America, 1700–1865* (New York: Oxford University Press, 1989).

46. Richard Henry Lee to Edmund Randolph, 16 October 1787, *DHRC*, 62.

47. For Madison and Washington's network, see Stuart Leibiger, *Founding Friendship: George Washington, James Madison, and the Creation of the American Republic* (Charlottesville: University Press of Virginia, 1999), chap. 3.

48. *Virginia Independent Chronicle*, 19 March 1788, *DHRC*, 504 (quotation); *DHRC*, 505, n. 1–2. For more about these newspapers, see *DHRC*, xliii–xliv.

49. Martin Oster to Comte de la Luzerne, 4 February 1788, *DHRC*, 344; Don Diego de Gardoqui to Conde de Floridablanca, 6 December 1787, *DHRC*, 205.

50. *Pennsylvania Gazette*, 17 October 1787, and *New York Packet*, 30 October 1787, both in *DHRC*, 70. See also Cyrus Griffin to Thomas FitzSimons, 18 February 1788, *DHRC*, 382.

51. "Landholder VI," *Connecticut Courant*, 10 December 1787, *DHRC*, 229–31; "Landholder VIII," *Connecticut Courant*, 24 December 1787, *DHRC*, 231, n. 3. "Landholder VIII" was not reprinted in Virginia.

52. William Shippen Jr. to Thomas Lee Shippen, 29 November 1787, *DHRC*, 183.

53. Robert Milligan to William Tilghman, 20 September 1787, *DHRC*, 13 (first quotation); Alexander Donald to Thomas Jefferson, 12 November 1787, *DHRC*, 155 (second quotation); George Washington to Marquis de Lafayette, 28 April–1 May 1788, *DHRC*, 768 (last quotation).

CHAPTER THREE: Spring 1788, Electing the Delegates

1. George Washington Diary, 17 March 1788, Founders Online, National Archives (founders.archives.gov). For the Virginia convention elections, see also Jürgen Heideking, *The Constitution before the Judgment Seat: The Prehistory and Ratification of the American Constitution, 1787–1791*, ed. John P. Kaminski and Richard Leffler (Charlottesville: University of Virginia Press, 2012), 211–20; F. Claiborne Johnston Jr., "Federalist, Doubtful, and Antifederalist: A Note on the Virginia Convention of 1788," *Virginia Magazine of History and Biography* 96 (1988): 333–44.

2. George Washington Diary, 18 March 1788 and 20 March 1788, Founders Online, National Archives (founders.archives.gov); James Madison to Eliza Trist House, 25 March 1788, *DHRC*, 603.

3. George Washington to Lafayette, 28 May 1788, Founders Online, National Archives (founders.archives.gov).

4. Littleton Waller Tazewell, "Sketches of His Own Family," 1823, *DHRC*, 623–26.

5. "Nov. Anglus," *Norfolk and Portsmouth Journal*, 30 January 1788, *DHRC*, 341.

6. Generally the ratification debates followed the referendum model. Pauline Maier, *Ratification: The People Debate the Constitution, 1787–1788* (New York: Simon & Schuster, 2010), 232–37. For the importance of public debates, including about how to vote, see also Max M. Edling, *A Revolution in Favor of Government: Origins of the U.S. Constitution and the Making of the American State* (New York: Oxford University Press, 2004), chap. 1.

7. George Washington, "Rules of Civility and Decent Behaviour in Company and Conversation," is widely available, in both print and digital formats. For conduct literature, see C. Dallett Hemphill, *Bowing to Necessities: A History of Manners in America, 1620–1860* (New York: Oxford University Press, 1999); Sarah E. Newton, *Learning to Behave: A Guide to American Conduct Books before 1900* (Westport, CT: Greenwood Press, 1994); Richard Bushman, *The Refinement of America: Persons, Houses, Cities* (New York: Knopf, 1992).

8. "An Old Planter," *Virginia Independent Chronicle*, 20 February 1788, *DHRC*, 394–95. For the persistence of elite control over Virginia state politics after ratification, see Richard R. Beeman, *The Old Dominion in the New Nation, 1788–1801* (Lexington: University Press of Kentucky, 1972); Charles Sydnor, *Gentlemen Freeholders: Political Practices in Washington's Virginia* (Chapel Hill: University of North Carolina Press, 1952); Brent Tarter, *The Grandees of Government: The Origins and Persistence of Undemocratic Politics in Virginia* (Charlottesville: University of Virginia Press, 2013).

9. "Cato Uticensis," *Virginia Independent Chronicle*, 17 October 1787, *DHRC*, 71.

10. Edmund Pendleton to James Madison, 29 January 1788, *DHRC*, 1776.

11. Olney Winsor to Mrs. Olney Winsor, 31 March 1788, *DHRC*, 523 (first quotation); Alexander White, *Winchester Virginia Gazette*, 29 February 1788, *DHRC*, 443–44; "A Virginian," *Norfolk and Portsmouth Journal*, 12 March 1788, *DHRC*, 481.

12. "An Impartial Citizen," *Petersburg Virginia Gazette*, 28 February 1788, *DHRC*, 431 (first quotation); "The State Soldier III," *Virginia Independent Chronicle*, 12 March 1788, *DHRC*, 488 (second quotation); Edward Carrington to James Madison, 10 February 1788, *DHRC*, 359 (last quotation).

13. Olney Winsor to unknown, 25 January 1788, *DHRC*, 325.

14. James Madison to George Washington, 9 December 1787, *DHRC*, 227. For an overview of the changing political culture, including the erosion of deference, see Gordon S. Wood, *The Radicalism of the American Revolution* (New York: Knopf, 1992).

15. "A Native of Virginia: Observations upon the Proposed Plan of Federal Government," 2 April 1788, *DHRC*, 657.

16. "A Native of Virginia: Observations upon the Proposed Plan of Federal Government," 2 April 1788, *DHRC*, 657; "A Freeholder," *Virginia Independent Chronicle*, 9 April 1788, *DHRC*, 719.

17. Edward Carrington to James Madison, 10 February 1788, *DHRC*, 360.

18. For the long history of Virginia gentlemen succeeding in fostering solidarity across class lines, see Edmund S. Morgan, *American Slavery, American Freedom: The Ordeal of Colonial Virginia* (New York: W. W. Norton, 1975).

19. "A Virginian," *Norfolk and Portsmouth Journal*, 12 March 1788, *DHRC*, 481 (first quotation); "A Native of Virginia: Observations upon the Proposed Plan of Federal Government," 2 April 1788, *DHRC*, 664 (second and third quotations); Alexander White, *Winchester Virginia Gazette*, 29 February 1788, *DHRC*, 443–44 (last quotation).

20. "A Ploughman," *Winchester Virginia Gazette*, 19 March 1788, *DHRC*, 509.

21. *Maryland Journal*, 1 January 1788, *DHRC*, 277. The issue of the *Virginia Herald* in which the letter was first published has not been found. It was, however, reprinted and credited in many papers, including the 1 January 1788 issue of the *Maryland Journal*.

22. *DHRC*, 276–77; George Washington to Charles Carter, 12 January 1788, *DHRC*, 278.

23. George Washington to Charles Carter, 12 January 1788 and 20 January 1788, *DHRC*, 278.

24. George Washington to Charles Carter, 22 January 1788, *DHRC*, 279; George Washington to James Madison, 5 February 1788, *DHRC*, 280.

25. James Madison to George Washington, 20 February 1788, *DHRC*, 280.

26. James Madison to George Washington, 20 February 1788, *DHRC*, 281; George Washington to Charles Carter, 12 January 1788, *DHRC*, 278.

27. George Washington to Caleb Gibbs, 28 February 1788, *DHRC*, 427; George Washington to John Jay, 3 March 1788, *DHRC*, 455.

28. "Valerius," *Virginia Independent Chronicle*, 23 January 1788, *DHRC*, 314–15. Lee shared his objections and proposed amendments in a 16 October 1787 letter to Edmund Randolph, which was subsequently and with Lee's encouragement published. See Richard Henry Lee to Edmund Randolph, 16 October 1787, *DHRC*, 59–67.

29. "Valerius," *Virginia Independent Chronicle*, 23 January 1788, *DHRC*, 316–18.

30. "Cassius," 12 March 1788, *Virginia Independent Chronicle*, 2 April 1788, *DHRC*, 643, 645; "Cassius," 28 March 1788, *Virginia Independent Chronicle*, 9 April 1788, *DHRC*, 714; "An Impartial Citizen," *Petersburg Virginia Gazette*, 28 February 1788, *DHRC*, 430. The Cassius letters were dated several days before they appeared in print.

31. Richard Henry Lee to Edmund Pendleton, 26 May 1788, *DHRC*, 881.

32. Martin Oster to Comte de la Luzerne, 4 February 1788, *DHRC*, 344.

33. For Randolph's conduct between October 1787 and the June convention, see John J. Reardon, *Edmund Randolph: A Biography* (New York: Macmillan, 1974), chap. 10.

34. Edmund Randolph to Beverley Randolph, 18 September 1787, *DHRC*, 11; *Virginia Independent Chronicle*, 26 September 1787, *DHRC*, 19. Reardon argued that Randolph wanted to get the letter right and that all the rumors about his actions in Philadelphia and about the Constitution "served to impose new burdens on him and complicate the drafting of his statement." Reardon, *Edmund Randolph*, 123.

35. Edmund Randolph to James Madison, 29 October 1787, *DHRC*, 133.

36. Edmund Randolph to James Madison, 29 October 1787, *DHRC*, 134.

37. Edmund Randolph to James Madison, 29 October 1787, *DHRC*, 133.

38. Meriwether Smith, Charles M. Thruston, John H. Briggs, and Mann Page Jr. to Edmund Randolph, 2 December 1787, *DHRC*, 195.

39. *DHRC*, 260–61.

40. Edmund Randolph, 27 December 1787, *DHRC*, 262.

41. Edmund Randolph, 27 December 1787, *DHRC*, 274, 262; *DHRC*, 274, n. 1 (regarding the Philadelphia meeting).

42. Edmund Randolph, 27 December 1787, *DHRC*, 274.

43. "A Plain Dealer," *Virginia Independent Chronicle*, 13 February 1788, *DHRC*, 364.

44. "A Plain Dealer," *Virginia Independent Chronicle*, 13 February 1788, *DHRC*, 364–65.

45. Lance Banning depicts Randolph as a moderate who reflected the middle path of Virginians eager for change to the Articles but skeptical about key elements of the Constitution. See Lance Banning, "1787 and 1776: Patrick Henry, James Madison, the

Constitution, and the Revolution," in Neil L. York, ed., *Toward a More Perfect Union: Six Essays on the Constitution* (Albany: State University of New York Press, 1989), 82–83. See also Reardon, *Edmund Randolph*; and Kevin R. C. Gutzman, "Edmund Randolph and Virginia Constitutionalism," *Review of Politics* 66 (2004): 469–97.

46. George Lee Turberville to Arthur Lee, 28 October 1787, *DHRC*, 127.

47. Banning, "1787 and 1776"; Lance Banning, *The Sacred Fire of Liberty: James Madison and the Founding of the Federal Republic* (Ithaca, NY: Cornell University Press, 1995), 261–64.

48. "The State Soldier V," *Virginia Independent Chronicle*, 2 April 1788, *DHRC*, 652 (first quotation); *Winchester Virginia Gazette*, 7 March 1788, *DHRC*, 470 (second quotation). For competing visions of state formation, see Edling, *A Revolution in Favor of Government*. For balancing liberty and power, see Bernard Bailyn, *Ideological Origins of the American Revolution* (Cambridge, MA: Harvard University Press, 1967); Gordon S. Wood, *The Creation of the American Republic, 1776–1787* (Chapel Hill: University of North Carolina Press, 1969).

49. James Madison to Thomas Jefferson, 9 December 1787, *DHRC*, 227. See also Jon Kukla, "A Spectrum of Sentiments: Virginia's Federalists, Antifederalists, and 'Federalists Who Are for Amendments,' 1787–1788," *Virginia Magazine of History and Biography* 96 (1988): 277–96.

50. "An Old Planter," *Virginia Independent Chronicle*, 20 February 1788, *DHRC*, 395.

51. James Madison to Edmund Randolph, 10 January 1788, *DHRC*, 289.

52. Edward Carrington to James Madison, 10 February 1788, *DHRC*, 360.

53. James Madison to George Nicholas, 8 April 1788, *DHRC*, 708.

54. James Madison to Edmund Randolph, 10 April 1788, *DHRC*, 731; Richard Henry Lee to Edmund Randolph, 16 October 1788, *DHRC*, 61.

55. James Madison to Archibald Stuart, 30 October 1787, *DHRC*, 135.

56. See, for example, George Washington to Bushrod Washington, 10 November 1787, *DHRC*, 152–54.

57. Edward Carrington to James Madison, 8 April 1788, *DHRC*, 706; Bishop James Madison to James Madison, 9 February 1788, *DHRC*, 357.

58. "A True Friend," 5 December 1787, *DHRC*, 217–20. The pamphlet was first printed in Richmond, and then reprinted, sometimes in slightly altered form, in several Virginia newspapers and in the *Philadelphia Independent Gazetteer*.

59. "An Impartial Citizen VI," *Petersburg Virginia Gazette*, 13 March 1788, *DHRC*, 495–96.

60. Slaveholders would have preferred, for their own political ambitions, to have slaves fully counted for purposes of representation. They wanted as much legislative advantage as possible. However, enslaved African Americans were not actually represented; rather, they were systematically denied civil rights in southern states. Antislavery delegates to the convention pointed out the hypocrisy of these southern demands, even as they sought a workable compromise. Interpreting this compromise has been the source of much scholarly debate. For further discussion, see François Furstenberg, *In the Name of the Father: Washington's Legacy, Slavery, and the Making*

of a Nation (New York: Penguin, 2006); David C. Hendrickson, *Peace Pact: The Lost World of the American Founding* (Lawrence: University Press of Kansas, 2003), chap. 26; Jack P. Greene, "The Constitution of 1787 and the Question of Southern Distinctiveness," in Greene, *Imperatives, Behaviors, and Identities: Essays in Early American Cultural History* (Charlottesville: University Press of Virginia, 1992), 327–47; David Waldstreicher, *Slavery's Constitution: From Revolution to Ratification* (New York: Hill and Wang, 2009).

61. "A Virginian," *Virginia Independent Chronicle*, 13 February 1788, *DHRC*, 367; "Republicus," *Kentucky Gazette*, 1 March 1788, *DHRC*, 450.

62. Harry Innes to John Brown, 20 February 1788, *DHRC*, 386. Innes's views did not damage his career after ratification. In 1789, President Washington appointed him as a US District Court judge.

63. Circular Letter, Fayette County, Kentucky, 29 February 1788, *DHRC*, 435.

64. In the summer of 1788, the Confederation Congress finally created a committee to consider the proposal for Kentucky statehood. In July, after Virginia and New Hampshire ratified and the Constitution passed, they then tabled all discussions of Kentucky statehood, leaving the question for the new Congress under the Constitution.

65. *Virginia Independent Chronicle*, 19 March 1788, *DHRC*, 504.

66. For a Federalist discussion of New Hampshire, see James Madison to George Washington, 3 March 1788, *DHRC*, 454.

67. George Washington to Henry Knox, 30 March 1788, *DHRC*, 521–22.

68. George Washington to John Langdon, 2 April 1788, Founders Online, National Archives (founders.archives.gov) (first quotation); George Washington to Benjamin Lincoln, 2 May 1788, *DHRC*, 780 (second quotation).

69. John Preston to John Brown, 10 February 1788, *DHRC*, 362.

70. James Madison to George Washington, 18 November 1787, *DHRC*, 167.

71. Edmund Randolph to James Madison, 3 January 1788, *DHRC*, 284; Edmund Pendleton to James Madison, 29 January 1788, *DHRC*, 1776; Tobias Lear to John Langdon, 3 April 1788, *DHRC*, 699 (last quotation). For additional warnings, see Edmund Randolph to James Madison, 3 January 1788, *DHRC*, 598–99; William Moore to James Madison, 31 January 1788, *DHRC*, 600; James Gordon Jr. to James Madison, 17 February 1788, *DHRC*, 600.

72. James Madison to Ambrose Madison, 8 November 1787, *DHRC*, 597; James Madison to George Washington, 20 February 1788, *DHRC*, 602.

73. James Madison to Eliza House Trist, 25 March 1788, *DHRC*, 603.

74. James Madison to Eliza House Trist, 25 March 1788, *DHRC*, 603 (quotation); James Duncanson to James Maury, 8 May 1788, *DHRC*, 604; Francis Taylor Diary, 24 March 1788, *DHRC*, 602.

75. James Duncanson to James Maury, 11 March 1788, *DHRC*, 479 (first quotation); Edward Carrington to James Madison, 8 April 1788, *DHRC*, 706 (second quotation); Edward Carrington to Thomas Jefferson, 24 April 1788, *DHRC*, 756 (last quotation).

76. *Maryland Journal*, 11 April 1788, *DHRC*, 735; *Philadelphia Federal Gazette*, 12 April 1788, *DHRC*, 737; *Philadelphia Independent Gazetteer*, 16 April 1788, *DHRC*, 738.

77. Edward Carrington to Thomas Jefferson, 24 April 1788, *DHRC*, 756; James Monroe to Thomas Jefferson, 10 April 1788, *DHRC*, 733 (including last quotation).

78. James Madison to Thomas Jefferson, 22 April 1788, *DHRC*, 745; George Mason to Thomas Jefferson, 26 May 1788, *DHRC*, 883.

79. George Washington to Lafayette, 28 May 1788, Founders Online, National Archives (founders.archives.gov).

CHAPTER FOUR: Summer 1788, Debating in Richmond

1. *Norfolk and Portsmouth Journal*, 21 May 1788, *DHRC*, 831 (first quotation); extract from a letter from Fairfax County, Virginia, 24 March 1788, *Providence United States Chronicle*, 24 April 1788, *DHRC*, 756–57.

2. Hugh Blair Grigsby, *The History of the Virginia Federal Convention of 1788: with some account of eminent Virginians of that era who were members of the body*, with a biographical sketch of the author and illustrative notes edited by R. A. Brock, 2 vols. (Richmond: Virginia Historical Society, 1890–91), 1:26–27. For additional explorations of the Virginia Ratification Convention, see Lance Banning, *The Sacred Fire of Liberty: James Madison and the Founding of the Federal Republic* (Ithaca, NY: Cornell University Press, 1995), chap. 8; Jürgen Heideking, *The Constitution before the Judgment Seat: The Prehistory and Ratification of the American Constitution, 1787–1791*, ed. John P. Kaminski and Richard Leffler (Charlottesville: University of Virginia Press, 2012), 311–20; Richard Labunski, *James Madison and the Struggle for the Bill of Rights* (New York: Oxford University Press, 2006), chaps. 4 and 5; Pauline Maier, *Ratification: The People Debate the Constitution, 1787–1788* (New York: Simon & Schuster, 2010), chaps. 9 and 10.

3. Alexander White to Mary Wood, 10–11 June 1788, *DHRC*, 1591.

4. For example, Federalist Richard Morris complained that his opponent in the Louisa County election, Anti-Federalist William White, won only by fraudulent votes. The Committee on Privileges and Elections heard depositions from witnesses that some voters were not property owners. White had prevailed at the close of polls by a slim margin, 199-195, but the committee disqualified fourteen White voters, reversing the outcome to 195-185 in Morris's favor. The convention as a whole overturned the committee's decision because it believed more evidence was necessary, but there was no time to gather it. White's election stood but not without controversy. *DHRC*, 594–95.

5. James Madison to Jonathan Elliot, ca. 15 November 1827, Founders Online, National Archives (founders.archives.gov).

6. Edmund Pendleton, 2 June 1788, *DHRC*, 911.

7. Grigsby, *History of the Virginia Federal Convention*, 1:34 (first quotation); Banning, *Sacred Fire of Liberty*, 235 (second quotation).

8. Grigsby, *History of the Virginia Federal Convention*, 1:75.

9. George Mason to Thomas Jefferson, 26 May 1788, Founders Online, National Archives (founders.archives.gov). For Mason's character and influence, see Brent

Tarter, "George Mason and the Conservation of Liberty," *Virginia Magazine of History and Biography* 99 (1991): 279–304; Peter Wallenstein, "Flawed Keepers of the Flame: The Interpreters of George Mason," *Virginia Magazine of History and Biography* 102 (1994): 229–60.

10. James Madison to Tench Coxe, 11 June 1788, *DHRC*, 1595.

11. William Grayson to Nathan Dane, 4 June 1788, *DHRC*, 1573.

12. Both Patrick Henry and James Madison claimed to represent Jefferson's views on the Constitution. James Madison, 12 June 1788, *DHRC*, 1223; Patrick Henry, 9 June 1788, *DHRC*, 1053.

13. George Washington to James Madison, 8 June 1788, *DHRC*, 1586 (first quotation); George Washington to Henry Knox, 17 June 1788, *DHRC*, 1633 (second quotation); James Breckenridge to John Breckinridge, 13 June 1788, *DHRC*, 1621.

14. Henry Lee to Alexander Hamilton, 16 June 1788, *DHRC*, 1631. For Anti-Federalist networks, see Saul Cornell, *The Other Founders: Anti-Federalism and the Dissenting Tradition in America, 1788–1828* (Chapel Hill: University of North Carolina Press, 1999), chap. 2.

15. Hugh Williamson to John Gray Blount, 3 June 1788, *DHRC*, 1572 (first quotation); James Duncanson to James Maury, 7 June 1788, *DHRC*, 1583 (second quotation); extract of a letter by a Virginia delegate, 13 June 1788, *Pennsylvania Packet*, 21 June 1788, *DHRC*, 1664 (last quotation). See also Henry Knox to Rufus King, 19 June 1788, *DHRC*, 1652. For speculation about Virginia before and during the convention, see *DHRC*, appendix 1, 1778–92.

16. Thomas Paine, *Common Sense*, in J. M. Opal, ed., *Common Sense and Other Writings* (New York: W. W. Norton, 2012); Edmund Randolph, 6 June 1788, *DHRC*, 988.

17. Patrick Henry, 4 June 1788, *DHRC*, 931.

18. Grigsby, *History of the Virginia Federal Convention*, 1:73.

19. Grigsby, *History of the Virginia Federal Convention*, 1:69; George Mason, 3 June 1788, *DHRC*, 914.

20. Richard Henry Lee to George Mason, 7 May 1788, *DHRC*, 785. See also Tarter, "George Mason and the Conservation of Liberty," 297. For Anti-Federalist concerns generally, see Cornell, *The Other Founders*, chaps. 2 and 3.

21. Grigsby, *History of the Virginia Federal Convention*, 1:76; Martin Oster to Comte da la Luzerne, 28 June 1788, *DHRC*, 1690 (quotation).

22. Congressional Resolution, 21 February 1787, in *Journals of the Continental Congress, 1774–1789*, 34 vols., ed. Worthington C. Ford et al. (Washington, DC: Government Printing Office, 1904–37), 32:74.

23. Edmund Pendleton, 4 June 1788, *DHRC*, 917.

24. For their relationship, see Grigsby, *History of the Virginia Federal Convention*, 1:105–6, 27–28.

25. James Madison to George Washington, 4 June 1788, *DHRC*, 1574.

26. Grigsby, *History of the Virginia Federal Convention*, 1:79, 246.

27. George Nicholas, 4 June 1788, *DHRC*, 920–21. Information about all state populations and congressional districts is available at www.census.gov.

28. George Nicholas, 4 June 1788, *DHRC*, 927.

29. Patrick Henry, 4 June 1788, *DHRC*, 929–30.

30. Patrick Henry, 4 June 1788, *DHRC*, 930–31. For the contested nature of the government, see also David C. Hendrickson, *Peace Pact: The Lost World of the American Founding* (Lawrence: University Press of Kansas, 2003).

31. Edmund Randolph, 4 June 1788, *DHRC*, 932. For Randolph's influence and constitutional views, see also Banning, *Sacred Fire of Liberty*, 246–63; Kevin R. C. Gutzman, "Edmund Randolph and Virginia Constitutionalism," *Review of Politics* 66 (2004): 469–97.

32. Edmund Randolph, 4 June 1788, *DHRC*, 933.

33. Edmund Randolph, 4 June 1788, *DHRC*, 936. Henry's condemnation of the preamble struck a nerve with the Federalists, and they returned to that point several times. See Edmund Pendleton, 5 June 1788, *DHRC*, 945; George Nicholas, 6 June 1788, *DHRC*, 999.

34. George Mason to John Mason, 13 March 1789, in Robert A. Rutland, ed., *The Papers of George Mason, 1725–1792*, 3 vols. (Chapel Hill: University of North Carolina Press, 1970), 3:1142.

35. George Mason, 4 June 1788, *DHRC*, 936.

36. George Mason, 4 June 1788, *DHRC*, 937–38.

37. George Mason, 4 June 1788, *DHRC*, 938–39. For representation, see Gordon S. Wood, *The Creation of the American Republic, 1776–1787* (Chapel Hill: University of North Carolina Press, 1969), chap. 5.

38. George Mason, 4 June 1788, *DHRC*, 939.

39. James Madison, 4 June 1788, *DHRC*, 940.

40. Edmund Pendleton, 5 June 1788, *DHRC*, 944.

41. Edmund Pendleton, 5 June 1788, *DHRC*, 947.

42. Edmund Pendleton, 5 June 1788, *DHRC*, 949.

43. Henry "Light-Horse Harry" Lee III represented Westmoreland County and voted in favor of ratification. Another Henry Lee, from Bourbon County in the Kentucky district, voted against ratification. Lee of Bourbon County never spoke during the proceedings, according to Robertson's notes.

44. Henry Lee, 5 June 1788, *DHRC*, 949.

45. Henry Lee, 5 June 1788, *DHRC*, 950.

46. Patrick Henry, 5 June 1788, *DHRC*, 951.

47. Patrick Henry, 5 June 1788, *DHRC*, 951–52.

48. Patrick Henry, 5 June 1788, *DHRC*, 951–53.

49. Patrick Henry, 5 June 1788, *DHRC*, 953–54.

50. Patrick Henry, 5 June 1788, *DHRC*, 954.

51. Patrick Henry, 5 June 1788, *DHRC*, 954.

52. Grigsby, *History of the Virginia Federal Convention*, 1: 119.

53. Patrick Henry, 5 June 1788, *DHRC*, 959–60, 963. See also Richard R. Beeman, *Patrick Henry: A Biography* (New York: McGraw Hill, 1974), 159–60.

54. Robertson's notes, 5 June 1788, *DHRC*, 964.

55. Patrick Henry, 5 June 1788, *DHRC*, 968; Edmund Randolph, 5 June 1788, *DHRC*, 968.

56. James Madison quoted in Samuel A. Otis to Theodore Sedgwick, 15 June 1788, *DHRC*, 970, n. 16.

57. Edmund Randolph, 6 June 1788, *DHRC*, 971.

58. Edmund Randolph, 6 June 1788, *DHRC*, 973.

59. Edmund Randolph, 6 June 1788, *DHRC*, 973, 975.

60. Edmund Randolph, 6 June 1788, *DHRC*, 972.

61. Edmund Randolph, 6 June 1788, *DHRC*, 976–79.

62. Edmund Randolph, 6 June 1788, *DHRC*, 983.

63. Edmund Randolph, 6 June 1788, *DHRC*, 984–86.

64. Edmund Randolph, 6 June 1788, *DHRC*, 987.

65. Edmund Randolph, 6 June 1788, *DHRC*, 988.

66. Edmund Randolph, 6 June 1788, *DHRC*, 988.

67. Robertson's notes, 6 June 1788, *DHRC*, 989; James Madison, 6 June 1788, *DHRC*, 989; Martin Oster to Comte de la Luzerne, 28 June 1788, *DHRC*, 1690; Marshall quoted in Grigsby, *History of the Virginia Federal Convention*, 1:97, n. 109. For Madison's influence and ideas, see Banning, *Sacred Fire of Liberty*; Labunski, *James Madison and the Struggle for the Bill of Rights*; Jack N. Rakove, *James Madison and the Creation of the American Republic*, 3rd ed. (New York: Pearson, 2007); Jack Rakove, *Revolutionaries: A New History of the Invention of America* (Boston: Houghton Mifflin Harcourt, 2010), chap. 8; Gordon S. Wood, *Revolutionary Characters: What Made the Founders Different* (New York: Penguin, 2006), chap. 5.

68. James Madison, 6 June 1788, *DHRC*, 989.

69. James Madison, 6 June 1788, *DHRC*, 990–97.

70. James Madison, 6 June 1788, *DHRC*, 995, 996.

71. George Nicholas, 6 June 1788, *DHRC*, 998–99.

72. George Nicholas, 6 June 1788, *DHRC*, 999.

73. George Nicholas, 6 June 1788, *DHRC*, 1003.

74. Francis Corbin, 7 June 1788, *DHRC*, 1013–15.

75. Patrick Henry, 7 June 1788, *DHRC*, 1016.

76. Edmund Randolph, 7 June 1788, *DHRC*, 1024–25.

77. Edmund Randolph, 7 June 1788, *DHRC*, 1025.

78. Robertson's notes, 7 June 1788, *DHRC*, 1030, 1032; James Madison, 7 June 1788, *DHRC*, 1028.

79. James Madison, 7 June 1788, *DHRC*, 1033–34.

80. James Madison, 7 June 1788, *DHRC*, 1034.

81. Patrick Henry, 7 June 1788, *DHRC*, 1035–36.

82. Patrick Henry, 7 June 1788, *DHRC*, 1041.

83. James Madison, 16 June 1788, *DHRC*, 1323; Edmund Pendleton, 16 June 1788, *DHRC*, 1325; Patrick Henry, 7 June 1788, *DHRC*, 1046–47.

84. For dueling, see Joanne B. Freeman, *Affairs of Honor: National Politics in the New Republic* (New Haven, CT: Yale University Press, 2001); Bertram Wyatt-Brown,

Southern Honor: Ethics and Behavior in the Old South (New York: Oxford University Press, 1982).

85. George Mason, 23 June 1788, *DHRC*, 1471; Henry Lee, 23 June 1788, *DHRC*, 1472; Patrick Henry, 24 June 1788, *DHRC*, 1478; Edmund Randolph, 24 June 1788, *DHRC*, 1487–88.

86. Patrick Henry, 7 June 1788, *DHRC*, 1041; Patrick Henry, 9 June 1788, *DHRC*, 1059 (first quotation); Edward Carrington to James Madison, 10 February 1788, *DHRC*, 360 (second quotation).

87. Adam Stephen, 23 June 1788, *DHRC*, 1467; Green Clay, 14 June 1788, *DHRC*, 1294; *DHRC*, 1298, n. 10. Though not specifically designated, the speaker was most likely Green Clay. The record gives only the last name, and there were two Clays from Kentucky who voted against ratification. The other man, Charles Clay, was a minister, and Robertson would likely have referred to him as Reverend Clay.

88. James Duncanson to James Maury, 7 June 1788, *DHRC*, 1583; George Nicholas, 10 June 1788, *DHRC*, 1128. See also Wood, *Creation of the American Republic*, 319–28.

89. James Madison to Thomas Jefferson, 12 July 1788, *DHRC*, 1704; James Breckenridge to John Breckinridge, 13 June 1788, *DHRC*, 1620.

90. William Grayson, 11 June 1788, *DHRC*, 1167.

91. George Nicholas, 10 June 1788, *DHRC*, 1128; James Madison, 11 June 1788, *DHRC*, 1142.

92. William Grayson, 12 June 1788, *DHRC*, 1191; George Mason, 16 June 1788, *DHRC*, 1317; James Madison, 16 June 1788, *DHRC*, 1318.

93. George Mason, 14 June 1788, *DHRC*, 1292 (first quotation); James Madison, 14 June 1788, *DHRC*, 1262; John Tyler, 14 June 1788, *DHRC*, 1263; James Madison, 14 June 1788, *DHRC*, 1265.

94. George Mason, 17 June 1788, *DHRC*, 1366 (quotation), 1367. See also James Monroe, 18 June 1788, *DHRC*, 1372.

95. James Monroe, 18 June 1788, *DHRC*, 1373–74.

96. James Madison, 18 June 1788, *DHRC*, 1376.

97. William Grayson, 24 June 1788, *DHRC*, 1498.

98. George Mason, 14 June 1788, *DHRC*, 1270–71; Patrick Henry, 9 June 1788, *DHRC*, 1065. For analysis of the military controversy, see Max M. Edling, *A Revolution in Favor of Government: Origins of the U.S. Constitution and the Making of the American State* (New York: Oxford University Press, 2003), part 2.

99. James Madison, 14 June 1788, *DHRC*, 1272–73; James Madison, 12 June 1788, *DHRC*, 1206.

100. Patrick Henry, 12 June 1788, *DHRC*, 1215.

101. John Marshall, 10 June 1788, *DHRC*, 1120. See also George Nicholas, 10 June 1788, *DHRC*, 1136. For analysis of taxation issues, see Edling, *A Revolution in Favor of Government*, part 3.

102. George Mason, 11 June 1788, *DHRC*, 1157; William Grayson, 12 June 1788, *DHRC*, 1185; George Mason, 11 June 1788, *DHRC*, 1156.

103. Patrick Henry, 9 June 1788, *DHRC*, 1051 (first quotation); James Madison to George Washington, 13 June 1788, *DHRC*, 1619.

104. Edmund Pendleton, 12 June 1788, *DHRC*, 1200.

105. Patrick Henry, 24 June 1788, *DHRC*, 1477. See also David Waldstreicher, *Slavery's Constitution: From Revolution to Ratification* (New York: Hill and Wang, 2009).

106. Grigsby, *History of the Virginia Federal Convention*, 1: 119.

107. George Mason, 17 June 1788, *DHRC*, 1338. For Mason's views on slavery, see also Wallenstein, "Flawed Keepers of the Flame," 243–47, 253.

108. Thomas Jefferson to Thomas Cooper, 10 September 1814, in J. Jefferson Looney, ed., *The Papers of Thomas Jefferson (Retirement Series)*, 7 vols. (Princeton, NJ: Princeton University Press, 2004–), 7:652; Patrick Henry, 18 January 1773, in William Wirt Henry, *Patrick Henry: Life, Correspondence and Speeches*, 3 vols. (New York: Charles Scribner's Sons, 1891), 1:152. For similar comments, see also James Madison to Edmund Randolph, 26 July 1785, in William T. Hutchinson et al., eds., *The Papers of James Madison, Congressional Series*, 17 vols. (Chicago: University of Chicago Press, 1962–77, vols. 1–10), 8:328; Thomas Jefferson to John Holmes, 22 April 1820, in Paul L. Ford, ed., *The Writings of Thomas Jefferson*, 10 vols. (New York: G. P. Putnam's Sons, 1899), 10:157. For analysis of the centrality of race in the early national era, see Lacy K. Ford, "Making the 'White Man's Country' White: Race, Slavery, and State-Building in the Jacksonian South," *Journal of the Early Republic* 19 (1999): 713–37.

109. James Madison, 17 June 1788, *DHRC*, 1338–39.

110. William Grayson, 21 June 1788, *DHRC*, 1444. For state sovereignty, see especially Hendrickson, *Peace Pact*.

111. James Madison, 20 June 1788, *DHRC*, 1417.

112. See also Banning, *Sacred Fire of Liberty*, chap. 8, especially 238.

113. Patrick Henry, 9 June 1788, *DHRC*, 1061; James Monroe, 10 June 1788, *DHRC*, 1106.

114. Patrick Henry, 9 June 1788, *DHRC*, 1064; James Monroe, 10 June 1788, *DHRC*, 1111.

115. Henry Lee, 16 June 1788, *DHRC*, 1321; Patrick Henry, 16 June 1788, *DHRC*, 1322.

116. James Monroe, 10 June 1788, *DHRC*, 1104; Patrick Henry, 14 June 1788, *DHRC*, 1284.

117. George Mason, 19 June 1788, *DHRC*, 1401. For Virginians' debates on the judiciary, see Maier, *Ratification*, 286–91.

118. Henry Lee, 9 June 1788, *DHRC*, 1074.

119. James Madison, 11 June 1788, *DHRC*, 1152.

120. James Madison, 11 June 1788, *DHRC*, 1152.

121. Patrick Henry, 9 June 1788, *DHRC*, 1055.

122. James Monroe, 10 June 1788, *DHRC*, 1113.

123. James Monroe, 10 June 1788, *DHRC*, 1104. For shared views, see also Lance Banning, "1787 and 1776: Patrick Henry, James Madison, the Constitution, and the

Revolution," in Neil L. York, ed., *Toward a More Perfect Union: Six Essays on the Constitution* (Albany: State University of New York Press, 1989), 59–89.

124. James Monroe, 10 June 1788, *DHRC*, 1115.

125. John Marshall, 10 June 1788, *DHRC*, 1119, 1127.

126. James Madison to Thomas Jefferson, 9 December 1787, *DHRC*, 227; George Mason, 11 June 1788, *DHRC*, 1162. For the three divisions, see also Jon Kukla, "A Spectrum of Sentiments: Virginia's Federalists, Antifederalists, and 'Federalists Who Are for Amendments,' 1787–1788," *Virginia Magazine of History and Biography* 96 (1988): 277–96. Historians disagree about the degree to which Mason's objections centered on the absence of a bill of rights. See Helen Hill Miller, *George Mason, Gentleman Revolutionary* (Chapel Hill: University of North Carolina Press, 1975), 250–64; Tarter, "George Mason and the Conservation of Liberty."

127. For example, see James Madison, 24 June 1788, *DHRC*, 1504.

128. Francis Corbin, 7 June 1788, *DHRC*, 1015; John Marshall, 10 June 1788, *DHRC*, 1125; George Nicholas, 10 June 1788, *DHRC*, 1132.

129. George Mason, 11 June 1788, *DHRC*, 1163; Patrick Henry, 9 June 1788, *DHRC*, 1070; George Mason, 11 June 1788, *DHRC*, 1159; Theodorick Bland to Arthur Lee, 13 June 1788, *DHRC*, 1617.

130. James Monroe, 10 June 1788, *DHRC*, 1112; Patrick Henry, 12 June 1788, *DHRC*, 1211.

131. George Mason, 11 June 1788, *DHRC*, 1158 (first quotation); Patrick Henry, 16 June 1788, *DHRC*, 1329 (second quotation).

132. Richard Beeman, *Plain, Honest Men: The Making of the American Constitution* (New York: Random House, 2009), 341–44.

133. George Nicholas, 16 June 1788, *DHRC*, 1334.

134. George Nicholas, 16 June 1788, *DHRC*, 1334.

135. Edmund Pendleton, 12 June 1788, *DHRC*, 1201; Edmund Randolph, 24 June 1788, *DHRC*, 1487; James Madison, 24 June 1788, *DHRC*, 1500.

136. George Wythe, 24 June 1788, *DHRC*, 1474; George Nicholas, 10 June 1788, *DHRC*, 1132; Edmund Randolph, 17 June 1788, *DHRC*, 1354; Edmund Randolph, 24 June 1788, *DHRC*, 1482.

137. Patrick Henry, 4 June 1788, *DHRC*, 930.

CHAPTER FIVE: Summer 1788, Deciding the Question and the Future

1. Judge Archibald Stuart, reminiscence of Patrick Henry, told to William Wirt, 1817, in William Wirt, *Sketches of the Life and Character of Patrick Henry* (Philadelphia: James Webster, 1817), 312 (first quotation); Spencer Roane Memorandum, [undated] in George Morgan, *The True Patrick Henry* (Philadelphia: J. B. Lippincott, 1907), 447 (second quotation); Stuart reminiscence of Patrick Henry, Wirt, *Sketches of the Life and Character of Patrick Henry*, 313 (last quotation). "The vasty deep" was a reference to Shakespeare's *Henry IV*.

2. John Dawson, 24 June 1788, *DHRC*, 1488–89.

3. John Dawson, 24 June 1788, *DHRC*, 1489.

4. John Dawson, 24 June 1788, *DHRC*, 1490–91.

5. John Dawson, 24 June 1788, *DHRC*, 1491.

6. John Dawson, 24 June 1788, *DHRC*, 1492, 1495.

7. John Dawson, 24 June 1788, *DHRC*, 1495.

8. James Madison, 24 June 1788, *DHRC*, 1499–1504; James Madison, 11 June 1788, *DHRC*, 1152 (last quotation).

9. Quoted in Pauline Maier, *Ratification: The People Debate the Constitution, 1787–1788* (New York: Simon & Schuster, 2010), 306.

10. James Madison, 24 June 1788, *DHRC*, 1499 (first quotation); James Madison, 25 June 1788, *DHRC*, 1518 (second quotation).

11. Benjamin Harrison, 25 June 1788, *DHRC*, 1518; James Monroe, 25 June 1788, *DHRC*, 1518–19.

12. Hugh Blair Grigsby, *The History of the Virginia Federal Convention of 1788: with some account of eminent Virginians of that era who were members of the body*, with a biographical sketch of the author and illustrative notes edited by R. A. Brock, 2 vols. (Richmond: Virginia Historical Society, 1890–91), 1:326.

13. James Innes, 25 June 1788, *DHRC*, 1520–21.

14. John Tyler, 25 June 1788, *DHRC*, 1525, 1528.

15. John Tyler, 25 June 1788, *DHRC*, 1524, 1529.

16. Zachariah Johnston, 25 June 1788, *DHRC*, 1534, 1530.

17. Patrick Henry, 25 June 1788, *DHRC*, 1537.

18. Bushrod Washington to George Washington, 7 June 1788, *DHRC*, 1581; James Madison to Rufus King, 13 June 1788, *DHRC*, 1619.

19. Patrick Henry, 20 June 1788, *DHRC*, 1424, 1419; George Nicholas, 23 June 1788, *DHRC*, 1467 (last quotation).

20. Patrick Henry, 25 June 1788, *DHRC*, 1537.

21. Patrick Henry, 25 June 1788, *DHRC*, 1537.

22. Spencer Roane to Philip Aylett, 26 June 1788, *DHRC*, 1713; George Washington to Tobias Lear, 29 June 1788, Founders Online, National Archives (founders.archives.gov).

23. Edmund Randolph, 25 June 1788, *DHRC*, 1537.

24. William Lee Miller, *The Business of May Next: James Madison and the Founding* (Charlottesville: University Press of Virginia, 1992), 215; *DHRC*, 907–8.

25. *DHRC*, 1513.

26. *DHRC*, 1543, n. 1.

27. Spencer Roane to Philip Aylett, 26 June 1788, *DHRC*, 1713 (first quotation); James Madison to Rufus King, 25 June 1788, *DHRC*, 1676; extract of letter from Richmond, 25 June 1788, *Pennsylvania Packet*, 2 July 1788, *DHRC*, 1698 (last quotation).

28. James Madison to Rufus King, 25 June 1788, *DHRC*, 1676; James Monroe to Thomas Jefferson, 12 July 1788, *DHRC*, 1705; *Philadelphia Independent Gazetteer*, 2 July 1788, *DHRC*, 1713, n. 2.

29. For various interpretations of Federalist/Anti-Federalist divisions, in and beyond Virginia, see Douglass Adair, "James Madison," in Trevor Colbourn, ed., *Fame and the Founding Fathers: Essays by Douglass Adair* (1974; repr., Indianapolis, IN: Liberty Fund, 1998), 194; Lance Banning, "1787 and 1776: Patrick Henry, James Madison, the Constitution, and the Revolution," in Neil L. York, ed., *Toward a More Perfect Union: Six Essays on the Constitution* (Albany: State University of New York Press, 1989), 59–89; Lance Banning, *The Sacred Fire of Liberty: James Madison and the Founding of the Federal Republic* (Ithaca, NY: Cornell University Press, 1995), 261; Stanley Elkins and Eric McKitrick, "The Founding Fathers: Young Men of the Revolution," *Political Science Quarterly* 76 (1961): 181–216; Richard E. Ellis, "The Persistence of Antifederalism after 1789," in Richard Beeman, Stephen Botein, and Edward C. Carter II, eds., *Beyond Confederation: Origins of the Constitution and American National Identity* (Chapel Hill: University of North Carolina Press, 1987), 295–314; Jürgen Heideking, *The Constitution before the Judgment Seat: The Prehistory and Ratification of the American Constitution, 1787–1791*, ed. John P. Kaminski and Richard Leffler (Charlottesville: University of Virginia Press, 2012), 271- 72; Woody Holton, *Unruly Americans and the Origins of the Constitution* (New York: Hill and Wang, 2007); James H. Huston, "Country, Court, and Constitution: Antifederalism and the Historians," *William and Mary Quarterly* 38 (1981): 337–68; Cecelia M. Kenyon, "Men of Little Faith: The Anti-Federalists on the Nature of Representative Government," *William and Mary Quarterly* 12 (1955): 3–43; Jon Kukla, "A Spectrum of Sentiments: Virginia's Federalists, Antifederalists, and 'Federalists Who Are for Amendments,' 1787–1788," *Virginia Magazine of History and Biography* 96 (1988): 277–96; Jackson Turner Main, *The Anti-Federalists: Critics of the Constitution, 1781–1788* (Chapel Hill: University of North Carolina Press, 1961), 28–32, 225–26, 249–81; Norman Risjord, "Virginians and the Constitution: A Multi-variant Analysis," *William and Mary Quarterly* 31 (1974): 613–32; Robert E. Thomas, "The Virginia Convention of 1788," *Journal of Southern History* 19 (1953): 63–72; Gordon S. Wood, *The Creation of the American Republic, 1776–1787* (Chapel Hill: University of North Carolina Press, 1969), 483–85.

30. Lance Banning offered a compelling commentary: "Men of comparable experience and intellect, responding to the same alarms and sharing many common values, were compelled to work a very difficult equation when presented with the Constitution." Banning, *Sacred Fire of Liberty*, 262. See also Banning, "1787 and 1776," 70, 81–82. Todd Estes recently compiled Banning's deeply influential essays on the founding era in an edited volume: *Founding Visions: The Ideas, Individuals, and Intersections that Created America* (Lexington: University Press of Kentucky, 2014).

31. Woody Holton made this point in *Unruly Americans*, 252–53. For the history of the Bill of Rights, see Banning, *Sacred Fire of Liberty*, chap. 9; Labunski, *James Madison and the Struggle for the Bill of Rights*, chaps. 8–9; Jack N. Rakove, *Original Meanings: Politics and Ideas in the Making of the Constitution* (New York: Knopf, 1996), chap. 10; Wood, *Creation of the American Republic*, 536–43.

32. James Madison to Alexander Hamilton, 27 June 1788, *DHRC*, 1688; James

Madison to George Washington, 27 June 1788, *DHRC*, 1688. See also Kukla, "A Spectrum of Sentiments." Some scholars think a bill of rights was not Mason's paramount concern. See, for example, Jeff Broadwater, *James Madison: A Son of Virginia and a Founder of the Nation* (Chapel Hill: University of North Carolina Press, 2012); Brent Tarter, "George Mason and the Conservation of Liberty," *Virginia Magazine of History and Biography* 99 (1991): 279–304. For a complete list of committee members, see *DHRC*, 1541.

33. *DHRC*, 1514–15; Convention proceedings, 27 June 1788, *DHRC*, 1556. For a complete list of the proposed amendments, see *DHRC*, 1551–56.

34. Convention proceedings, 27 June 1788, *DHRC*, 1558.

35. Grigsby, *History of the Virginia Federal Convention*, 1:354. For changes in political culture in the early nineteenth century, see Gordon S. Wood, *The Radicalism of the American Revolution* (New York: Knopf, 1992), part 3.

36. Grigsby, *History of the Virginia Federal Convention*, 1:355.

37. "A Spectator of the Meeting," *Virginia Independent Chronicle*, 9 July 1788, *DHRC*, 1560.

38. "A Spectator of the Meeting," *Virginia Independent Chronicle*, 9 July 1788, *DHRC*, 1560.

39. *DHRC*, 1562, n. 1.

40. *Massachusetts Centinel*, 26 July 1788, *DHRC*, 1561; *Carlisle Gazette*, 24 September 1788, *DHRC*, 1561.

41. David Meade Randolph, "Anecdote of Patrick Henry," c. 1792, *DHRC*, 1562.

42. *DHRC*, 1673.

43. *New York Independent Journal*, 2 July 1788, *DHRC*, 1723; *DHRC*, 1723.

44. *Virginia Journal*, 3 July 1788, *DHRC*, 1716; George Washington to Tobias Lear, 29 June 1788, Founders Online, National Archives (founders.archives.gov).

45. *Winchester Virginia Gazette*, 2 July 1788, *DHRC*, 1722 (quotation); *DHRC*, 1713, 1729–36. For additional reports, see *Maryland Journal*, 1 July 1788, *DHRC*, 1718–19; *Virginia Journal*, 3 July 1788, *DHRC*, 1716–17.

46. *New York Journal*, 3 July 1788, *DHRC*, 1725.

47. *DHRC*, 1747.

48. *Virginia Centinel*, 2 July 1788, *DHRC*, 1728; *Norfolk and Portsmouth Journal*, 9 July 1788, *DHRC*, 1742.

49. Speech by John O'Conner, *Norfolk and Portsmouth Journal*, 16 July 1788, *DHRC*, 1738–39. For Anti-Federalist influences, see Saul Cornell, *The Other Founders: Anti-Federalism and the Dissenting Tradition in America, 1788–1828* (Chapel Hill: University of North Carolina Press, 1999); Holton, *Unruly Americans*; Ellis, "The Persistence of Antifederalism."

50. Richard Henry Lee to John Lamb, 27 June 1788, *DHRC*, 826.

51. *Virginia Gazette and Independent Chronicle*, 28 June 1788, *DHRC*, 1691–93.

52. Patrick Henry, 25 June 1788, *DHRC*, 1537. See also Lance Banning, "Republican Ideology and the Triumph of the Constitution, 1789–1793," *William and Mary Quarterly* 31 (1974): 167–88.

53. James Madison to Alexander Hamilton, 27 June 1788, *DHRC*, 1688; James Madison to Thomas Jefferson, 24 July 1788, *DHRC*, 1707.

54. Nathaniel Gorham to George Washington, 5 July 1788, Founders Online, National Archives (founders.archives.gov).

55. George Washington Diary, 4 July 1788, Founders Online, National Archives (founders.archives.gov). For Washington and slavery, see François Furstenberg, *In the Name of the Father: Washington's Legacy, Slavery, and the Making of a Nation* (New York: Penguin, 2006); Philip D. Morgan, "'To Get Quit of Negroes': George Washington and Slavery," *Journal of American Studies* 39 (2005): 403–29.

56. John Jay to George Washington, 4–8 July 1788, Founders Online, National Archives (founders.archives.gov); George Washington to Charles Cotesworth Pinckney, 28 June 1788, Founders Online, National Archives (founders.archives.gov); Jack Rakove, *Revolutionaries: A New History of the Invention of America* (Boston: Houghton Mifflin Harcourt, 2010), 392. For New York's convention, see Maier, *Ratification*, chaps. 12–13. The voting process in New York was very complicated. This final vote tally included the state's ratification form and requested amendments.

57. George Washington to John Langdon, 20 July 1788, *DHRC*, 1757.

58. George Washington to Thomas Jefferson, 31 August 1788, *DHRC*, 1760.

59. George Washington to Benjamin Lincoln, 29 June 1788, Founders Online, National Archives (founders.archives.gov).

Epilogue

1. Patrick Henry, 25 June 1788, *DHRC*, 1537.

2. Richard Henry Lee to Theodorick Bland, 15 October 1788, in Richard H. Lee, ed., *Memoir of the Life of Richard Henry Lee, and His Correspondence with the most distinguished men in America and Europe, illustrative of their characters, and of the events of the American Revolution*, 2 vols. (Philadelphia: H. C. Carey and I. Lea, 1825), 2:95; Richard Henry Lee to Patrick Henry, 28 May 1789, *Memoir of the Life of Richard Henry Lee*, 2: 97.

3. For Patrick Henry's efforts, see *DHRC*, 1761–68. For the persistence of the Anti-Federalist influences, see Saul Cornell, *The Other Founders: Anti-Federalism and the Dissenting Tradition in America, 1788–1828* (Chapel Hill: University of North Carolina Press, 1999); Richard E. Ellis, "The Persistence of Antifederalism after 1789," in Richard Beeman, Stephen Botein, and Edward C. Carter II, eds., *Beyond Confederation: Origins of the Constitution and American National Identity* (Chapel Hill: University of North Carolina Press, 1987), 295–314.

4. Madison defeated Monroe 1308 to 972. Richard Labunski, *James Madison and the Struggle for the Bill of Rights* (New York: Oxford University Press, 2006), 174.

5. Brent Tarter, "George Mason and the Conservation of Liberty," *Virginia Magazine of History and Biography* 99 (1991): 301.

6. Richard Henry Lee to Patrick Henry, 14 September 1789, *Memoir of the Life of Richard Henry Lee*, 2:98.

7. Richard Henry Lee and William Grayson to Virginia House of Delegates, 28 September 1789, *Memoir of the Life of Richard Henry Lee*, 2:100.

8. For the debate over the Bill of Rights in Virginia, see Labunski, *James Madison and the Struggle for the Bill of Rights*, 241–56.

9. Quoted in William G. Morgan, "The Congressional Nominating Caucus of 1816: The Struggle against the Virginia Dynasty," *Virginia Magazine of History and Biography* 80 (1972): 461.

10. For an overview of this factional division, see Gordon S. Wood, *Empire of Liberty: A History of the Early American Republic, 1789–1815* (New York: Oxford University Press, 2009), chaps. 2–4.

11. Many differences exist between the factions of the 1790s and modern political parties, most important, support for the very idea of parties. Today, Americans see the two-party system as a valid and central part of government: electoral and legislative processes rely on political parties. But both Federalists and Republicans disdained the idea of parties and denied their legitimacy.

12. Alexander Hamilton to Edward Carrington, 26 May 1792, in Harold C. Syrett, ed., *The Papers of Alexander Hamilton*, 27 vols. (New York: Columbia University Press, 1961–87), 11:429; Thomas Jefferson to George Washington, 9 September 1792, in Julian P. Boyd et al., eds., *The Papers of Thomas Jefferson*, 41 vols. (Princeton, NJ: Princeton University Press, 1950–), 24:352. To understand the roles and influence of the press, see Jeffrey L. Pasley, *"The Tyranny of Printers": Newspaper Politics in the Early American Republic* (Charlottesville: University Press of Virginia, 2001).

13. James Madison, 6 April 1796, in William T. Hutchinson et al., eds., *The Papers of James Madison, Congressional Series*, 17 vols. (Chicago: University of Chicago Press, 1962–77, vols. 1–10; Charlottesville: University Press of Virginia, 1977–91, vols. 11–17), 16:295–96; Preamble to Constitution; Patrick Henry, 4 June 1788, *DHRC*, 931.

Suggested Further Reading

Primary sources revealing the debates over the Constitution are voluminous and wide-ranging. Thankfully, most are readily accessible, too. The starting point for any investigation of the ratification debates is the remarkable editorial project, John P. Kaminski et al., eds., *The Documentary History of the Ratification of the Constitution* (Madison: State Historical Society of Wisconsin). The Virginia materials run more than 1,800 pages. Included in the *DHRC* is the fascinating transcription of the Virginia Ratification Convention by David Robertson, originally published as *Debates and Other Proceedings of the Convention of Virginia* (Petersburg, VA: Hunter and Prentiss, 1788–89). The actions of the Confederation Congress can be traced in Worthington C. Ford et al., eds., *Journals of the Continental Congress, 1774–1789*, 34 vols. (Washington, DC: Government Printing Office, 1904–37). Jonathan Elliot, ed., *The Debates in the Several State Conventions, on the Adoption of the Federal Constitution*, 5 vols. (Philadelphia: J. B. Lippincott, 1901), remains valuable for understanding the creation of the Constitution. Hugh Blair Grigsby compiled the first history of the Virginia Ratification Convention in the nineteenth century. His work was published as *The History of the Virginia Federal Convention of 1788: with some account of eminent Virginians of that era who were members of the body*, with a biographical sketch of the author and illustrative notes edited by R. A. Brock, 2 vols. (Richmond: Virginia Historical Society, 1890–91). All of these materials are accessible in print form at major libraries, and Ford's and Elliot's works are also available digitally through the Library of Congress (memory.loc.gov).

Starting in the mid-twentieth century, the National Archives and the National Historical Publications and Records Commission (NHPRC) entered into a decades-long partnership with leading university presses to publish comprehensive modern editions of the writings of important members of the founding generation. *The Papers of George Washington*, from the University of Virginia Press (1976–), and *The Papers of James Madison*, first from the University of Chicago Press (1962–77) and then the University of Virginia Press (1977–), are stunning efforts of scholarship in and of themselves, and they have enabled countless studies of the founding era. As a part of this same initiative, equally fine editorial projects center on Thomas Jefferson, Benjamin Franklin, John Adams, and others. *The Papers of George Washington* includes his diaries and five chronological series. *The Papers of James Madison* is divided into four chronological series. Both are ongoing and now part of the "American Founding Era" collection of Rotunda, an extraordinary digital project from the University of Virginia

Press (rotunda.upress.virginia.edu). The primary source collections on Rotunda, most of which require subscription access, include a word-searchable digital edition of *The Documentary History of the Ratification of the Constitution*. The letterpress editions of the NHPRC-funded papers projects are now also complemented with an open access digital platform through the National Archives: Founders Online (founders.archives .gov). Today, many of the writings of George Washington and James Madison are just a click away. A list of all the NHPRC-partnered editorial projects is also available on the National Archives website.

Both Mount Vernon and Montpelier, Washington's and Madison's respective homes, are popular museums and important centers for historical study. The Robert H. Smith Center for the Constitution at Madison's estate, Montpelier, and the Fred W. Smith National Library for the Study of George Washington at Mount Vernon support research, fund programming, and provide access to rich collections of artifacts, art, and print sources. Readers will enjoy visiting the websites (mountvernon.org and montpelier.org) and, hopefully, the homes and libraries, too.

George Mason and Patrick Henry were far less prolific than George Washington and James Madison and less vigilant about preserving their papers. A first-rate collection of Mason's writings is Robert A. Rutland, ed., *The Papers of George Mason, 1725–1792*, 3 vols. (Chapel Hill: University of North Carolina Press, 1970). Henry's papers have not been comprehensively updated since William Wirt Henry, *Patrick Henry: Life, Correspondence and Speeches*, 3 vols. (New York: Charles Scribner's Sons, 1891). Some of his most influential speeches and writings can be read in James M. Elson, ed., *Patrick Henry in His Speeches and Writings and in the Words of His Contemporaries* (Lynchburg, VA: Warwick House Publishers, 2007).

Additional print volumes of primary sources open up the world of the founders generally and the creation of the Constitution in particular. A comprehensive edition of the decades-long and illuminating correspondence between James Madison and Thomas Jefferson is provided by James Morton Smith, ed., *The Republic of Letters: The Correspondence between Thomas Jefferson and James Madison, 1776–1826*, 3 vols. (New York: W. W. Norton, 1995). Earlier versions of James Madison's writings, while incomplete in many ways, contain some materials not yet available through the comprehensive UVA Press project. Gaillard Hunt edited nine volumes of *The Writings of James Madison* (New York: G. P. Putnam's Sons, 1900–10). See also William C. Rives and Philip R. Fendell, eds., *Letters and Other Writings of James Madison*, 4 vols. (Philadelphia: J. B. Lippincott, 1865). Crucial letters of Richard Henry Lee are available in Richard H. Lee, ed., *Memoir of the Life of Richard Henry Lee, and His Correspondence with the most distinguished men in America and Europe, illustrative of their characters, and of the events of the American Revolution*, 2 vols. (Philadelphia: H. C. Carey and I. Lea, 1825).

Historians have debated the origins and the character of the American Republic since the late eighteenth century. Gordon S. Wood has written widely about the founding era and with great influence, both among scholars—many of whom challenge his ideas—and the reading public. His dissertation, published as *The Creation of the American Republic, 1776–1787* (Chapel Hill: University of North Carolina Press, 1969), redefined scholarly conversations about the American Revolution, alongside his mentor Bernard Bailyn's *The Ideological Origins of the American Revolution* (Cambridge, MA: Harvard University Press, 1967). Wood offered a sweeping overview of the Revolution in the Pulitzer Prize–winning *The Radicalism of the American Revolution* (New York: Knopf, 1992). His *Empire of Liberty: A History of the Early American Republic, 1789–1815* (New York: Oxford University Press, 2009) carried into the early national era. And *Revolutionary Characters: What Made the Founders Different* (New York: Penguin, 2006) centered on the lives and contributions of leading members of the revolutionary generation. Jack Rakove, who has also been deeply influential in the field, authored a similarly conceived study: *Revolutionaries: A New History of the Invention of America* (Boston: Houghton Mifflin Harcourt, 2010). Alongside Wood and Rakove, Lance Banning wrote extensively about the founding era, and with remarkable sophistication and nuance. His intellectual biography of James Madison, *The Sacred Fire of Liberty: James Madison and the Founding of the Federal Republic* (Ithaca, NY: Cornell University Press, 1995), is essential reading for anyone studying the Constitution. Banning developed his interpretations in a number of influential articles, including "Republican Ideology and the Triumph of the Constitution, 1789–1793," *William and Mary Quarterly* 31 (1974): 167–88. One of Banning's former graduate students, Todd Estes, recently compiled those articles in a single edited volume: *Founding Visions: The Ideas, Individuals, and Intersections that Created America* (Lexington: University Press of Kentucky, 2014).

Important overviews of this era include Robert Middlekauff, *The Glorious Cause: The American Revolution, 1763–1789*, 2nd rev. ed. (New York: Oxford University Press, 2005); Gary Nash, *The Unknown American Revolution: The Unruly Birth of Democracy and the Struggle to Create America* (New York: Viking, 2005); John Ferling, *A Leap in the Dark: The Struggle to Create the American Republic* (New York: Oxford University Press, 2003); and Stanley Elkins and Eric McKitrick, *The Age of Federalism* (New York: Oxford University Press, 1993).

The single best account of the Philadelphia Convention is Richard Beeman's lively and engaging *Plain, Honest Men: The Making of the American Constitution* (New York: Random House, 2009). The most significant interpretive studies of the creation of the Constitution include Jack Rakove, *Original Meanings: Politics and Ideas in the Making of the Constitution* (New York: Knopf, 1996); Max M. Edling, *A Revolution in Favor of Government: Origins of the U.S. Constitution and the Making of the American State* (New York: Oxford University Press, 2003); and David C. Hendrickson, *Peace Pact: The Lost World of the American Founding* (Lawrence: University Press of Kansas, 2003). Woody Holton offered an interpretation centered on class and economic interests in *Unruly Americans and the Origins of the Constitution* (New York: Hill and Wang, 2007). Jack P. Greene explored the sectional tensions in Philadelphia in "The Constitution of 1787 and the Question of Southern Distinctiveness," in Greene, *Imperatives, Behaviors, and Identities: Essays in Early American Cultural History* (Charlottesville: University Press of Virginia, 1992), 327–47. William E. Nelson, "Reason and Compromise in the Establishment of the Federal Convention," *William and Mary Quarterly* 44 (1987): 458–84, explained the mindset of the framers of the Constitution.

Pauline Maier's *Ratification: The People Debate the Constitution, 1787–1788* (New York: Simon & Schuster, 2010) is an engaging and comprehensive (nearly 500 pages) account of the ratification process in all the states. A group of historians debated the interpretations Maier embedded in her narrative in a critical forum devoted to the book in the *William and Mary Quarterly* 69 (2012): 361–403. Todd Estes is writing a book about the public dimensions of ratification—the contest "out of doors." He shared some of his ideas in "The Constitution Goes Public: Politics and the Ratification Debates," *Reviews in American History* 41 (2013): 213–19. Additional important studies of ratification include Michael Allen Gillespie and Michael Lienesch, eds., *Ratifying the Constitution* (Lawrence: University Press of Kansas, 1989); and Jürgen Heideking, *The Constitution before the Judgment Seat: The Prehistory and Ratification of the American Constitution, 1787–1791*, which was posthumously edited by John P. Kaminski and Richard Leffler (Charlottesville: University of Virginia Press, 2012).

The clearest investigation into the values and influence of Anti-Federalists is Saul Cornell, *The Other Founders: Anti-Federalism and the Dissenting Tradition in America, 1788–1828* (Chapel Hill: University of North Carolina Press, 1999). Notable earlier interpretations include Cecelia M. Kenyon, "Men of Little Faith: The Anti-Federalists on the Nature of Representative Government," *William and Mary Quarterly* 12 (1955): 3–43; and Jackson Turner Main, *The Anti-Federalists: Critics of the Constitution, 1781–1788* (Chapel Hill: University of North Carolina Press, 1961). Like Cornell, Richard E. Ellis charted the influence of Anti-Federalists after 1788. See Ellis, "The Persistence of Antifederalism after 1789," in Richard Beeman, Stephen Botein, and Edward C. Carter II, eds., *Beyond Confederation: Origins of the Constitution and American National Identity* (Chapel Hill: University of North Carolina Press, 1987).

The Constitution sanctioned slavery, and slavery was a foundational element of the revolutionary era. Any enquiry into the role of slavery in the American Republic still starts with Edmund S. Morgan, *American Slavery, American Freedom: The Ordeal of Colonial Virginia* (New York: W. W. Norton, 1975). Books about this crucial, still timely subject are numerous. Among the most recent significant interpretations are François Furstenberg, *In the Name of the Father: Washington's Legacy, Slavery, and the Making of a Nation* (New York: Penguin, 2006); Alan Taylor, *The Internal Enemy: Slavery and War in Virginia, 1772–1832* (New York: W. W. Norton, 2013); and David Waldstreicher, *Slavery's Constitution: From Revolution to Ratification* (New York: Hill and Wang, 2009).

To learn more about the politics and culture of Virginia in the revolutionary and early national eras, in addition to Morgan, *American Slavery, American Freedom*, see Charles Sydnor, *Gentlemen Freeholders: Political Practices in Washington's Virginia* (Chapel Hill: University of North Carolina Press, 1952); Richard R. Beeman, *The Old Dominion in the New Nation, 1788–1801* (Lexington: University Press of Kentucky, 1972); Woody Holton, *Forced Founders: Indians, Debtors, Slaves, and the Making of the American Revolution in Virginia* (Chapel Hill: University of North Carolina Press, 1999); Michael A. McDonnell, *The Politics of War: Race, Class, and Conflict in Revolutionary Virginia* (Chapel Hill: University of North Carolina Press, 2007); and Brent Tarter, *The Grandees of Government: The Origins and Persistence of Undemocratic Politics in Virginia* (Charlottesville: University of Virginia Press, 2013).

Biography is a popular and enriching way to learn about the past. Since so much of the formal debates in Richmond were driven by a handful of men, it is important to know about their lives. And they are fascinating. In addition to Banning's *The Sacred Fire of Liberty*, important biographies of James Madison include Jack N. Rakove, *James Madison and the Creation of the American Republic*, 3rd ed. (New York: Pearson, 2007), a highly readable and brief overview; Drew R. McCoy, *The Last of the Fathers: James Madison and the Republican Legacy* (Cambridge: Cambridge University Press, 1989); Richard Labunski, *James Madison and the Struggle for the Bill of Rights* (New York: Oxford University Press, 2006); and Jeff Broadwater, *James Madison: A Son of Virginia and a Founder of the Nation* (Chapel Hill: University of North Carolina Press, 2012).

For Patrick Henry's life and career, start with Richard R. Beeman, *Patrick Henry: A Biography* (New York: McGraw Hill, 1974), and see also Kevin J. Hayes, *The Mind of a Patriot: Patrick Henry and the World of Ideas* (Charlottesville: University of Virginia Press, 2008); Thomas S. Kidd, *Patrick Henry: First among Patriots* (New York: Basic Books, 2011); Henry Mayer, *A Son of Thunder: Patrick Henry and the American Republic* (New York: Franklin Watts, 1986); and David A. McCants, *Patrick Henry, the Orator* (Westport, CT: Greenwood Press, 1990).

The best biography of George Mason is Jeff Broadwater, *George Mason, Forgotten Founder* (Chapel Hill: University of North Carolina Press, 2006). Peter R. Henriques provided a revealing approach in "An Uneven Friendship: The Relationship between George Washington and George Mason," *Virginia Magazine of History and Biography* 97 (1989): 185–204. Additional important studies of Mason include Helen Hill Miller, *George Mason, Gentleman Revolutionary* (Chapel Hill: University of North Carolina Press, 1975); Brent Tarter, "George Mason and the Conservation of Liberty," *Virginia Magazine of History and Biography* 99 (1991): 279–304; and Peter Wallenstein, "Flawed Keepers of the Flame: The Interpreters of George Mason," *Virginia Magazine of History and Biography* 102 (1994): 229–60.

There are more good biographies about George Washington than I have space to list. Among the best are Ron Chernow, *Washington: A Life* (New York: Penguin, 2010); Joseph J. Ellis, *His Excellency: George Washington* (New York: Knopf, 2004); and Don Higginbotham, *George Washington: Uniting a Nation* (Lanham, MD: Rowman & Littlefield, 2002). Stuart Leibiger studied Madison and Washington's close, complicated relationship in *Founding Friendship: George Washington, James Madison, and the Creation of the American Republic* (Charlottesville: University Press of Virginia, 1999).

Additional good biographies of key players in the Virginia debates include John J. Reardon, *Edmund Randolph: A Biography* (New York: Macmillan, 1975); Jean Edward

Smith, *John Marshall: Definer of a Nation* (New York: Henry Holt, 1996); and Harlow Giles Unger, *The Last Founding Father: James Monroe and the Nation's Call to Greatness* (Philadelphia: Da Capo Press, 2009).

Several scholars have offered interpretations of the ratification debates in Virginia, most importantly Lance Banning and Jon Kukla. See Lance Banning, "Virginia: Sectionalism and the General Good," in Gillespie and Lienesch, *Ratifying the Constitution*; Lance Banning, "1787 and 1776: Patrick Henry, James Madison, the Constitution, and the Revolution," in Neil L. York, ed., *Toward a More Perfect Union: Six Essays on the Constitution* (Albany: State University of New York Press, 1989), 59–89; and Jon Kukla, "A Spectrum of Sentiments: Virginia's Federalists, Antifederalists, and 'Federalists Who Are for Amendments,' 1787–1788," *Virginia Magazine of History and Biography* 96 (1988): 277–96. Kevin R. C. Gutzman explored Edmund Randolph's role in "Edmund Randolph and Virginia Constitutionalism," *Review of Politics* 66 (2004): 469–97. And Robert W. Smith made a compelling case for reading the contest in an international context in "Foreign Affairs and the Ratification of the Constitution in Virginia," *Virginia Magazine of History and Biography* 122 (2014): 40–63. Additional approaches include F. Claiborne Johnston Jr., "Federalist, Doubtful, and Antifederalist: A Note on the Virginia Convention of 1788," *Virginia Magazine of History and Biography* 96 (1988): 333–44; Norman Risjord, "Virginians and the Constitution: A Multi-variant Analysis," *William and Mary Quarterly* 31 (1974): 613–32; and Robert E. Thomas, "The Virginia Convention of 1788," *Journal of Southern History* 19 (1953): 63–72.

The ratification contest in Virginia touches on many important topics that historians have explored with rich detail. For example, a perceptive analysis of conceptions of liberty is offered in Michal Jan Rozbicki, *Culture and Liberty in the Age of the American Revolution* (Charlottesville: University of Virginia Press, 2011). There is an extensive literature on women in the era of the American Revolution. The best recent book and an excellent place to start exploring this subject is Rosemarie Zagarri, *Revolutionary Backlash: Women and Politics in the Early American Republic* (Philadelphia: University of Pennsylvania Press, 2007). David Waldstreicher, *In the Midst of Perpetual Fetes: The Making of American Nationalism, 1776–1820* (Chapel Hill: University of North Carolina Press, 1997), provides a lively and important study of popular political practices. And Jeffrey L. Pasley, *"The Tyranny of Printers": Newspaper Politics in the Early American Republic* (Charlottesville: University Press of Virginia, 2001), presents an engrossing examination of newspapers. These fine books exemplify the vibrant and capacious research advanced by historians of the American Republic.

Index

Adams, John, 158
Adams, Samuel, 60
advocates for ratification. *See* Federalists
African Americans and public debate, 27–28.
    See also slavery
Alexandria, Virginia, 150
amendments issue: Anti-Federalists and, 44,
    48–49; Federalists and, 44; first Congress
    and, 156–57; Harrison on, 137–38; R. Lee
    and, 156; Madison on, 137; in Massachusetts,
    57; Monroe on, 138; previous vs. subsequent,
    41, 81, 137; E. Randolph on, 106; in Virginia,
    80–82, 130–31; work on, 146–47. *See also*
    bill of rights
American exceptionalism, 83, 115, 130
Anti-Federalists: amendments issue and, 44,
    48–49; beliefs of, 23, 120; bill of rights and,
    56, 131–32; case presented by, 145; conse-
    quences of campaign of, 80–81; corruption
    concerns of, 72–73, 122; in defeat, 142, 144,
    152–53; influence of, 25; localism theme of,
    52; in New York, 58; in Pennsylvania, 55;
    political deference and, 68–69; rebuke of,
    84; referendum approach to elections of,
    72–73; slavery and, 85; timing of ratification
    decision and, 45, 47; in Virginia, 30, 33–34;
    virtual representation and, 45; Washington
    and, 70, 75. *See also* Henry, Patrick; Lee,
    Richard Henry; Mason, George
armies, standing, 33–34, 110, 123–24
Articles of Confederation: decision to abandon,
    12; failures of, 4, 44; Federalist view of, 109;
    gridlock and, 51; E. Randolph on, 113. *See
    also* Confederation Congress

bill of rights: Anti-Federalists and, 56, 131–32;
    R. Lee and, 60; Madison and, 156; Mason

and, 17–18; for Virginia, 5; Virginia conven-
    tion and, 132–33
Bill of Rights, ratification of, 157–58
Blair, John, 12, 19, 66
Boston, news of ratification received in, 151
Breckinridge, James, 39, 100, 121
Breckinridge, John, 46

Carrington, Edward: Constitution and, 19–20,
    22; on election of representatives, 91; on
    Henry, 53, 72; on Massachusetts ratification
    convention, 56; on public opinion, 81–82;
    Washington and, 75
Carrington, Paul, 83
Carter, Charles, 73, 74
civic culture, polarization of, 29–30. *See also*
    Anti-Federalists; Federalists
class, in debate, 72
Clay, Green, 120
Clinton, George, 58
communication: by horse and rider, 149–50;
    by networks of correspondence, 59–61
Confederation Congress: Constitution and,
    19–23; Kentucky statehood proposal and,
    179n64; R. Lee and, 14; Madison and, 16;
    negotiations with Spain by, 50; news of rati-
    fication received by, 149–50. *See also* Articles
    of Confederation
Connecticut, 4, 62
Constitution: Confederation Congress and, 19–
    23; convention to debate, 40–44; publica-
    tion and distribution of, 24; ratification of, 4,
    5–6, 149–50; support for, and Washington,
    5. *See also* amendments issue; Philadelphia
    Convention; state ratification conventions;
    Virginia Ratification Convention
Constitution Day, 5